I0810612

IMAGES
of America

SCHROEDER'S DEPARTMENT STORE

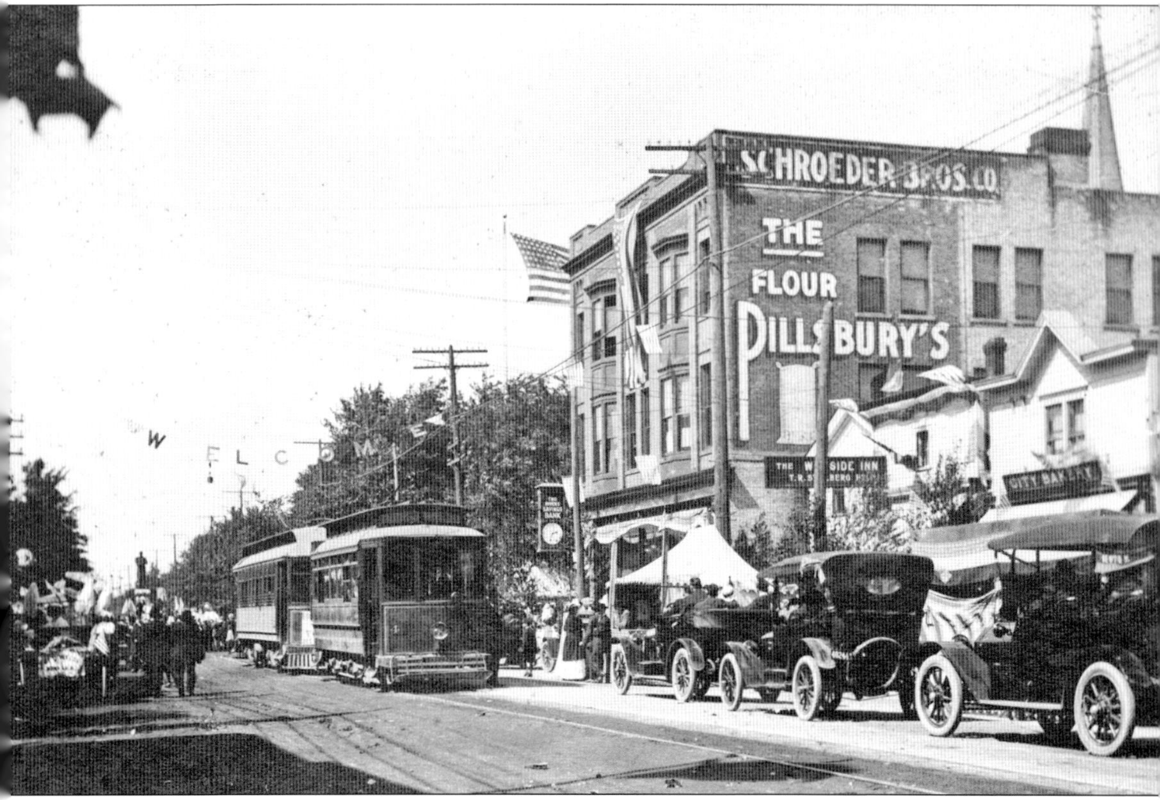

Downtown Two Rivers was a busy place during the 1920s. The trolley ran north and south on Washington Street, making its way around the Central Park Statue of the Civil War solider. In later years, the trolley was removed, and the soldier was moved to Central Park. (Courtesy of Schroeder's Department Store.)

On the Cover: In 1933, Two Rivers Savings Bank merged with the Tisch Mills State Bank and Mishicot State Bank. Due to this merger, a larger location was necessary. In 1935, Two Rivers Savings bank moved into the Empire Building. Local residents still referred to this bank as the "Red Bank" because of the original location inside Schroeder's red-brick storefront. (Courtesy of the Schroeder Brothers Company.)

IMAGES
of America

Schroeder's Department Store

A.J. Schroeder and Theresa Kronforst
Foreword by Tim Schroeder

ARCADIA
PUBLISHING

ISBN 978-1-4671-2898-8

Published by Arcadia Publishing
Charleston, South Carolina

Printed in the United States of America

Library of Congress Control Number: 2017960990

For all general information, please contact Arcadia Publishing:
Telephone 843-853-2070
Fax 843-853-0044
E-mail sales@arcadiapublishing.com
For customer service and orders:
Toll-Free 1-888-313-2665

Visit us on the Internet at www.arcadiapublishing.com

Bryan, Connor, and Norah, you are my heaven on earth.
Being with you reminds me what life is all about.

—A.J. Schroeder

This book is dedicated to my dad for showing me the ledge
and to Nathan for constantly talking me off it.

—Theresa Kronforst

Contents

Foreword

In 1891, Peter and Joseph Schroeder had a dream of establishing a retail store to serve the needs of the growing Two Rivers community. That opportunity came when the B. Mayer Mercantile (on the corner of Eighteenth and Washington Streets) went out of business. The two brothers purchased the building and the business, and on that day, Schroeder Brothers Company was born.

Not long after, brothers Frank and John Schroeder joined the growing firm. By 1899, more space was needed to accommodate the growing business. The four brothers' father agreed to help finance their desired three-story building. And just before the Christmas season of that same year, the brothers moved the business to its current location on the corner of Seventeenth and Washington Streets.

Over the next 118 years, that original generation and the three succeeding it have diversified the business according to the needs of the community. They adapted to the ever-changing retail climate both locally and nationally. At one time or another, Schroeder's Department Store carried groceries, appliances, custom-made draperies, and piece goods. That first generation even operated a bank located in the corner of where now resides the Red Bank Coffeehouse. Locals referred to it as the "Red Bank" because of the red-bricked Schroeder Building.

That first generation was followed by a second—Joseph's sons Neal, Hilary, and Gary—and the second by a third—Gary's son John and Hilary's son Tim. And in 2008, a fourth generation—John's daughters, Amanda and Theresa—took over the reins of running the business.

Now "downsized" to primarily carrying ladies and men's clothing and footwear, Amanda and Theresa sought out local businesses to fill the empty spaces. In 2012, their first tenant, the Read Apple Toy Store, came in. Today, a yarn, quilt, and gift shop all occupy space in the large Schroeder Building.

And although Schroeder's will always be Schroeder's, this new, young generation promotes Schroeder's as the Two Rivers Marketplace.

—Tim Schroeder

ACKNOWLEDGMENTS

I would like to express my appreciation to Julie Schroeder. She was able to provide photographs and information necessary to complete this book. I am grateful she very seldom throws anything away.

To Jeff Dawson and the staff at the Lester Library. Thank you for your encouragement and smiles while Theresa got motion sick looking through 126 years of microfilm for nuggets of information.

Thank you to my godfather, Tim Schroeder, for writing the foreword and providing historical details about his father's generation and filling in some gaps with the third generation.

A special thank-you to the staff at Arcadia Publishing; Angel Hisnanick provided constant support and encouragement throughout the writing process.

A sincere appreciation goes to my sister, Theresa. It was her investigations and thorough reading of our Schroeder Brothers Company minute books that provided endless amount of information and a glimpse into the past 126 years. She lets me play and create here at Schroeder's, and she keeps me tethered to reality.

Finally, to my husband, Bryan. You gave up many evenings listening to me stress about writing this book. Thank you for your constant encouragement and keeping the refrigerator well stocked with beer.

—A.J. Schroeder

INTRODUCTION

Peter J. Schroeder immigrated to the United States from Koblenz, Germany. He brought the knowledge of blacksmithing to Chicago and moved north to Two Creeks, Wisconsin. He was the first blacksmith to settle in Two Creeks. He married Angeline Rollinger and created a homestead. He had eight children: Peter, Joseph, Katherine, John, Mary, Theresa, Frank, and Frances.

Theresa Kronforst and A.J. Schroeder found conflicting reports of when exactly Schroeder's Department Store started. According to the newspaper records of the time, it states Schroeder's mercantile began in the B. Mayer building in March 1890. Peter and Joseph purchased the stock of goods and rented the store at this time. In early 1891, with financial help from their father, Peter Joseph, the name of the business was changed to Schroeder Brothers Company. The building was located at the northwest corner of Eighteenth and Washington Streets. The conflict steps in with the Occupational Monograph 69, Series 1991 of *The Schroeder Brothers Company of Two Rivers, 1891–1991: A Family Tradition of Retail Business* by Georgia M. Fay, great-granddaughter of John Schroeder, one of the four brothers who began the store more than a century ago. As the monograph states, "Peter began his own mercantile in Two Rivers in 1891." Joseph Schroeder joined his brother in 1892, John Schroeder joined in 1893, and finally, Frank Schroeder joined in 1896.

The story starts with Peter Schroeder. Peter Schroeder left the family farm and worked in Manitowoc for three years at a mercantile. In 1891, with financial help from his father, he started Schroeder's in the B. Mayer building. He was instrumental in starting the Two Rivers Savings Bank and was founding officer of the E.J. Vodra Canning Company. Peter was mayor of Two Rivers from 1901 to 1904 and school commissioner from 1896 to 1904. He married Ida Schwantes.

Peter Schroeder bought the old Albert Wehausen Flouring Mill in 1895. The mill was located at the foot of the West Twin River. Two Rivers was a trading center for farmers of the area. According to the Monograph 69, by Georgia M. Fay, she stated that it was common for 15 to 20 carloads of hay to be piled by the railroad tracks waiting to be picked up. Wheat, rye, barley, and oats were received and transported by rail and boat. Schroeder Brothers Company operated the mill until 1964, when it was sold to the Twin Rivers Cooperative.

Joseph joined his older brother Peter in 1892. Prior to joining the family business, he was in the Coast Guard in Chicago and was a lumberjack in northern Wisconsin. He served 25 years as a justice of the peace and was a Two Rivers police judge. He married Mary Ann Short and had one daughter, Helen. Mary Ann passed away in 1898. In 1900, Joseph married Isabella Wolfe and had seven children: Cornelius ("Neal"), Hilary, Claude, Honoratus ("Pete"), Margaret ("Mousy"), Katherine ("Kitty"), and Gregory ("Gary").

John joined Peter and Joseph in 1893. In 1904, the year Schroeder Brothers Company incorporated, John became vice president and later the president of the Two Rivers Savings Bank. John married Elizabeth Bingen, and they had 10 children: Oscar, Mary, Elizabeth, Anna, Hubert, John, Louis, Raymond, Paul, and Gertrude.

Frank attended the Spencerian Business College of Milwaukee before joining his brothers in 1896. Frank held title of treasurer when Schroeder's incorporated and was a cashier in the Two

Rivers Savings Bank. Frank married Ervine Delille, and they had five children: Joseph, Frances, Mildred, Genevieve, and Elaine.

Joseph Schroeder's three sons, Neal, Hilary, and Gary, represented the second generation and worked at Schroeder Brothers Company from 1928 until the 1980s.

Neal joined in the 1920s, and his name first appears in minutes from the Schroeder Brothers Company board meeting in June 1929, where he received shares from his mother. He married Margaret Rodgers and had four daughters: Elizabeth ("Betty"), Marilyn, Joann ("Joan"), and Catherine ("Kay").

Hilary started working in the 1920s, and his name also appears at the same time as Neal's in regard to shares being distributed from his mother. He married Agnes Glysch and had four children: Nancy, Joseph, Tim, and Christine.

Gary began helping at the store in the doctor's quarters at the young age of 10. He would sleep overnight in the doctor's quarters, answer phone calls, and deliver medicine to patients. He first appears in the board minutes in February 1935. He married Bernice "Connie" Conway and had seven children: Peter, Michael, James, Mary Lou, John, Gregory, and Julie.

During the 1970s through 2008, the third generation ran the show. John Schroeder, son of Gary, and Timothy Schroeder, son of Hilary, were the men in charge.

John Schroeder came back to work in 1972. He was instrumental in bringing the Main Street Program to Two Rivers in 1996. The purpose of the Two Rivers Main Street Program is to improve the community's quality of life by strengthening the downtown as the center of the community. John served on several organizational boards, such as Two Rivers Main Street, Rogers Street, Two Rivers Business Association (TRBA), and the Lions Club. He married Jean Shesta and had three daughters: Amanda ("A.J."), Theresa, and Elizabeth ("Liz").

Tim Schroeder was summoned back in 1973 and was also instrumental in recruiting Two Rivers to be a part of the Main Street Program in 1996. He is still active in the Two Rivers Rotary Club, coaches Roncalli High School Cross Country, and is an active member at St. Peter the Fisherman Catholic Church. John and Tim would flip-flop president and vice president titles throughout their tenure at Schroeder's. Tim married Karen Rademacher and had two children: Timothy and Veronica.

Currently, the fourth generation—daughters of John C. Schroeder, A.J., and Theresa—manage day-to-day operations. Like most of the children of business owners, a kid helps out from an early age. A.J. and Theresa started at the young age of 10, waiting on customers at the yearly sidewalk sale in August. They would have to slide a chair to the counter to run people's credit card transactions.

A.J. started full-time at Schroeder's in 2002. She assumed management duties in 2004. It was not until the death of her dad in 2008 that she inherited any ownership of the business. A.J. served on several community organizations, such as the Optimist Club, Rogers Street Fishing Village, Two Rivers Business Association, and Two Rivers Main Street. Theresa and A.J. swap titles of vice president and president on the Board of Schroeder's. A.J. is married to Bryan Ashenbrenner, and they have two children: Connor and Norah.

Theresa worked part-time in the Red Bank Coffeehouse, women's and men's apparel, and footwear until 2008. In 2009, she took management of the Red Bank Coffeehouse and the office duties at Schroeder's. In 2015, Theresa became manager/buyer of the men's apparel department. Theresa serves on community organization boards such as Manitowoc Area Visitor and Convention Bureau and Two Rivers Main Street. She is married to Nathan Kronforst, stepmother to Madison and Samantha, and has one child: Clara.

In 2012, A.J. met with Pam Duveneck, owner of the Read Apple a local book and kids learning store, about cross promoting each other's business. A.J. mentioned, "I would love to get into toys, but I do not have the time." Pam said, "I'd love to get into toys, but I don't have the space." They laughed and that September, the Read Apple was leasing 1,000 square feet from Schroeder's. Keith Duveneck recalls, "It was a marketplace concept, similar to places in Toronto where his oldest daughter, Anikka calls home." A.J. was more than willing to lease the usable space to businesses that complimented Schroeder's men's and women's apparel and footwear. She put her superpowers to work.

In March 2013, A.J. welcomed a yarn shop, the next business to the marketplace concept. Linda Hansen took ownership in 2012 and renamed her yarn shop Intertwined Yarn Shop. She specializes in fibers, patterns, classes and boutique items. Open seven days a week, Linda offers service and a unique blend of fibers for her cliental. She leases 1,500 square feet of the Schroeder second floor adjacent to the alterations department.

The next two shops happened almost at the same time. In July 2014, on another crazy Monday for A.J., Holly Anderson called A.J. to chat about moving her primitive gift shop, Home Sweet Home Décor, into a space outside the Red Bank Coffeehouse. Tuesday, Sarah Gallagher, the Quilt Shop of Two Rivers, called and was interested in the doctor's quarters of the Schroeder Building. By September, Home Sweet Home Décor was moved in, and by December, the Quilt Shop of Two Rivers was home also. The Two Rivers Marketplace concept was a real working model.

The fifth generation, Connor, Norah, and Clara, are shareholders and hang out in the store while their moms work. Connor can be seen cleaning windows and delivering packages during the summer months.

The family has been 126 years in business and are still growing and changing. Four generations have put their stamp on their years at the business. It is still family owned and operated and honors the idea of the founding brothers to offer quality products and knowledgeable service at a reasonable price.

One

The Beginning

As a person walks around the building they are greeted with fashionable apparel and footwear, while the displays honor bits of the past. Crates from the grocery store, adding machines from the bank, advertising signs from the 1960s, and pictures from the past surround the daily buzz of activity. Peter Joseph Schroeder immigrated here with a knowledge of blacksmithing and Clydesdales. He settled in Two Creeks, married, and had eight children. His children were all successful in different fields: teaching, business, and religious devotion. His four sons created a lasting legacy for many generations with the creation of Schroeder's Department Store in 1891. In 1899, a fine three-story structure being 50 by 80 feet was erected. Peter Schroeder was a prominent figure in the city of Two Rivers who had connections with industrial and financial development. He was director of the Two Rivers Knitting Mills and a shareholder in the Two Rivers Improvement Company and Two Rivers Coal Company. He was a far-sighted and forward-thinking man of his generation. He served as mayor of Two Rivers for eight years, four years as county board supervisor, and was a member of the Catholic Order of Foresters. As mayor, he ran the city in a businesslike manner, avoiding useless expenditures, instead promoting progress and achievement. Joseph followed a different path from his brother and left home for Chicago and served in the life-saving service. He moved to northern Wisconsin and worked eight winters as a lumberjack near Lake Superior. He moved home in 1892 and joined Peter at the general store. Joseph served the public as a police judge and justice of the peace; in both positions, he was known to be strict but fair and impartial. Frank was fortunate to attend the Spencerian College of Milwaukee, Wisconsin. In 1896, he moved back to Two Rivers to work with his brothers. He was a member of St. Joseph's Society of Two Rivers and the Knights of Columbus of Manitowoc. The foundation of Schroeder's rests with a family devoted to business in Two Rivers, Wisconsin.

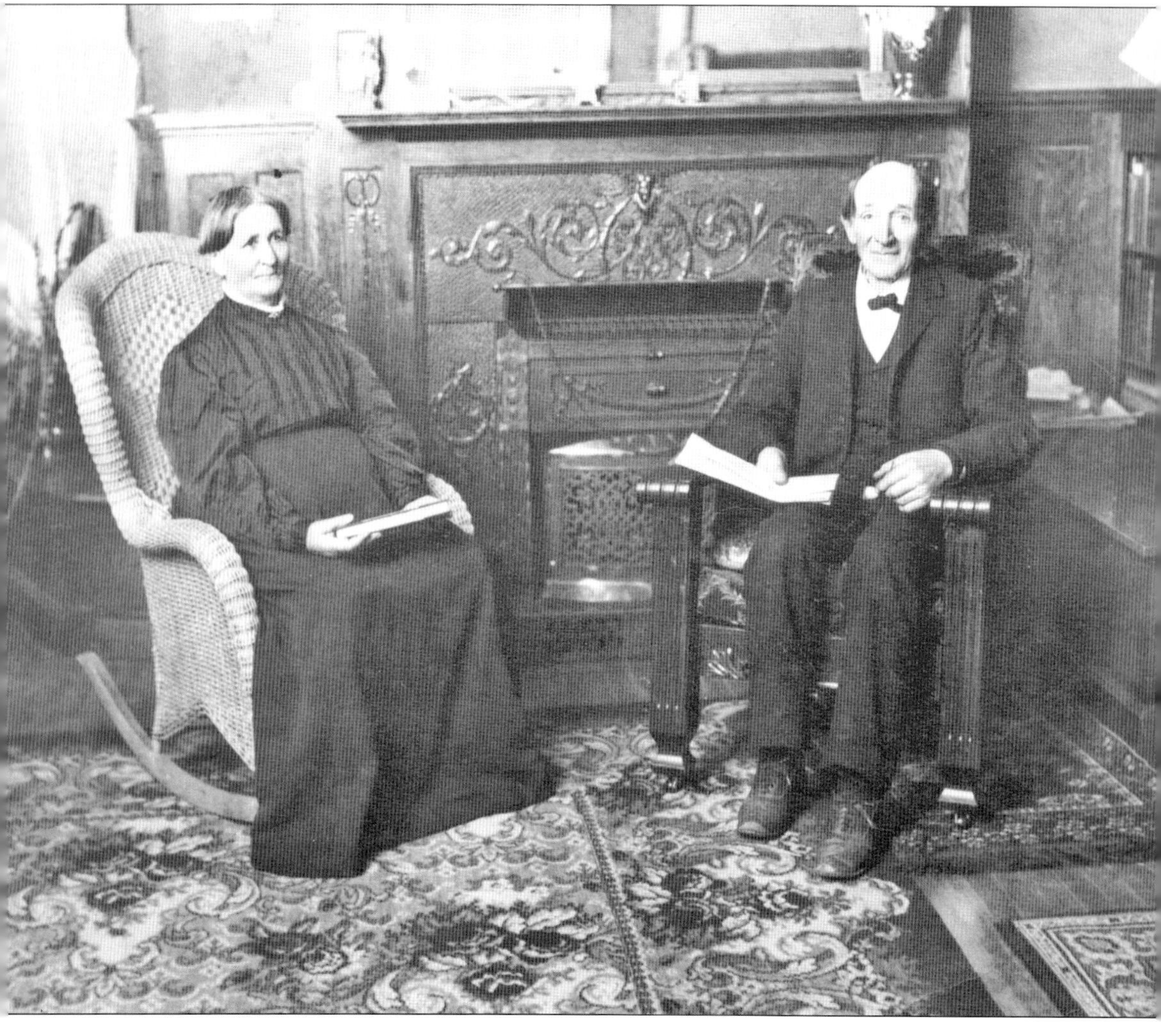

Angeline (Rollinger) and Peter Joseph Schroeder relax in front of the fireplace in their Two Rivers home. P.J. Schroeder (1831–1917) immigrated to the United States from Germany and settled in Two Creeks in 1857. Angeline Rollinger, immigrated with her family in 1856 and also settled in the Two Creeks area. They married in 1859, bought farmland in the township of Two Creeks, and raised eight children. It was with P.J. Schroeder's financial help that the sons were able to start their own mercantile business in Two Rivers. (Courtesy of Schroeder's Department Store.)

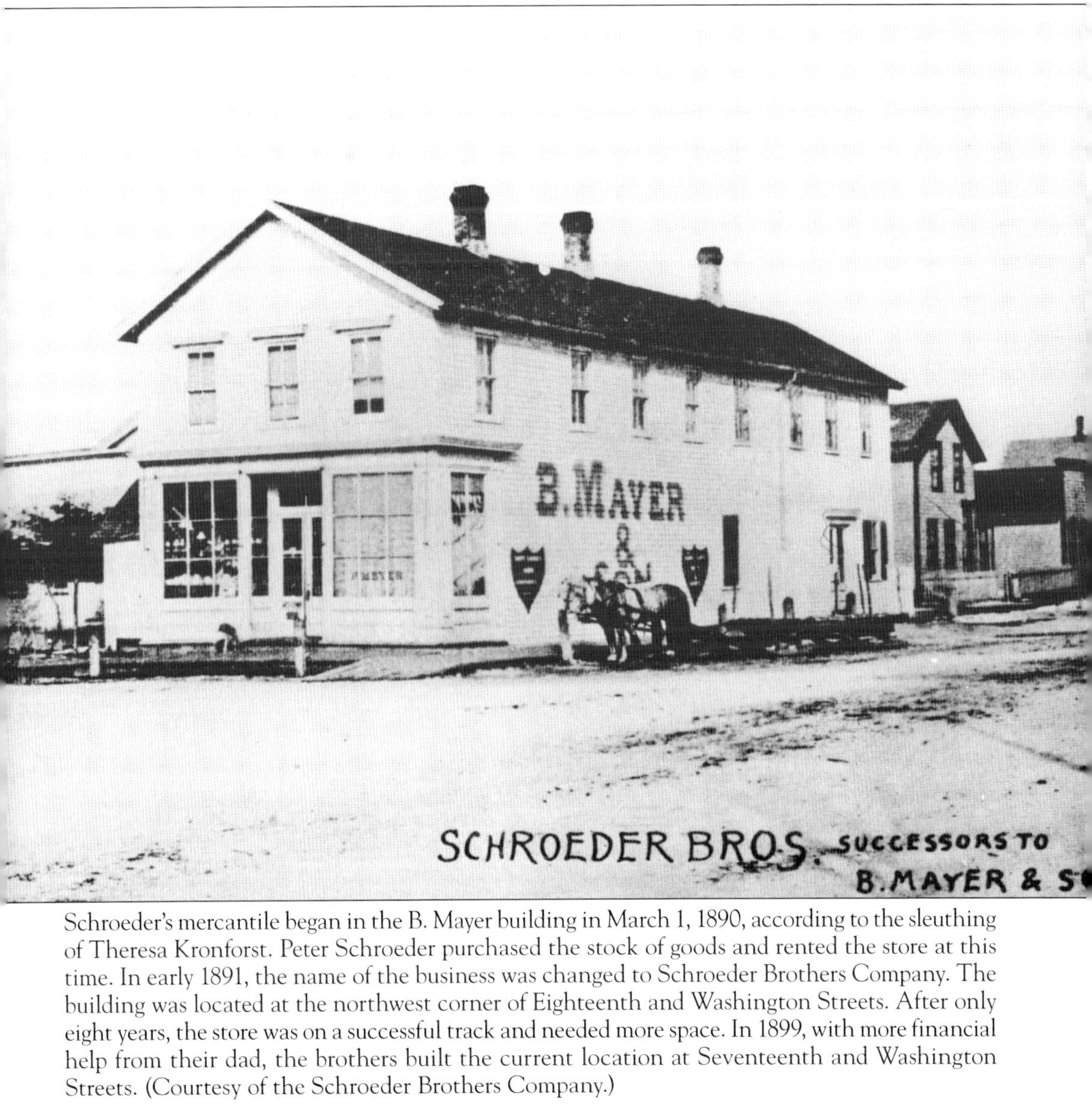

Schroeder's mercantile began in the B. Mayer building in March 1, 1890, according to the sleuthing of Theresa Kronforst. Peter Schroeder purchased the stock of goods and rented the store at this time. In early 1891, the name of the business was changed to Schroeder Brothers Company. The building was located at the northwest corner of Eighteenth and Washington Streets. After only eight years, the store was on a successful track and needed more space. In 1899, with more financial help from their dad, the brothers built the current location at Seventeenth and Washington Streets. (Courtesy of the Schroeder Brothers Company.)

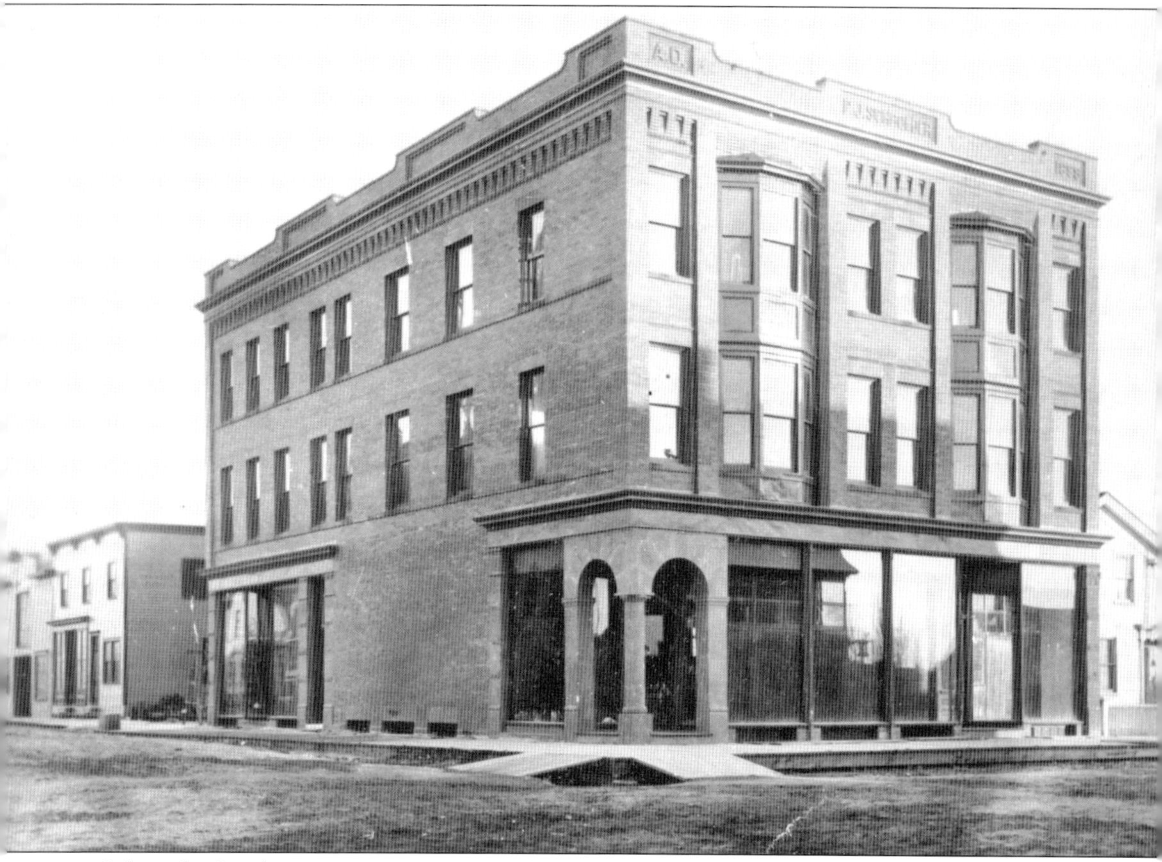

Schroeder Brothers Company is pictured here soon after completion in 1899. Reported in the October 24, 1899, newspaper, in front and near the top of the Schroeder Building, cut in solid red sandstone, is P.J. Schroeder's name. On December 26, 1899, the store was officially lit. A gas-engine was used to power the 500-candlepower lights. It was stated in the *Two Rivers Reporter* that it was the "Best Lighted Store in Manitowoc County." On February 29, 1904, Schroeder's Department Store incorporated to become Schroeder Brothers Company, Inc. After 12 years of accepting farmers' goods and giving credit on account at the general store, the federal government sent a letter to Peter Schroeder explaining he was running a bank and should cease and desist his activities. His response was to incorporate, and on March 14, 1904, the first Schroeder board meeting took place. At that time, Peter Schroeder was elected president and John J. Schroeder elected vice president, while Joseph S. Schroeder was secretary and Frank Schroeder was the treasurer. (Courtesy of Schroeder's Department Store.)

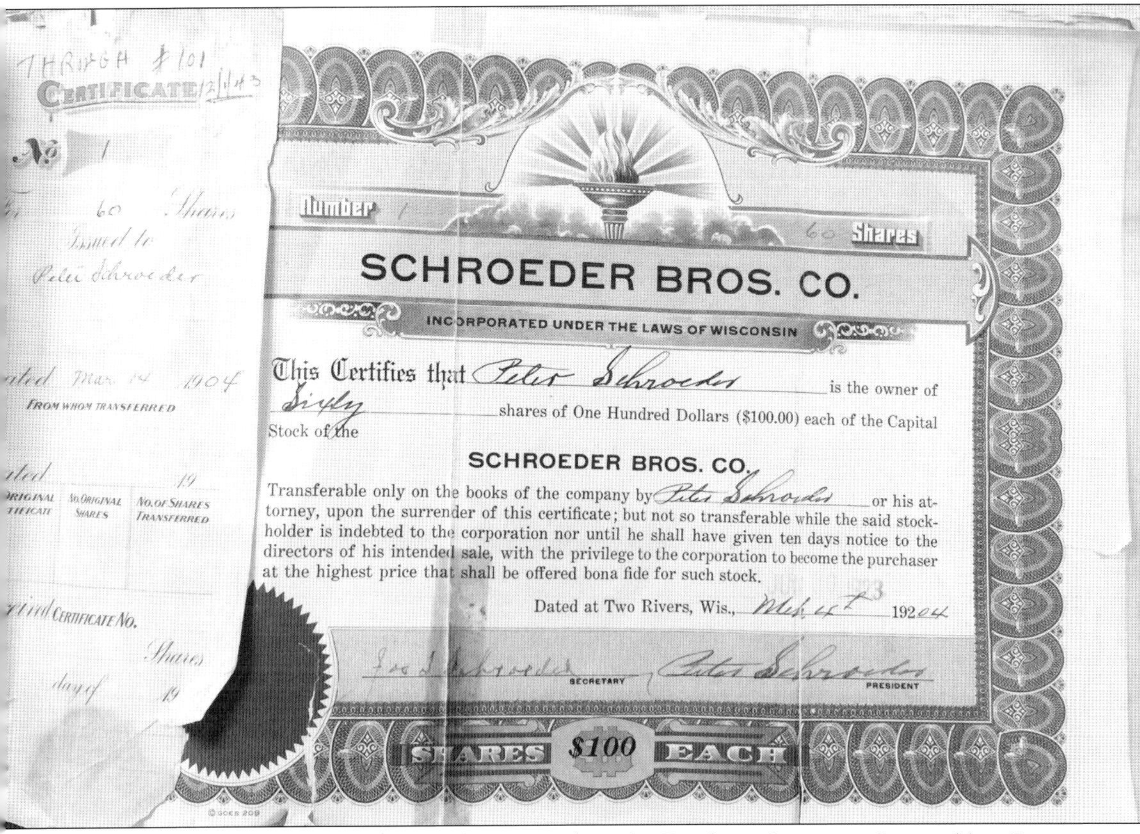
THRUGH #101 CERTIFICATE 12/1/43
No. 1
For 60 Shares
Issued to
Peter Schroeder
Dated Mar 14 1904
FROM WHOM TRANSFERRED
Dated 19
ORIGINAL CERTIFICATE | No. ORIGINAL SHARES | No. OF SHARES TRANSFERRED
Received Certificate No.
Shares
day of 19

Number 1
60 Shares
SCHROEDER BROS. CO.
INCORPORATED UNDER THE LAWS OF WISCONSIN
This Certifies that Peter Schroeder is the owner of Sixty shares of One Hundred Dollars ($100.00) each of the Capital Stock of the
SCHROEDER BROS. CO.
Transferable only on the books of the company by Peter Schroeder or his attorney, upon the surrender of this certificate; but not so transferable while the said stockholder is indebted to the corporation nor until he shall have given ten days notice to the directors of his intended sale, with the privilege to the corporation to become the purchaser at the highest price that shall be offered bona fide for such stock.
Dated at Two Rivers, Wis., Mch 14th 1904
Jos. J. Schroeder SECRETARY
Peter Schroeder PRESIDENT
SHARES $100 EACH

Pictured are the first 60 shares to help form Schroeder Brothers Company, Inc., sold to Peter Schroeder, the founder of Schroeder's Department Store. At the first board meeting Peter was elected to serve as president of the board of directors. At this meeting, shares in the corporation were distributed. Peter received 60 shares, Joseph received 80 shares, John received 60 shares, and Frank received 30 shares. Other shareholders at this time were Peter Beth, husband to Catherine Schroeder, the daughter of Peter Joseph and Angeline Schroeder; he received 30 shares. (Courtesy of Schroeder's Department Store.)

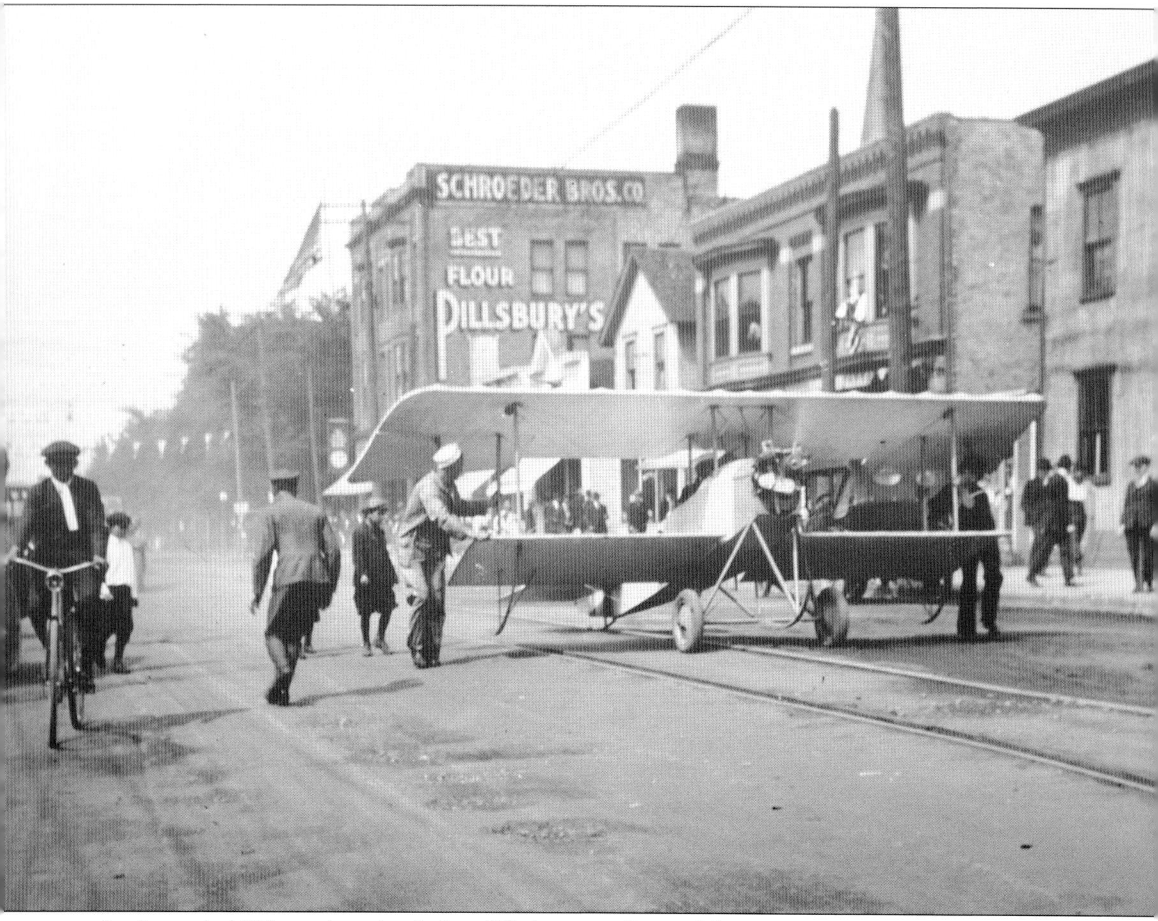

In the early 1900s, a plane landed on Washington Street. This image captures the plane getting ready to take off for the skies over Two Rivers. Schroeder's clock is visible in the background of the photograph. (Courtesy of Schroeder's Department Store.)

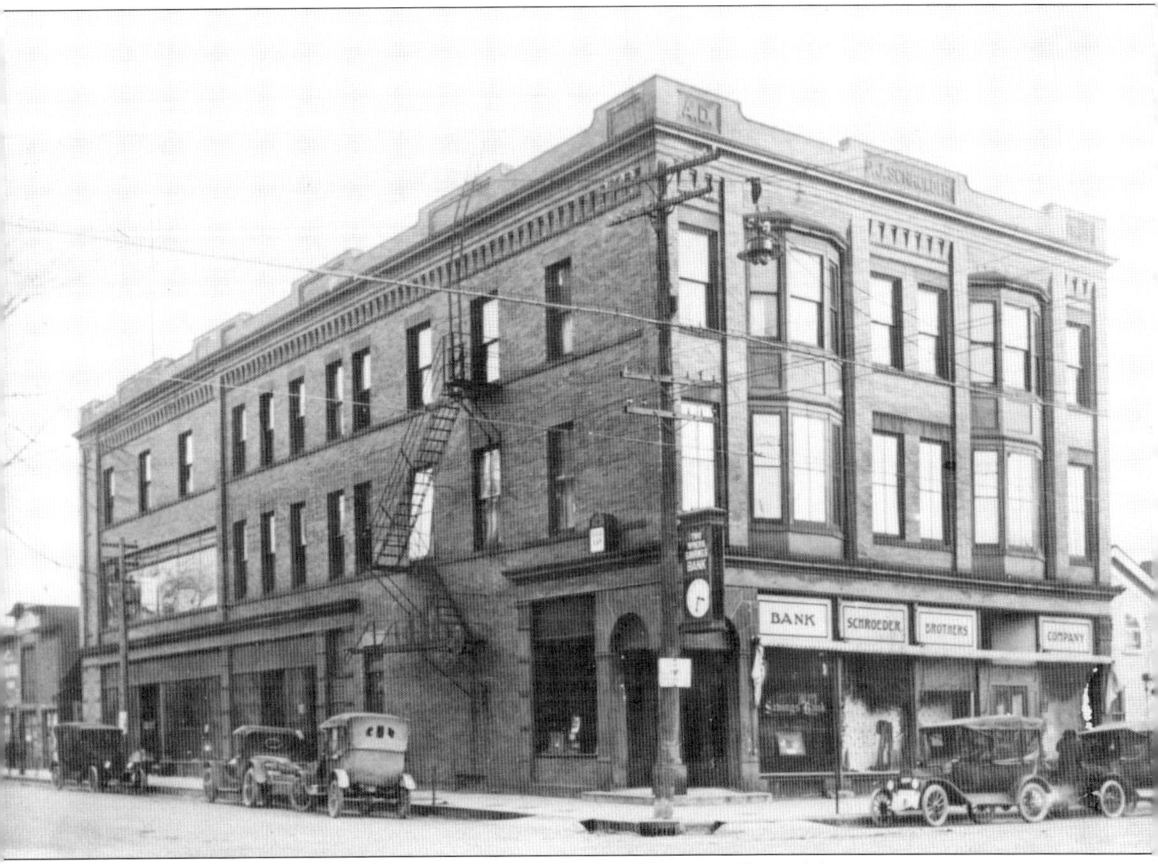

This photograph, taken in 1916, shows the 1912 addition. This addition was necessary to accommodate more customers, and it moved the bank to the northwest corner of the building for a more secure location. The children's clothing department was in that corner from 1899 to 1918. The addition of 1912 gave Schroeder Brothers Company more room to expand. The front entrance of Schroeder's was moved from the corner to the front of Washington Street. The northwest corner floor was reinforced to hold the safe for the Two Rivers Savings Bank, and bank operations moved in. In the back addition, a mezzanine was created overlooking the entire first floor. The office was moved there and a trolley system was set to handle all sales transactions. The 1912 addition created a larger space for the grocery department to move to the far east part of the building. (Courtesy of Schroeder's Department Store.)

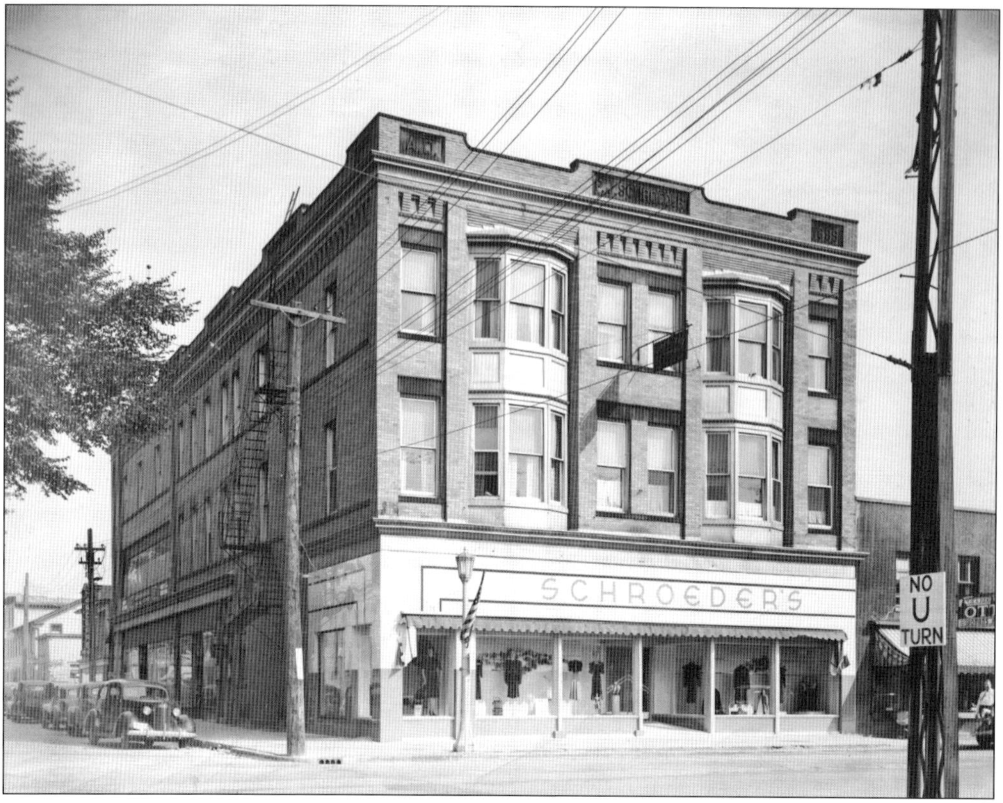

In 1933, Two Rivers Savings Bank merged with the Tisch Mills State Bank and Mishicot State Bank. Due to this merger, a larger location was necessary. In 1935, Two Rivers Savings Bank moved into the Empire Building. Local residents still referred to this bank as the "Red Bank" because of the original location inside Schroeder's red-brick store. As soon as the bank moved out, remodeling took place and made room for new departments. Rugs, linoleum, draperies, and appliances were all added. (Courtesy of Schroeder's Department Store.)

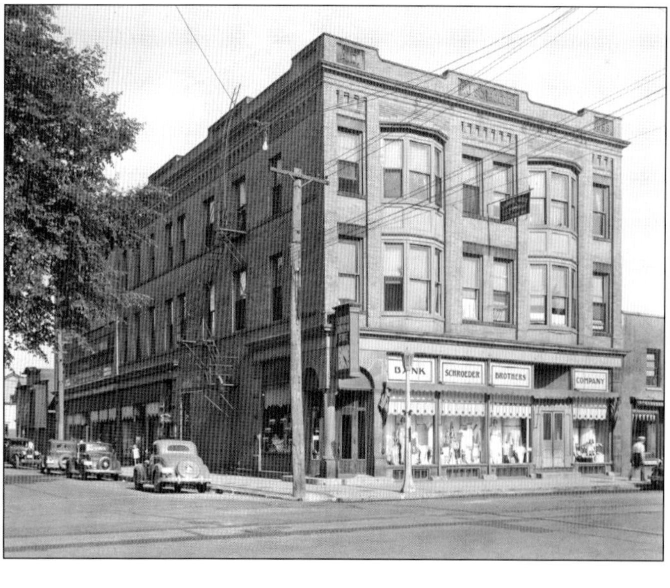

This 1930s photograph was donated to Schroeder's by customer Brandon Gauthier. He found it online from a lady in Milwaukee. She acquired the image from an architect Sylvester Schmitt, a local of Two Rivers. The bank recently moved out, but the upper glass sign remained. The window on Seventeenth Street displayed housewares and was no longer home to the Two Rivers Savings Bank. (Courtesy of Vassar Studio and Schroeder's Department Store.)

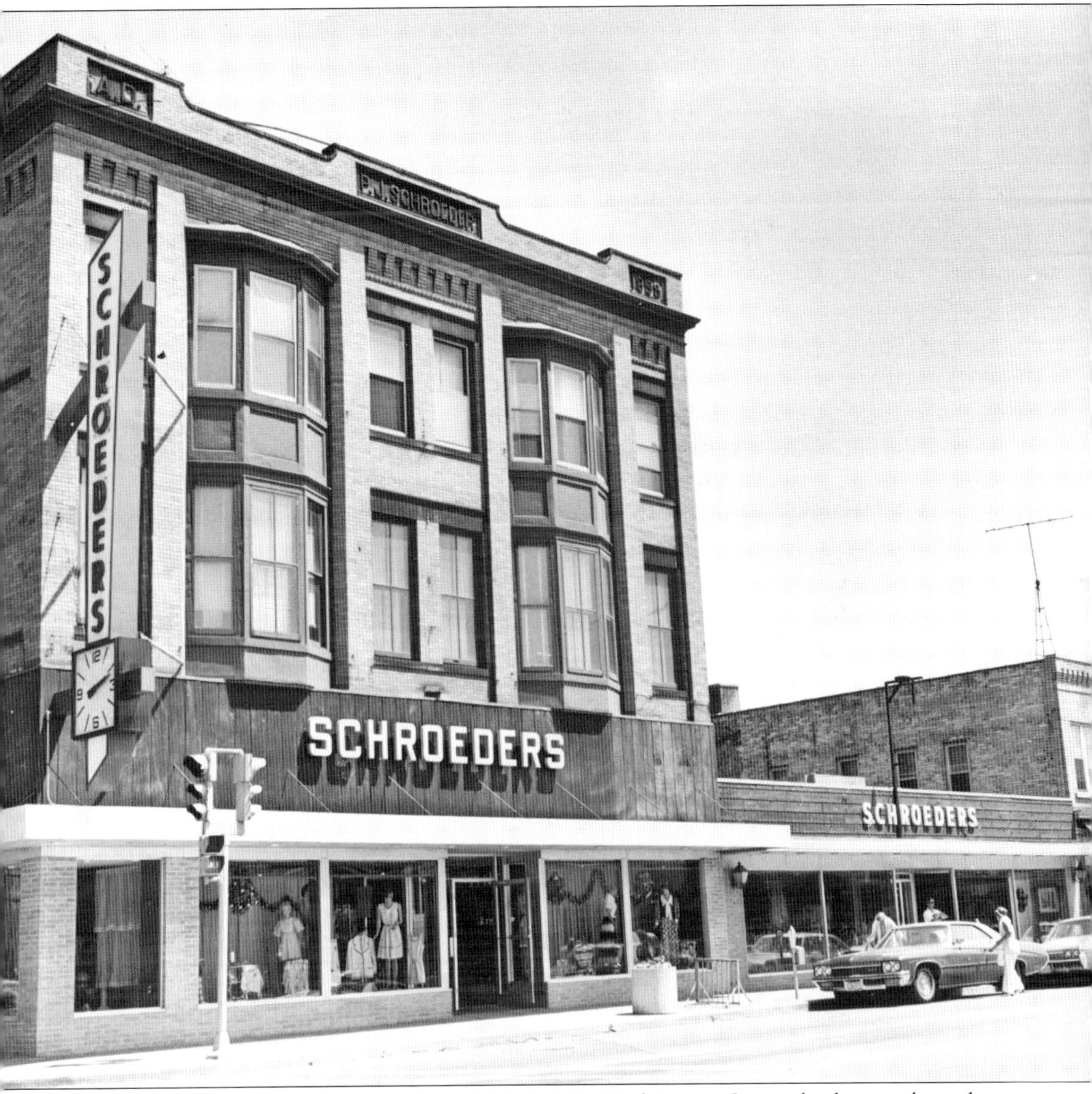

Schroeder's Department Store in the spring of 1975. Washington Street display windows show children's and women's clothing, plus window treatments, footwear, and lingerie were displayed in the windows on the far right. (Courtesy of Schroeder's Department Store.)

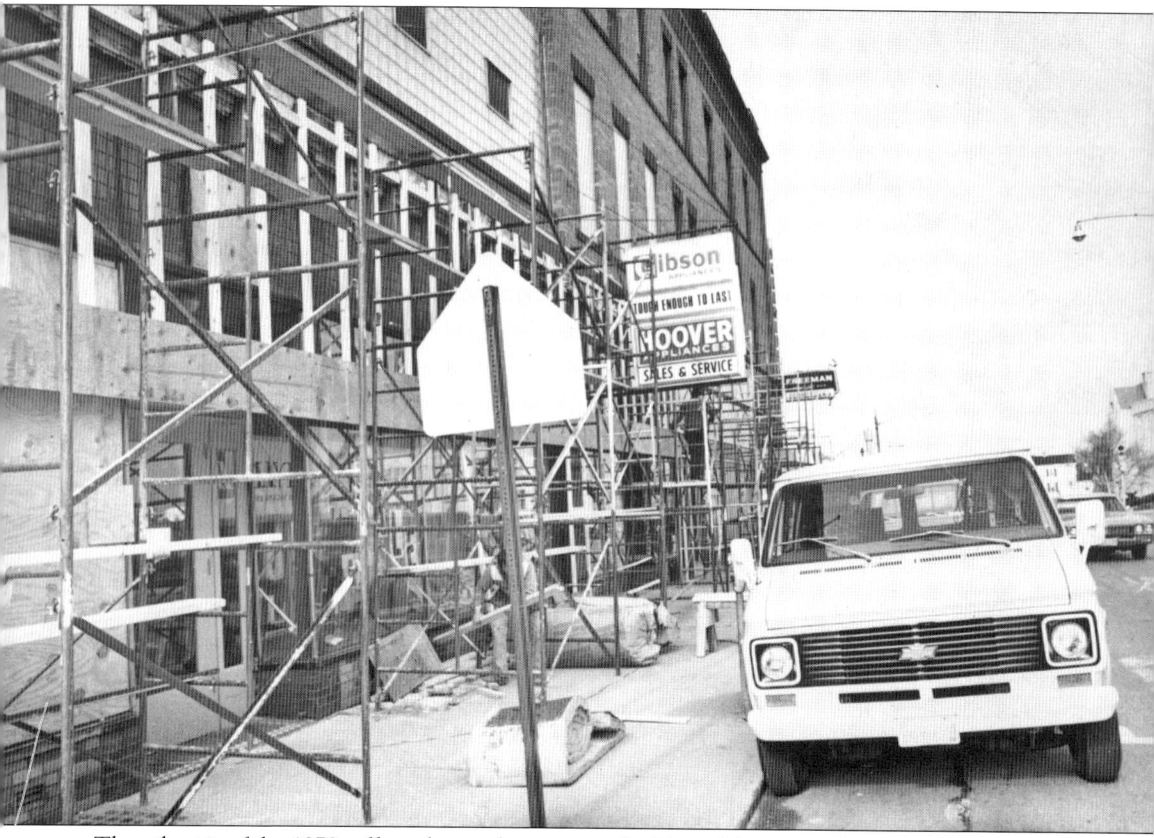

The oil crisis of the 1970s affected every business in the United States, and the Schroeder Building was no different. Large floor-to-ceiling windows, high uninsulated tin ceilings, and poor lighting all contributed to the remodeling changes at Schroeder's. The original tin ceilings were covered with insulated ceiling tiles, and new florescent lights were installed for better electricity conservation. The top halves of the second- and third-floor windows were covered up to conserve energy. The Seventeenth Street side of the building was also remodeled, and the original brick was covered with insulation and wood siding, all in response to the high cost of heating and cooling. (Courtesy of the Schroeder Brothers Company.)

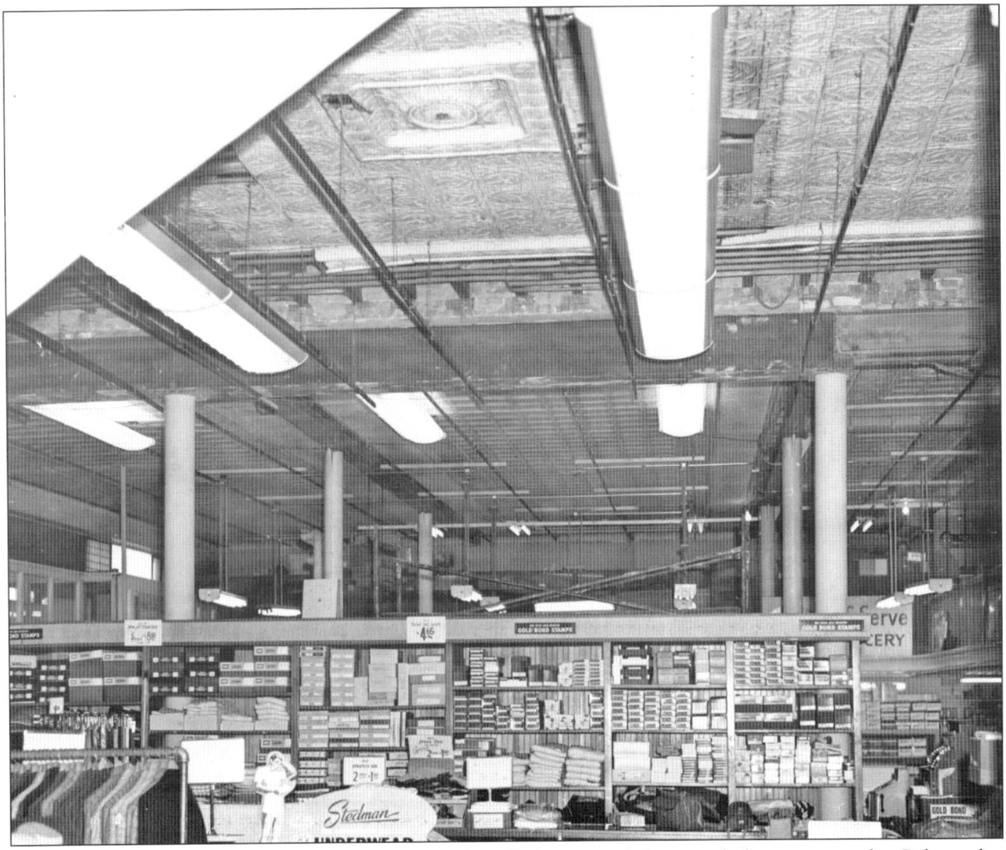

The energy crisis of the 1970s was the cause for all the remodeling and changing at the Schroeder Building. The Seventeenth Street side facade of the building was covered up to make the store easier and cheaper to heat and cool. The large display windows and entrances were reconfigured so the store would lose less heat. During the energy crisis, this remodel shows the beautiful tin ceilings getting ready to be covered up with insulated ceiling tiles for energy conservation. (Courtesy of the Schroeder Brothers Company.)

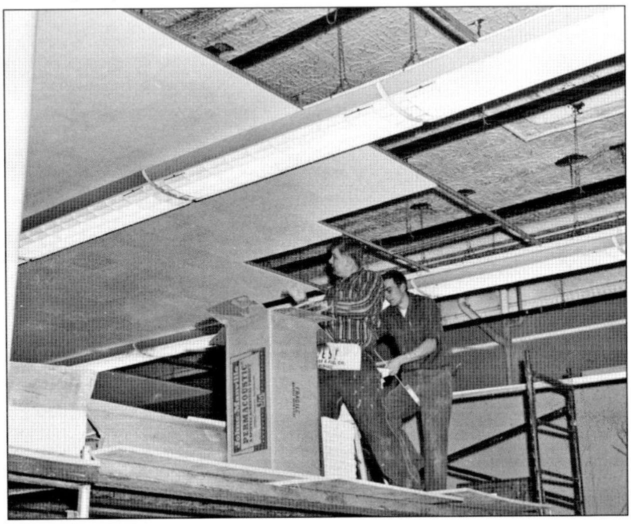

Remodeling experts fit tiles and change over the lighting fixtures throughout the first floor of the Schroeder Building. It was a costly solution to save money on heating. (Courtesy of the Schroeder Brothers Company.)

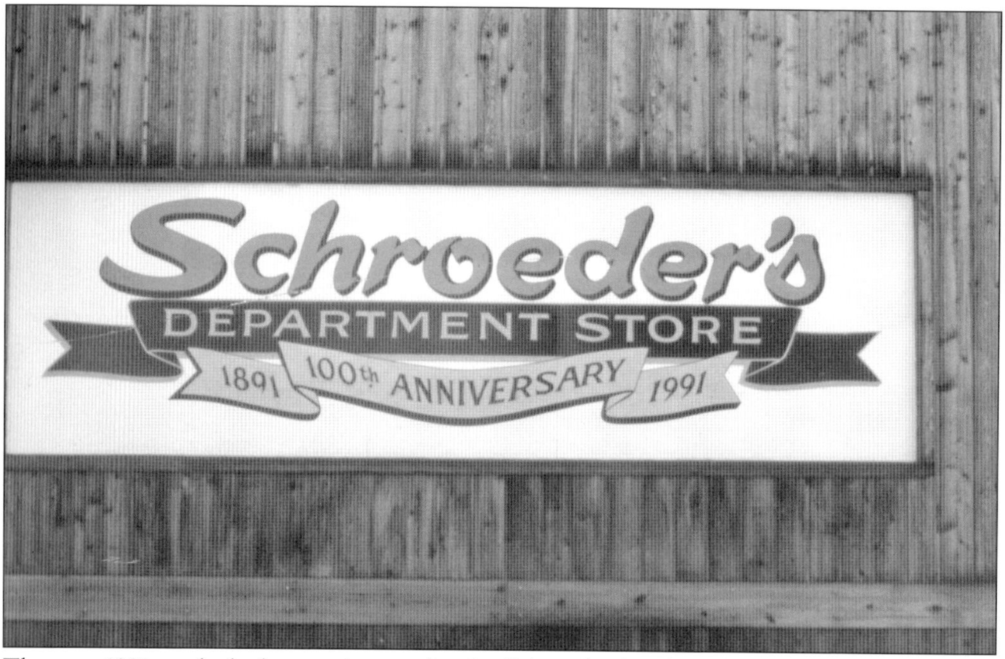

The year 1991 marked a huge milestone for the Schroeder family and the business. Schroeder's celebrated its 100th anniversary in 1991 with a new sign on the back of the building. At the same time, John Schroeder also photographed the side and front of the building. The store promoted all the new remodeling efforts underway inside the different departments in a February 1991 advertisement in the *Herald Times Reporter*. (Courtesy of Schroeder's Department Store.)

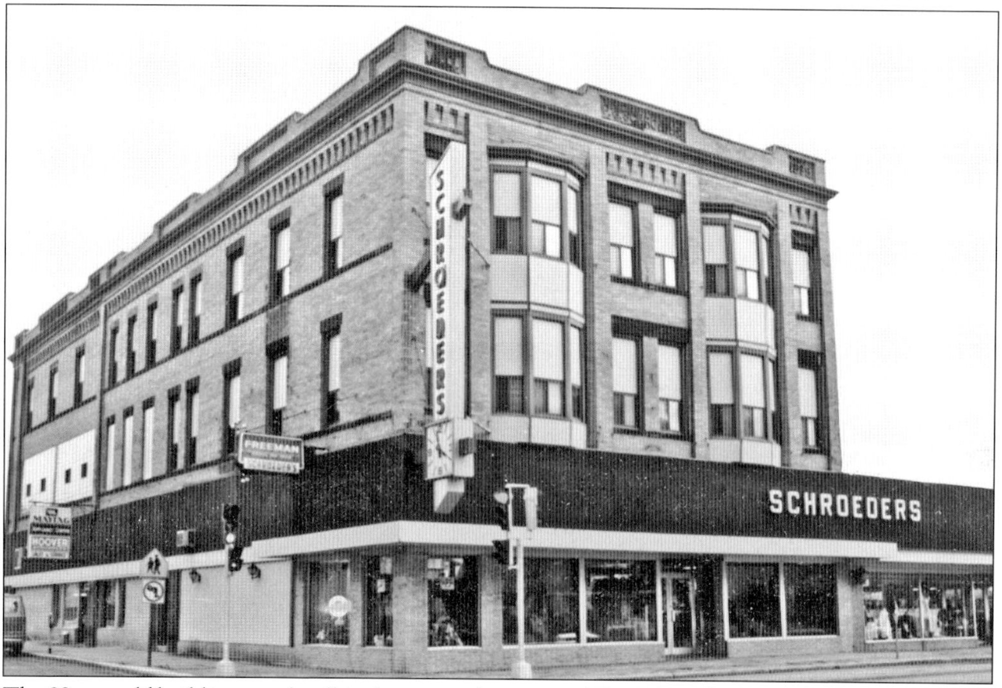

The 92-year-old building stands tall in the quaint downtown. The Schroeder family celebrated 100 years in business at the Washington Street location. (Courtesy of Schroeder's Department Store.)

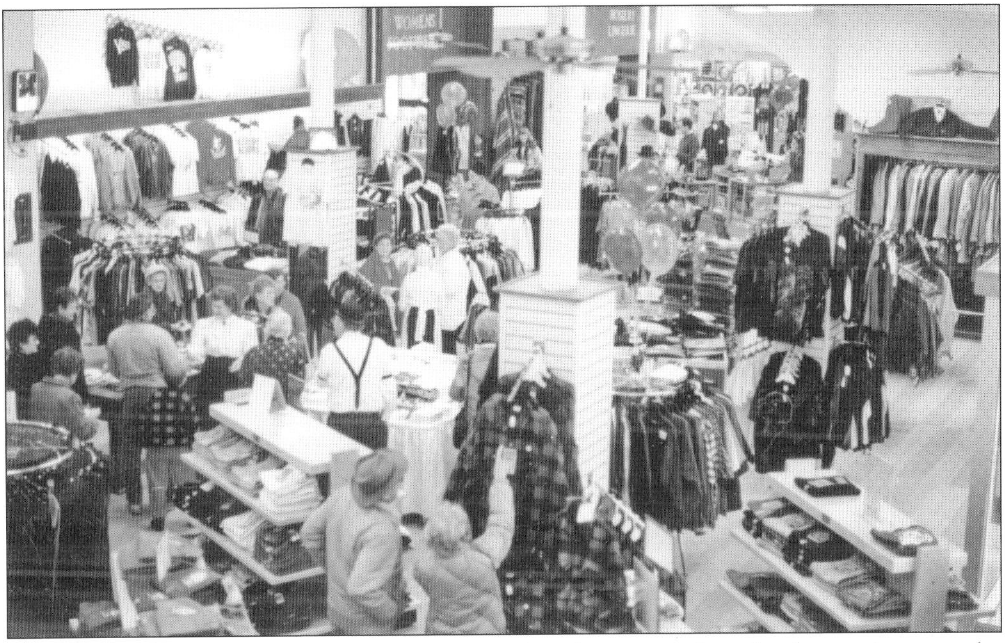

The 100th anniversary was a momentous occasion. In preparations for the anniversary, the Schroeder retail space underwent a small remodel. The men's department had the large support pillars wrapped in slatwall for a better use of selling space. The Two Rivers Historical Society served cake, and there were huge sales storewide. (Courtesy of Schroeder's Department Store.)

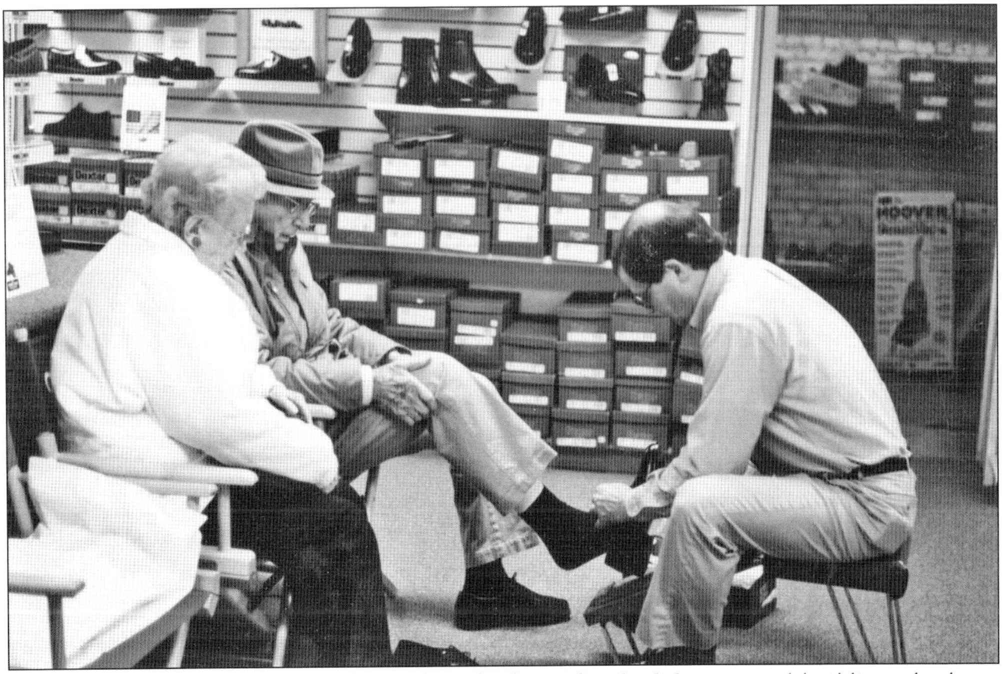

In the men's shoe department, located in the lower level of the original building, the large bookcases used to hold shoes were removed, and slatwall was put up for better displaying of footwear. John is pictured here, helping a customer with a purchase of shoes. (Courtesy of Schroeder's Department Store.)

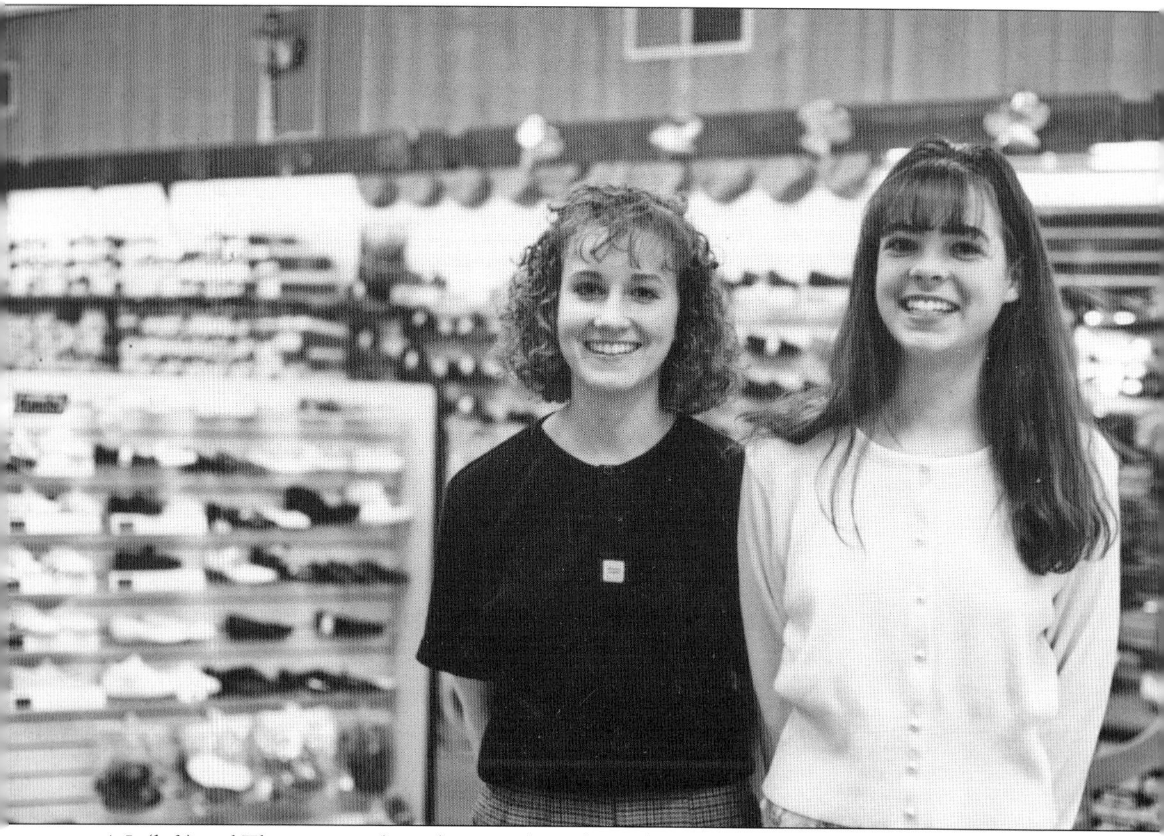

A.J. (left) and Theresa pose for a photograph in the updated women's footwear department. In 1991, three generations of Schroeders were working at the store: managers Tim and John Schroeder; John's daughters A.J., Theresa, and Liz, fourth-generation workers; and Gary Schroeder, second-generation (retired), was hauling garbage for Schroeder's and served a position on the Schroeder's Board of Directors. (Courtesy of Schroeder's Department Store.)

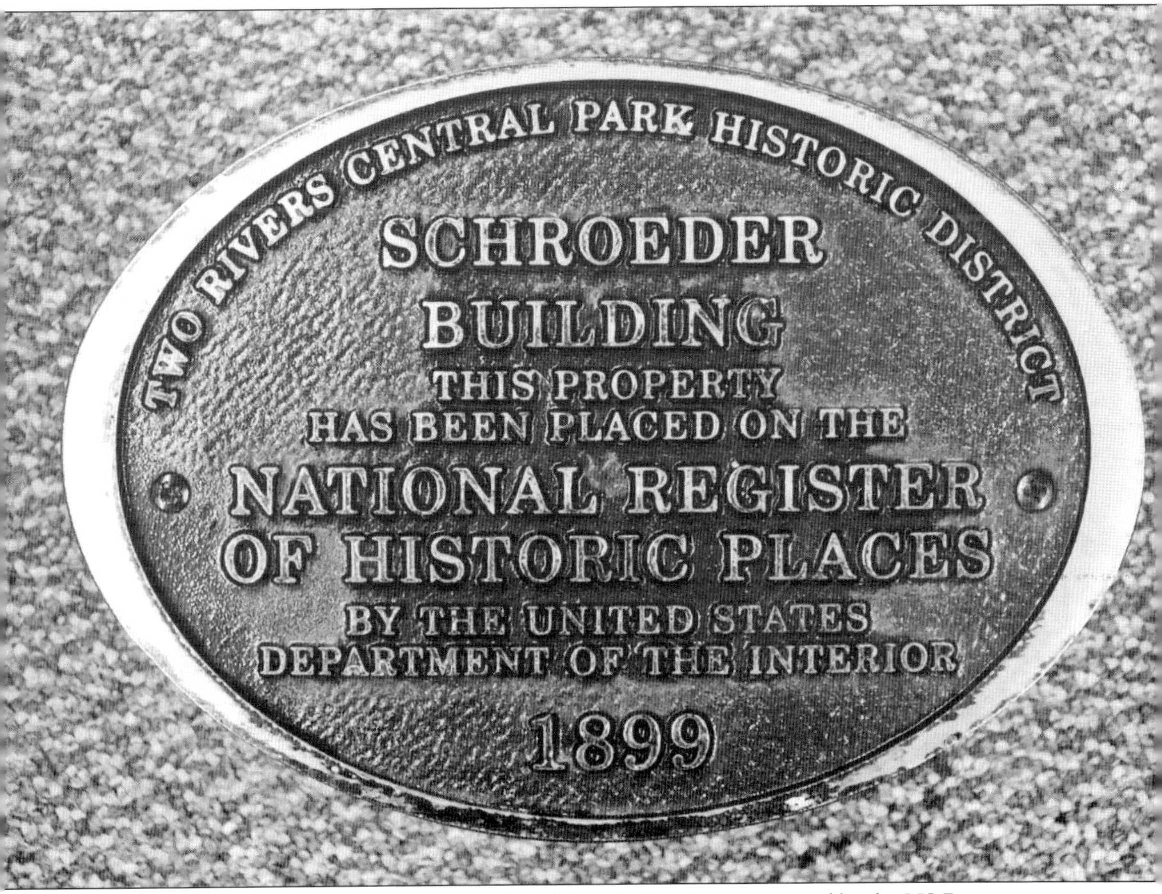

On August 1, 2000, the Two Rivers Central Park Historic District was created by the US Department of the Interior. The historic district, as stated in the application, is a two-and-one-half-block section in a small city in northeastern Wisconsin. The pictured plaque was on the corner of the Schroeder Building. (Courtesy of Julie Schroeder.)

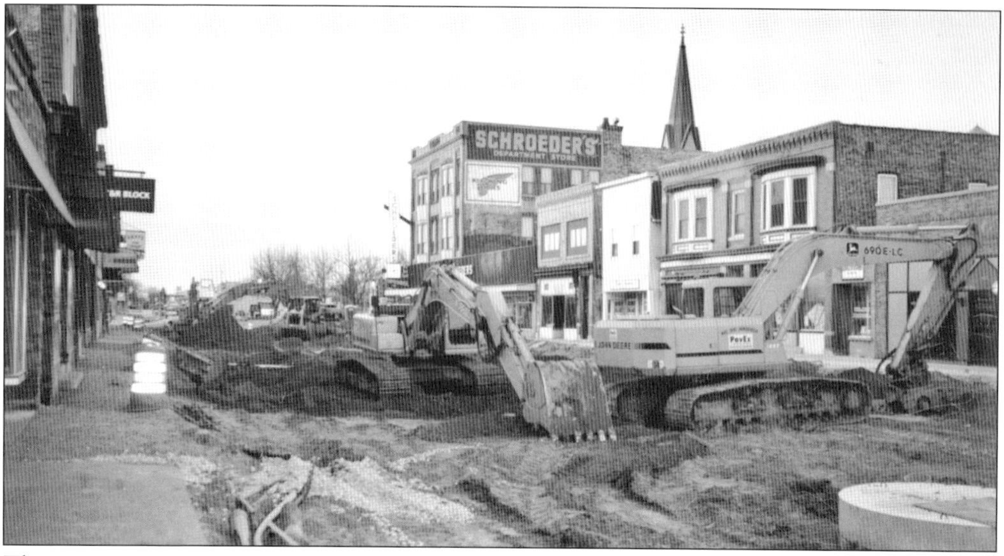

The year 2005 was a big year for Schroeder's and the city of Two Rivers. Major upgrades to Highway 42 (Washington Street) were long overdue. The last time any improvements were made was in 1955. This view and the one below looks north on downtown Two Rivers, Wisconsin. The entire previous year, John and Tim Schroeder attended city meetings to discuss the streetscape and target dates of the street project. The entire downtown underwent a total renovation. Lateral plumbing, electrical lines, and Wi-Fi cables were all replaced with 2005 technology. (Courtesy of Schroeder's Department Store.)

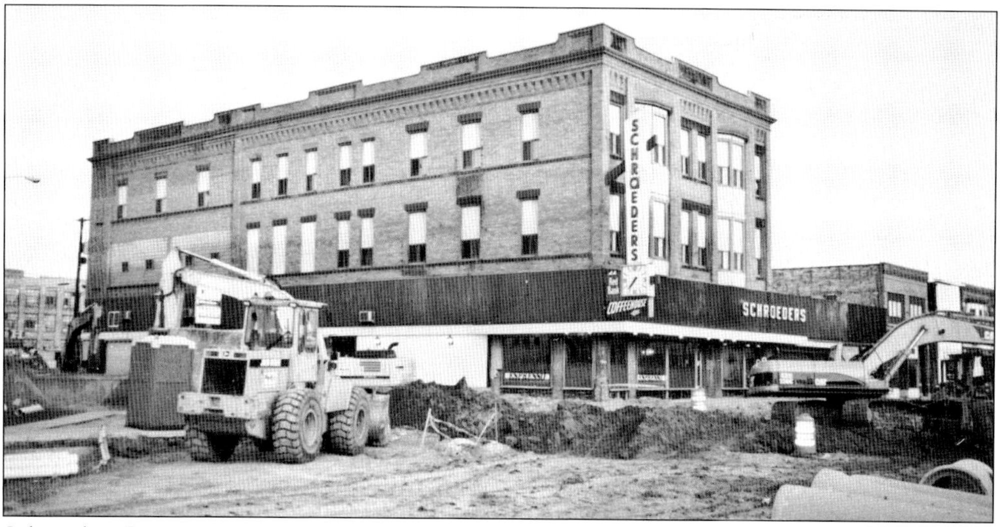

Schroeder's Department Store was fortunate to have several different entrances and a rear parking lot for customers to access the store. Schroeder's received a facelift, not by the choice of John Schroeder but due to the removal of the sidewalks around the store. Early one morning, a crew started removing the sidewalks on Washington Street in front of Schroeder's, but little did anyone realize that the front brick facade was resting on the sidewalk and was not braced. In removing the sidewalk, the bricks fell into the tunnels of Schroeder's. Schroeder's tunnels went along the front of the original building and wrapped around onto Seventeenth Street. So, the Schroeder Building received new sidewalks and a new brick facade in the summer of 2005. This image shows the missing brick facade. (Courtesy of Schroeder's Department Store.)

Two

Many Facets of Schroeder's

In the early stages of the Schroeder business, the Schroeder brothers focused on a few different businesses. Some business dealings helped stimulate traffic in Schroeder's Department Store. Since 1891, each managing generation put its stamp in the store. Peter Schroeder was moved to open a bank after contact from the federal government in the early 1900s. Finally, in 1979, all Schroeder ownership of the bank was sold. Peter also invested in a mill northwest of the train depot in Two Rivers, Wisconsin. Up until the 1970s, customers could visit the mill and buy bulk bird food, rabbit food, and grains. Bulk coffee beans were a popular commodity available at the Schroeder Mill and the grocery department at Schroeder's. The Two Rivers Cooperative purchased the mill from Schroeder Brothers Company, Inc., in 1964.

Since then, the store has seen many services and products come and go. With this in mind, A.J. wanted to help Two Rivers by creating a business incubator inside her family's building. Starting a business and maintaining a business is a tough venture, and A.J. sought out businesses that would complement her business model and drive more foot traffic in her building. The Schroeder Building offers 20,000 square feet of retail space. Schroeder's Department Store only uses 9,000 square feet and rents out the remainder to four other businesses. While the monetary rent helps cover overhead costs like utilities and taxes, the other businesses all complement each other and share the customer base. It is a one-stop shop for many of the customers that cross the threshold into the century-old building. All six businesses are women owned.

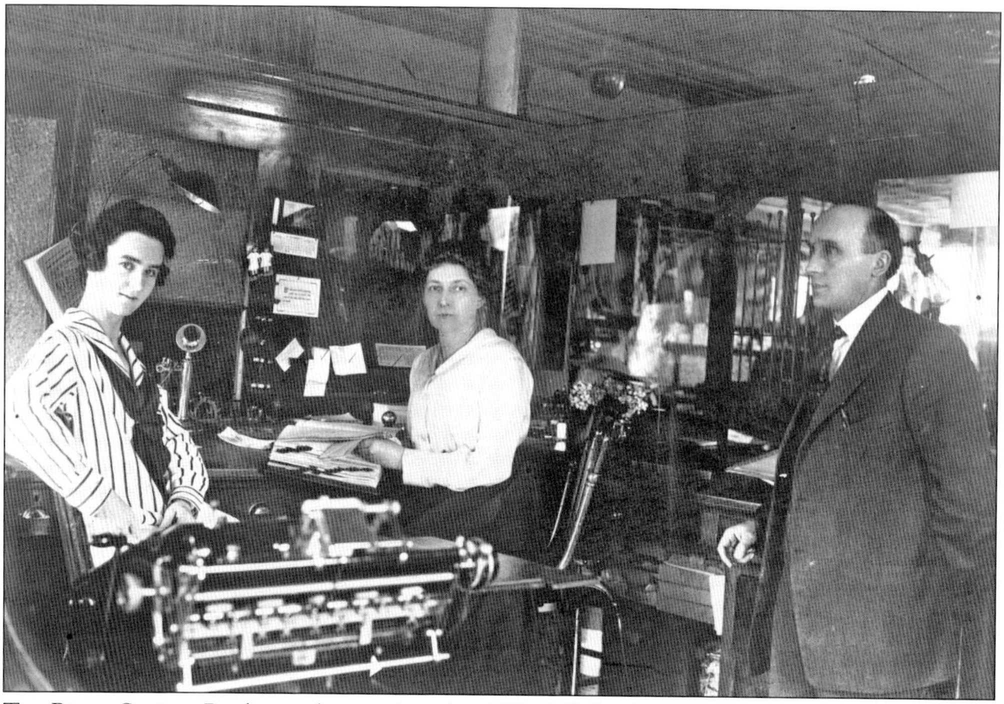

Two Rivers Savings Bank was chartered on April 27, 1902. Little documentation is found this early in the Schroeder's history. During the grocery department era, the men would take the farmers' goods like eggs, milk, and butter, and in exchange for the goods, he would give the farmers credit on account. The federal government contacted Peter Schroeder and informed him he was running a bank. In true Schroeder fashion, he started the Two Rivers Savings Bank. This photograph captures three of Two Rivers Savings Bank employees in September 1918. (Courtesy of Naidl Photography and the Schroeder Brothers Company)

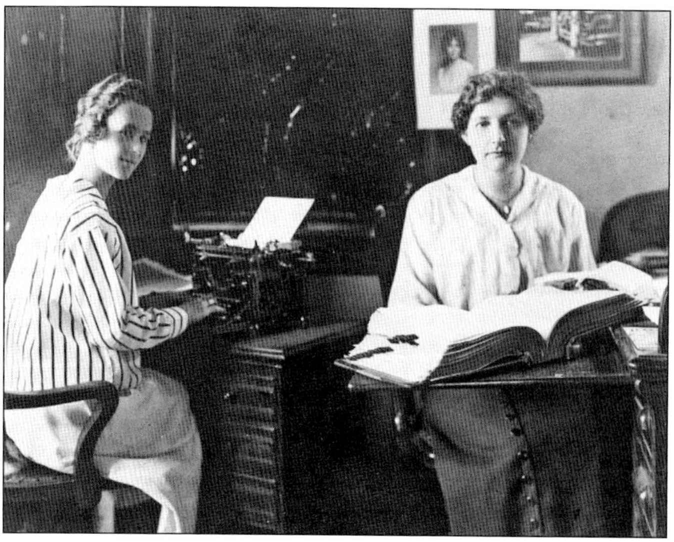

The Two Rivers Savings Bank was located in northwest corner of the Schroeder Building. The Red Bank Coffeehouse now occupies this corner. The Two Rivers Savings Bank was nicknamed the "Red Bank," and the "White Bank" occupies the corner of Sixteenth and Washington Streets. In later years, the bank moved to the corner of Washington and Eighteenth Streets in the Empire Building. (Courtesy of Schroeder's Department Store.)

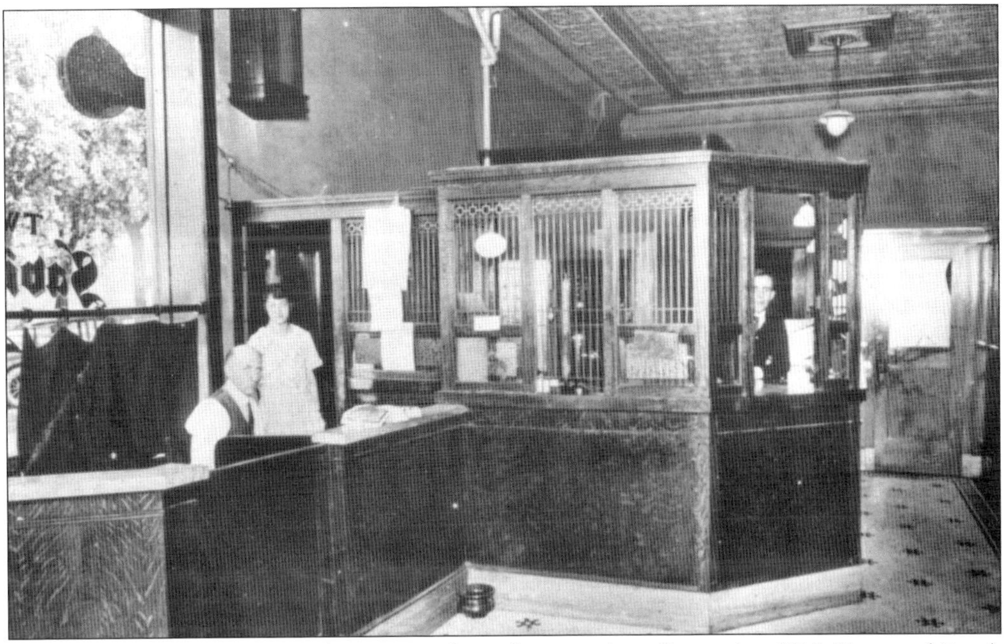

Two Rivers Savings Bank employees pose for a photograph in September 1918. Peter and Frank Schroeder managed the bank for three decades, and each held executive seats on the board of directors. In 1935, the Two Rivers Savings Bank merged with the Tisch Mills State Bank and Mishicot State Bank and moved to the Empire Building located on the northeast corner of Eighteenth and Washington Streets. The Schroeder family sold its stock in the Two Rivers Savings Bank in 1979. (Courtesy of Naidl Photography and the Schroeder Brothers Company.)

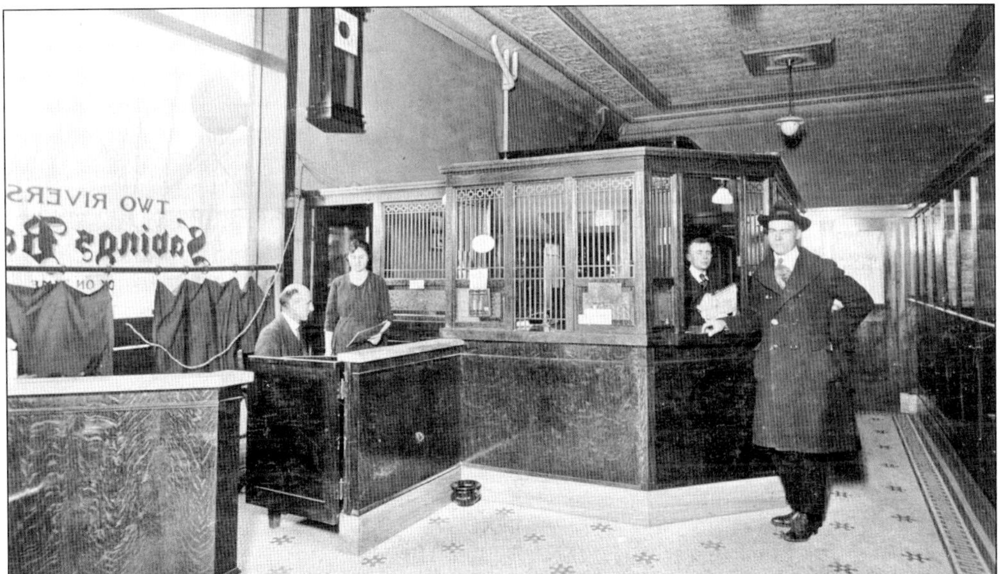

This is a view of the bank from the front corner entrance. This corner entrance was covered up in the 1930s, and Schroeder's created a central entrance to the building. The original entrance is covered up behind the current facade. This photograph shows the bank teller with a customer visiting the counter. (Courtesy of the Schroeder Brothers Company.)

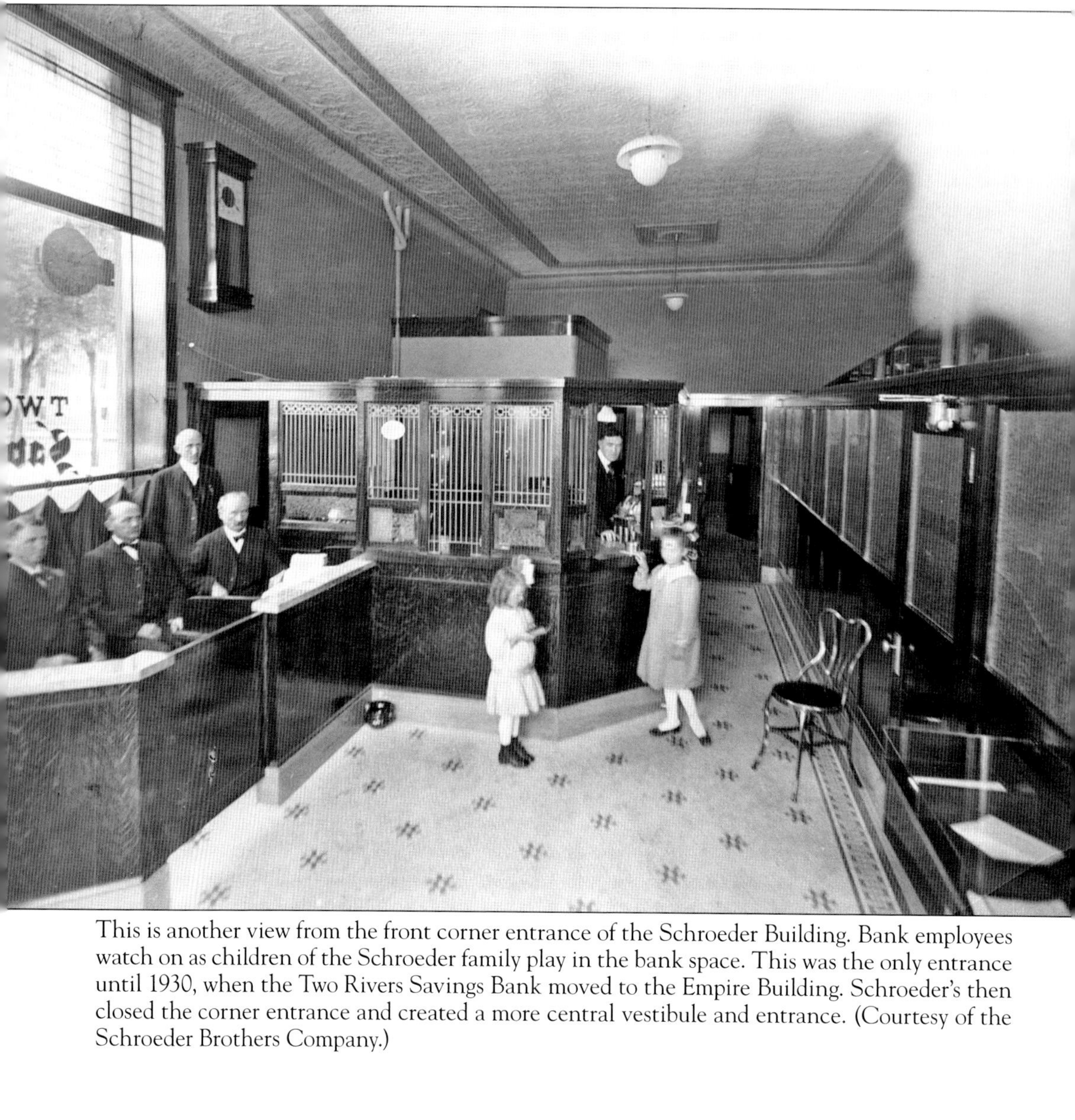

This is another view from the front corner entrance of the Schroeder Building. Bank employees watch on as children of the Schroeder family play in the bank space. This was the only entrance until 1930, when the Two Rivers Savings Bank moved to the Empire Building. Schroeder's then closed the corner entrance and created a more central vestibule and entrance. (Courtesy of the Schroeder Brothers Company.)

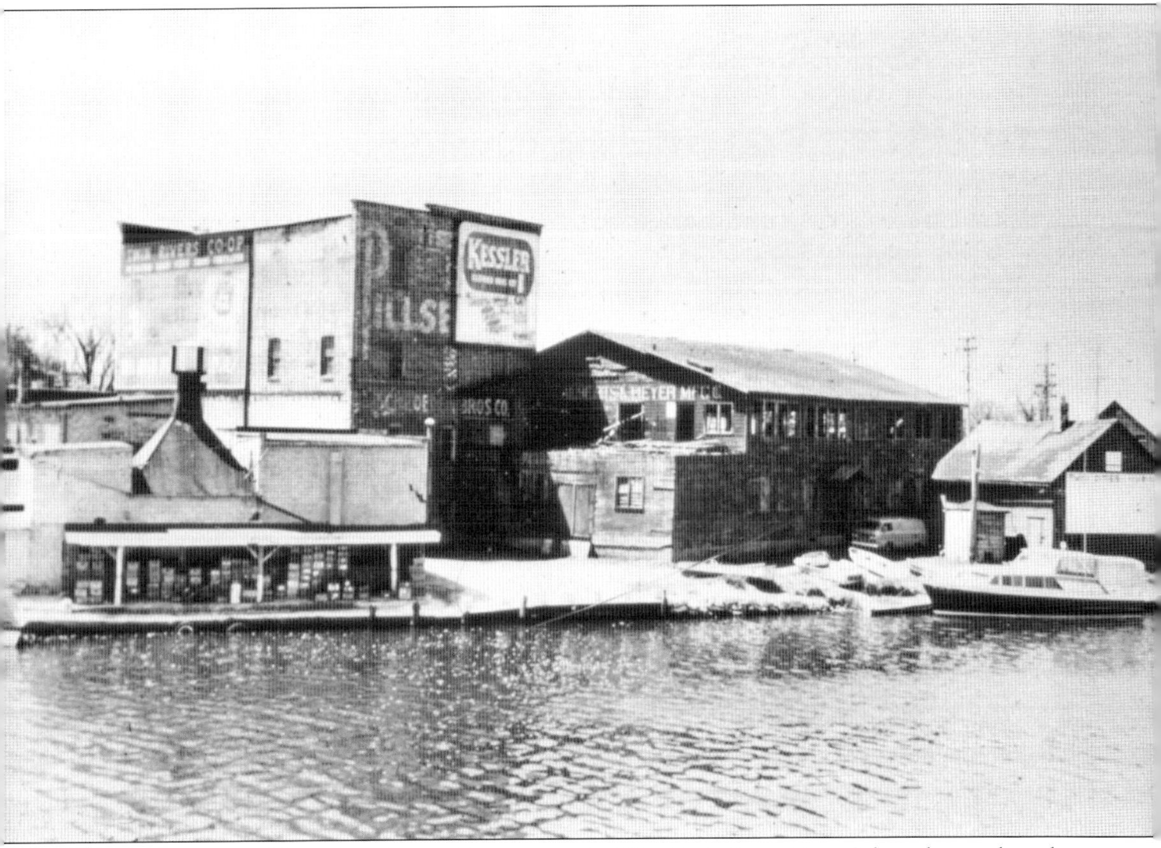

This is a river view of the Schroeder Mill located on the West Twin River. Peter Schroeder purchased the mill in 1895 and was a popular place for local farmers to sell their goods. The railroad tracks were adjacent to the mill, and it was common to see loads of barley, corn, and flour waiting to be shipped out of town. (Courtesy of Schroeder's Department Store.)

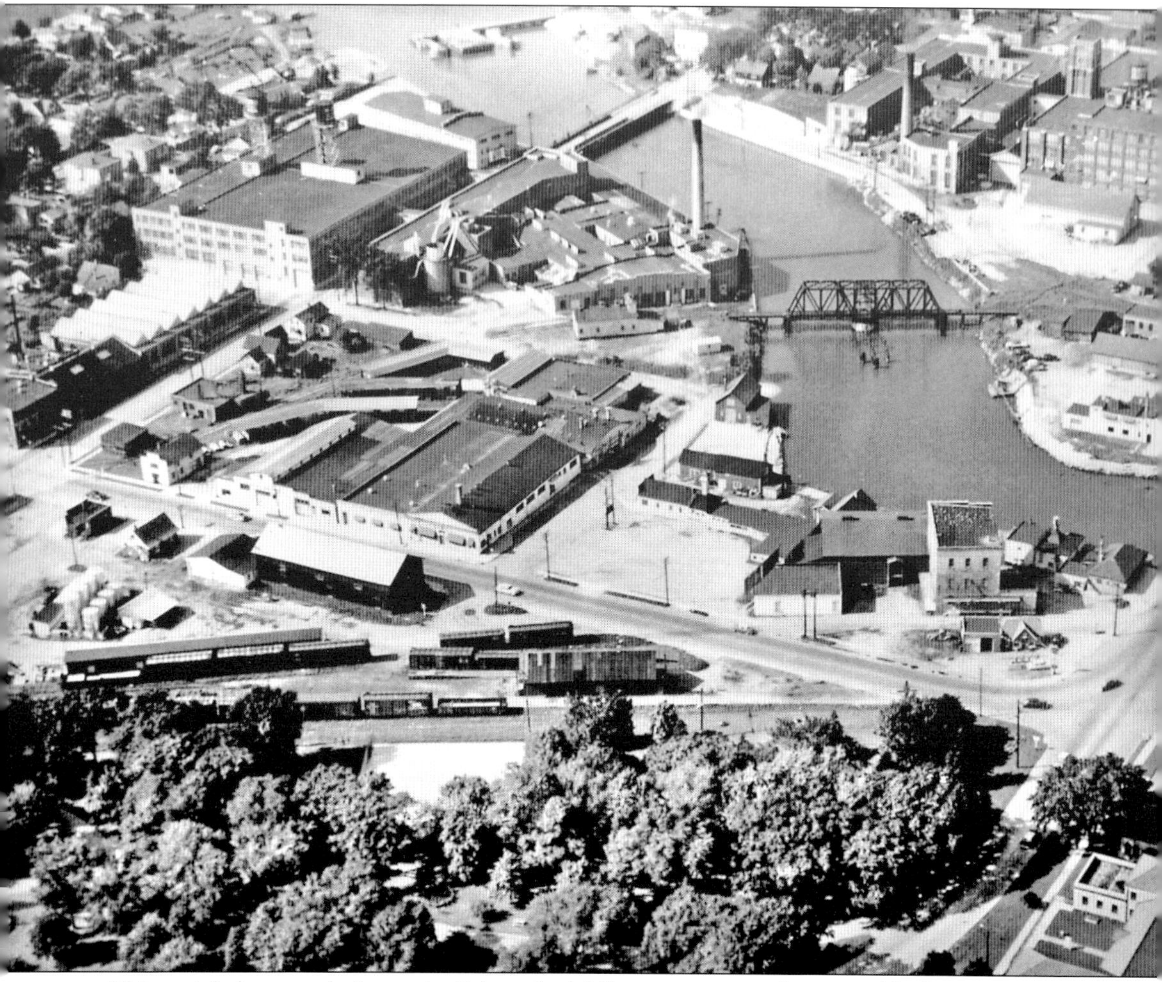

This aerial photograph shows the Schroeder Mill encompassing the entire block on the river. In the background, the railroad bridge is awaiting the arrival of the train. The train delivered goods to the mill and hauled the farmers' products out. (Courtesy of Schroeder's Department Store.)

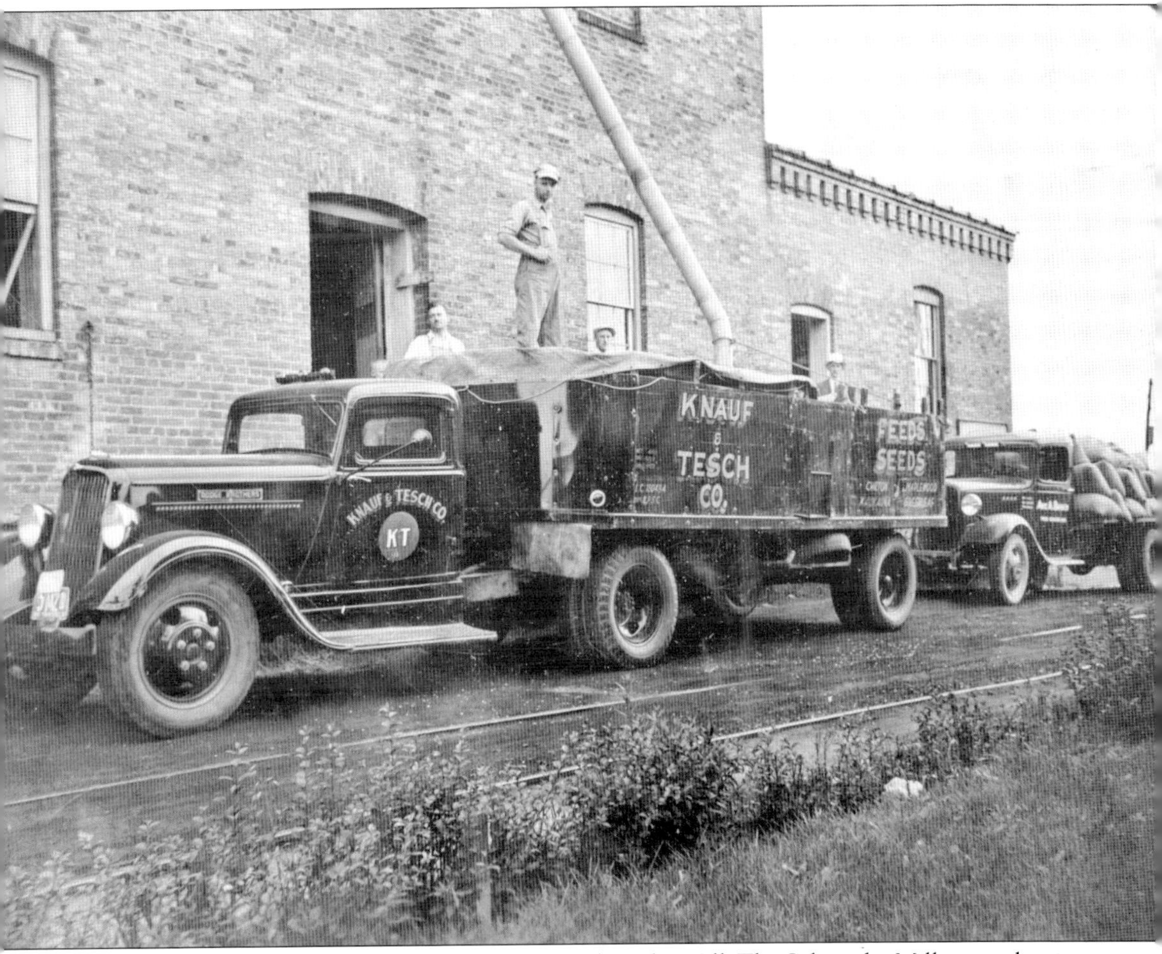

These trucks are loaded up with product from the Schroeder Mill. The Schroeder Mill was a place for farmers to sell and buy products. In addition to selling items at the mill, Schroeder's would also sell some items in the Schroeder's grocery department. Coffee, flour, and animal feeds were all common purchases at the mill. (Courtesy of Schroeder's Department Store.)

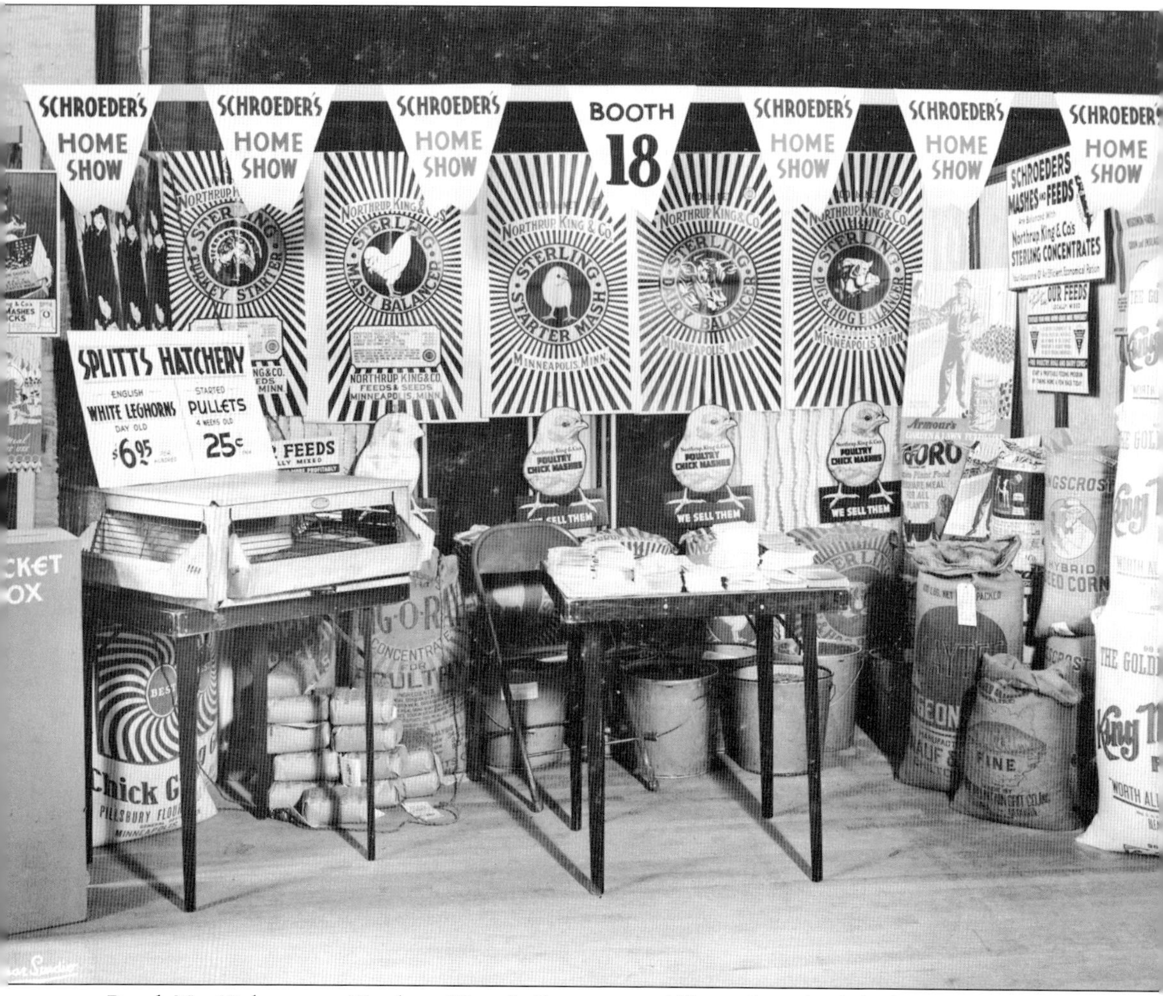

Booth No. 18 showcases Northrup King & Company and Kaytee brands of chicken feed. Schroeder's Department Store was a big supplier to farmers of the Two Rivers area, and in return farmers brought in goods to sell at Schroeder's. The Home Show was held at the J.E. Hamilton Community House. (Courtesy of Vassar Studio and the Schroeder Brothers Company.)

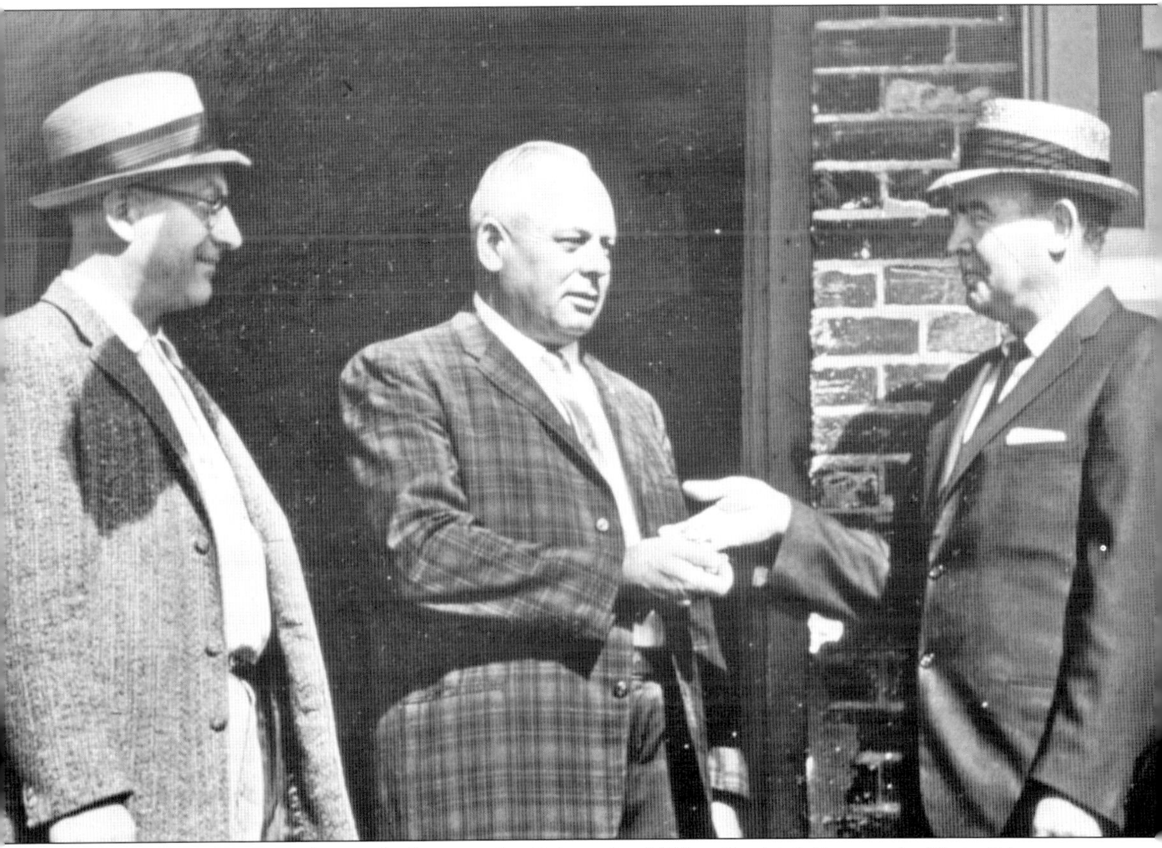

Hilary Schroeder turned over the keys to the Schroeder Mill to Fredrick Strutz, the Twin Rivers Cooperative president in 1964. The mill offered the new buyers a molasses mixer for feed and the needed facility for added growth. (Courtesy of the *Two Rivers Reporter*.)

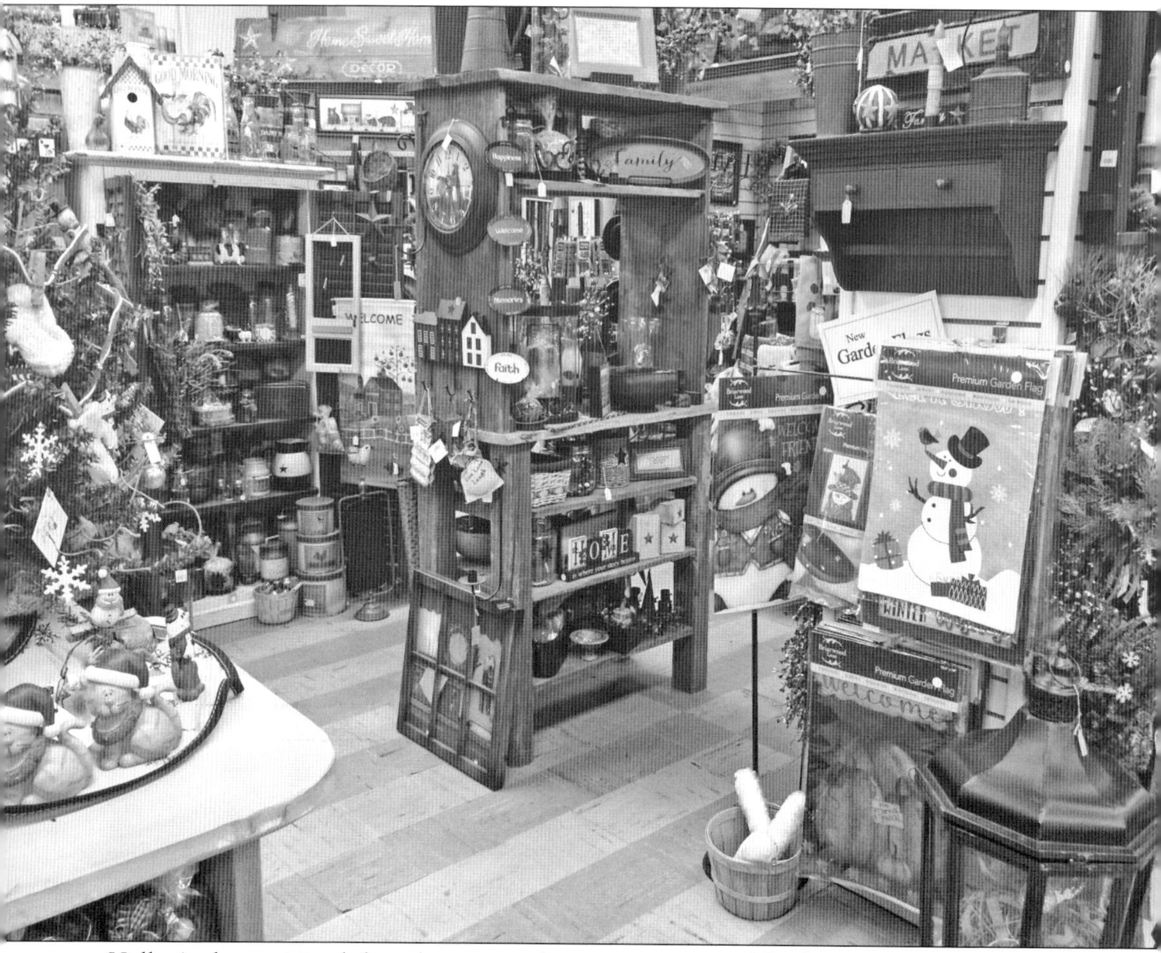

Holly Anderson joined the other women business owners in fall of 2014. She features a variety of primitive home decorating, seasonal décor, and candles and waxes. (Courtesy of Schroeder's Department Store.)

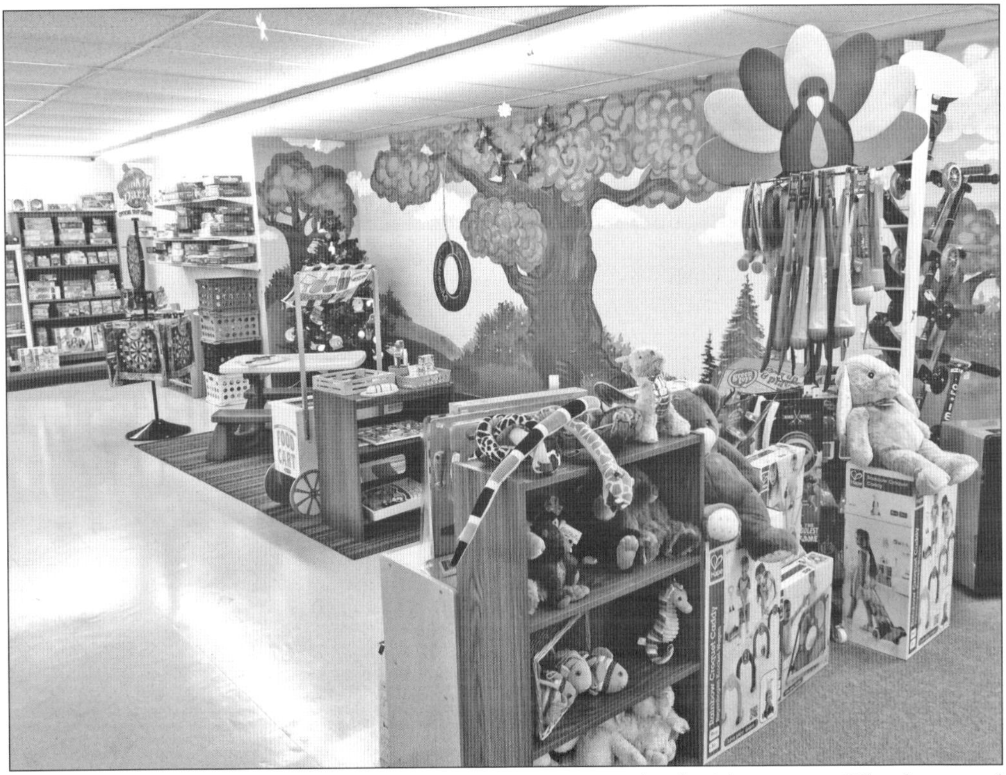

Pam Duveneck reached out to A.J. as a way to cross promote each other's businesses. What happened next was a leap of faith. Pam expanded several times while leasing space from Schroeder's. She went from a space of 1,000 square feet, to 1,700 square feet in a lower level to finding her forever home with 3,000 square feet. (Courtesy of Schroeder's Department Store.)

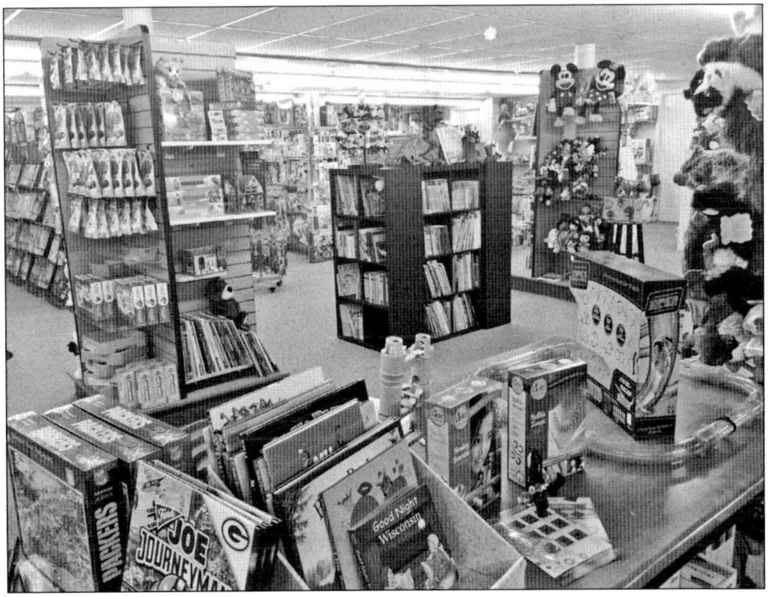

This is another photograph of the Read Apple, which features games and puzzles for all ages and toys. Pam Duveneck's first career was as a kindergarten teacher and she used that knowledge to help her customers buy unique, quality toys. (Courtesy of Schroeder's Department Store.)

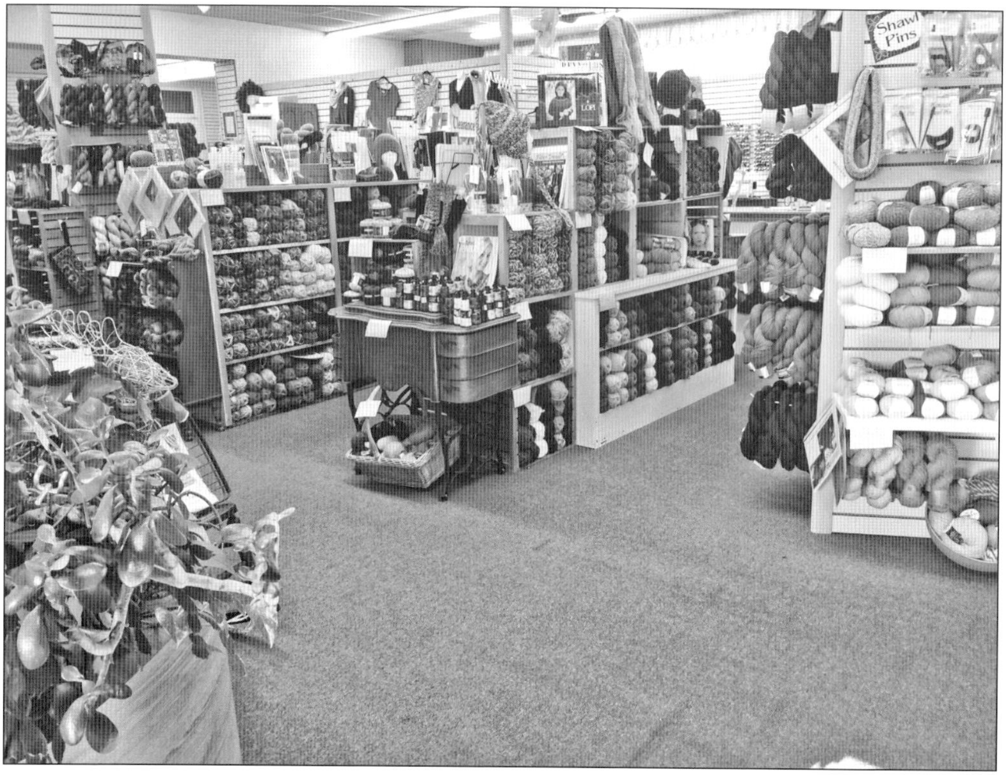

Linda Hansen was able to purchase Intertwined Yarn Shop in 2012. Linda has a diverse retail background, and her mom once owned a yarn and quilt shop in Door County, Wisconsin. She brings her love of creativity to all she meets. She actively participates in the annual Fiber Frolics and offers lessons and classes. (Courtesy of Schroeder's Department Store.)

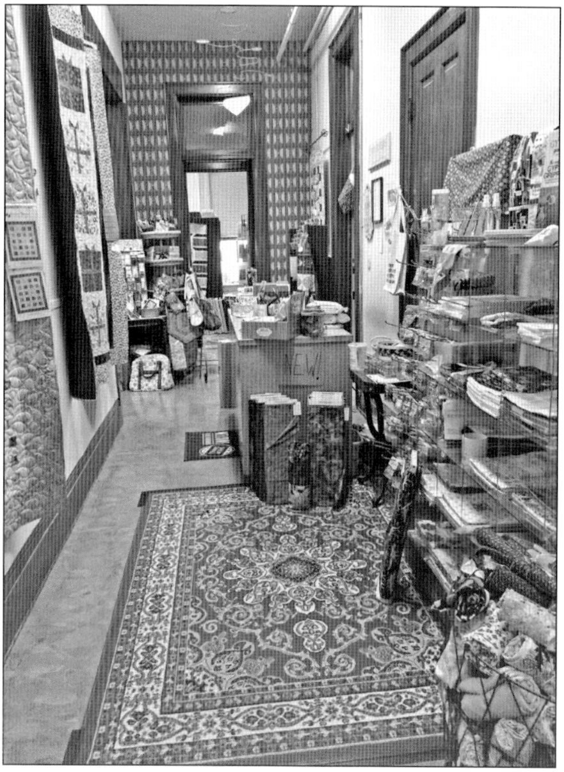

The Quilt Shop of Two Rivers calls the doctor's quarters its home at Schroeder's. Three local doctors called on patients in this space until the 1960s. Sarah Gallagher restored the space and created a quilt shop. She manages to use every nook and cranny of the space, and people from all over the Midwest visit and shop her unique selections of fabric. (Courtesy of Schroeder's Department Store.)

Three

Departments Here and Gone

It was always a struggle to let a department close at Schroeder's, but if it meant they could better serve another area of business, the managers cut ties to that area. Never an easy choice, but many factors were examined and a decision was made. Many decades would sometimes pass before a department was cut. Primary factors were sales and costs; however, opinions of the board of directors and managers also played a huge part. During many board meetings, discussions about the profitability of groceries, appliances, and window treatments would take place. As Theresa Kronforst would review the minute books for board meetings, discussions took place over many meetings about how to increase profit in the grocery department. The board of directors was typically made up of family members, but sometimes, local non-family members were invited to serve on the board of directors. Having a variety of different backgrounds and viewpoints would help owners and managers constantly think outside the box to solve a problem. A decision to close a department was never taken lightly. Schroeder's began its general store with groceries, hardware, apparel, and footwear. It expanded to offering appliances, draperies, children's apparel and footwear, fabrics, and gifts. Currently, the Schroeder team is focused on selling quality men's and women's apparel and footwear. They continue to offer an alterations department that can fix and alter almost any type of clothing—and if one purchases a pair of pants from Schroeder's and needs them shortened, the alteration is free. Purchase an item somewhere else, and they will alter it for a nominal fee. In addition to apparel and footwear, Schroeder's owns and operates the Red Bank Coffeehouse, which opened in November 1997. At the end of the day, Schroeder's attributes their success to good leadership and great employees. Many times, one can hear A.J. say, "Treat the customer how you would want to be treated." Knowledge of products, friendliness, and service are all very important to the Schroeder model of success. A person does not get that from big-box stores or online. Schroeder's still offers knowledgeable, friendly service with every product it sells. Whether it is a cup of nitro coffee or a pair of jeans, hemming a suit, or selling a pair of casual shoes, the staff at Schroeder's knows their products. They also volunteer heavily in the community, send their kids to school in Two Rivers, and shop in the local businesses.

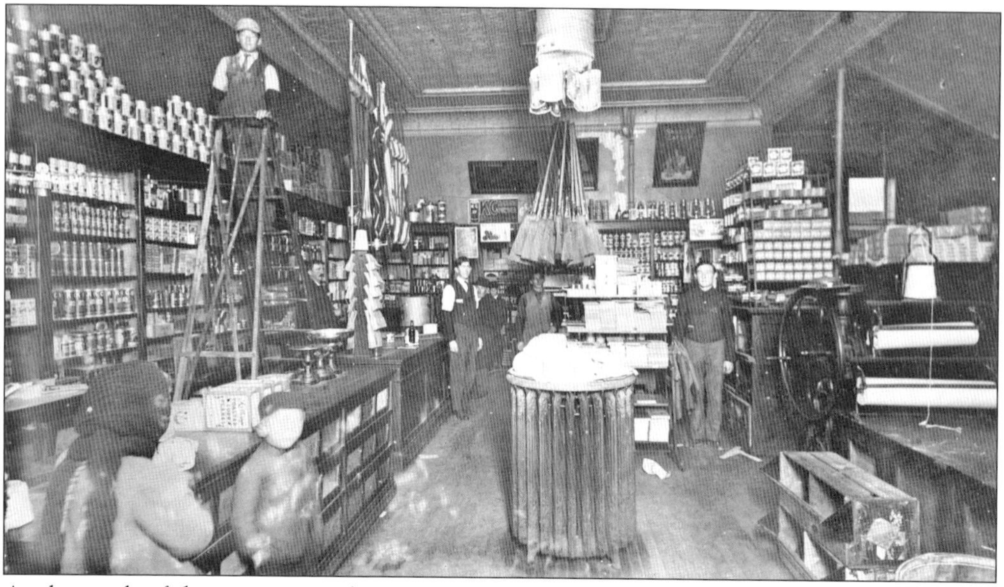

As the needs of the customer and community changed, so did the departments at Schroeder's. After the 1912 addition to the east of the original building, more room was created to add and expand a few areas of Schroeder's. The grocery department was a part of Schroeder's since its opening in 1891. This interior photograph showcases the large grocery department. Farmers from the area would bring in their produce, and Schroeder's would give them credit in the store. Gary Schroeder remembers a delivery of bananas arriving and a tarantula crawling out a day later. (Courtesy of Schroeder's Department Store.)

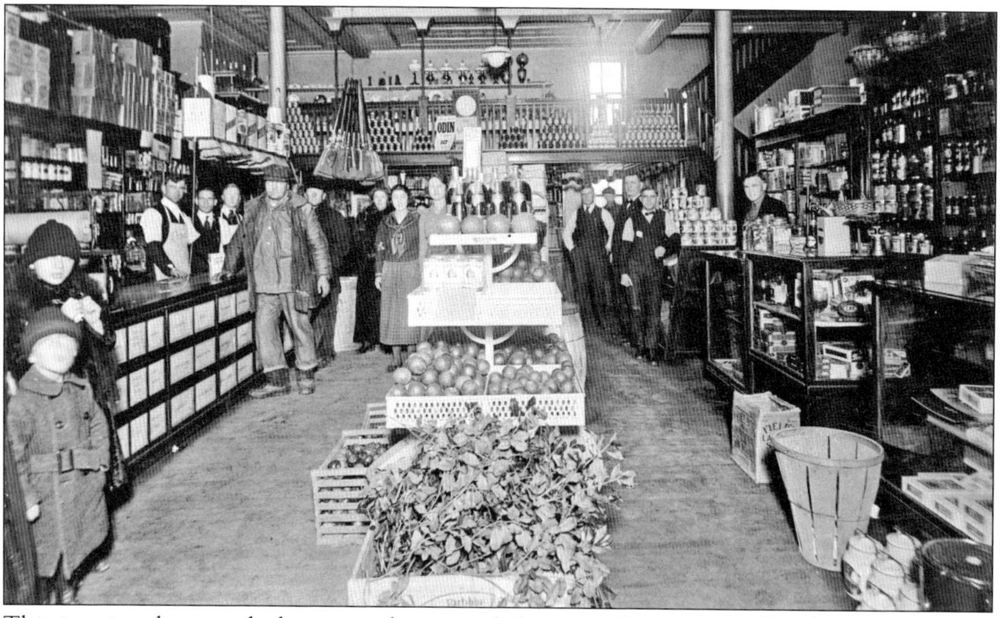

This interior photograph showcases the expanded grocery department after the 1912 addition. The addition gave more room to add more grocery selection. More vegetables and fruits, bulk candies, and canned goods. In 1938, there was discussion on how to improve the sales in the grocery department. They focused on cutting deliveries and having customers carry as much as they can at the time of purchase. (Courtesy of Schroeder's Department Store.)

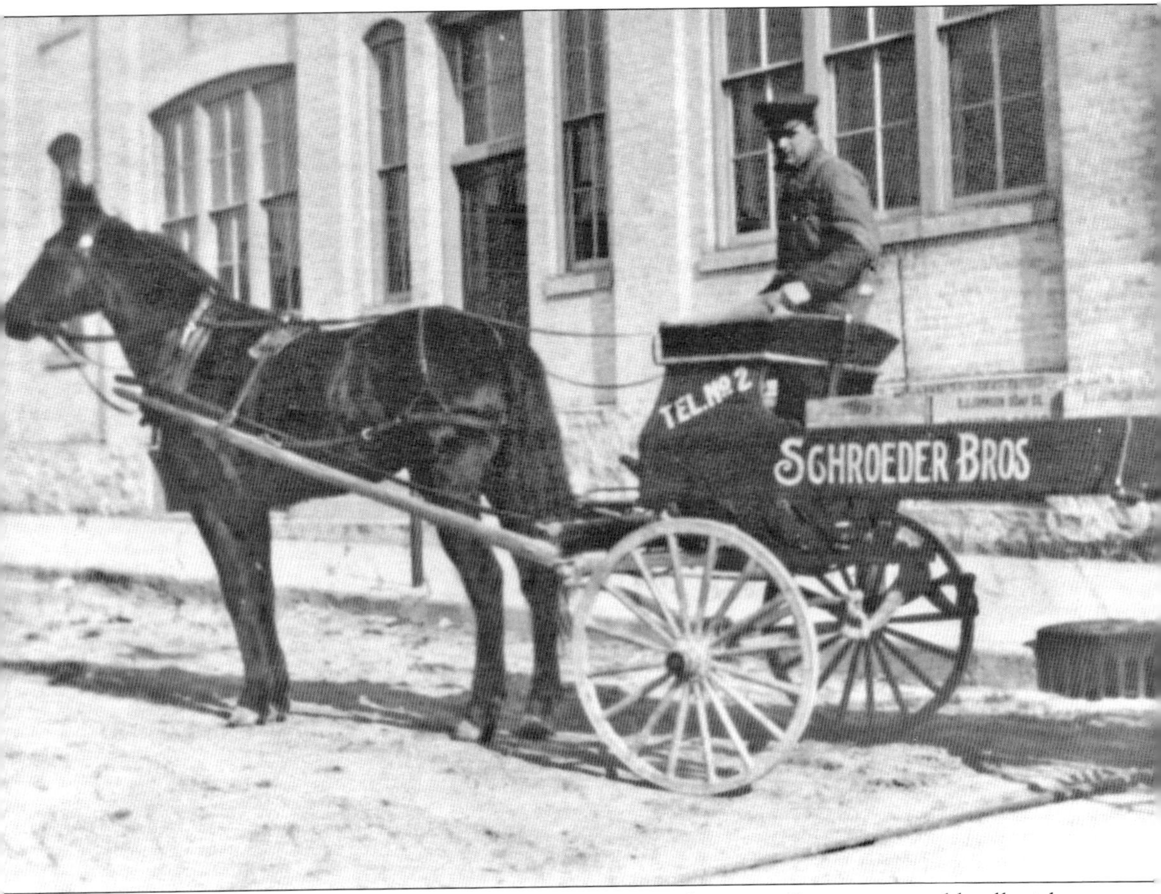

Goods and groceries were originally delivered by horse and wagon. Customers would call with the list of groceries, and an employee would deliver the groceries. Schroeder's stables were behind the building. Schroeder's phone number was No. 2, the brewery was No. 1, and fire/police was No. 3. (Courtesy of Schroeder's Department Store.)

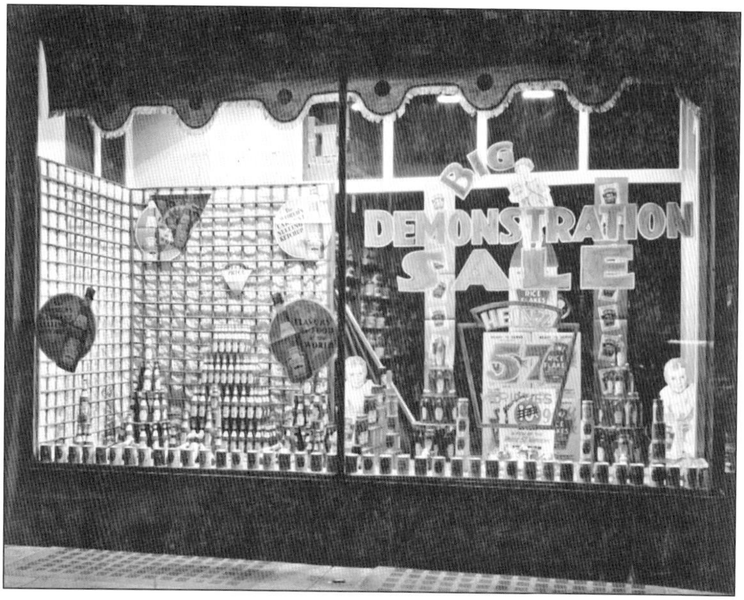

This image of the Schroeder's Department Store Seventeenth Street display window was captured by the Braun Studio of Two Rivers, Wisconsin. A painted sign on the window announced a big demonstration sale with a large Heinz ketchup bottle display. (Courtesy of the Paul J. Braun Studio and Schroeder's Department Store)

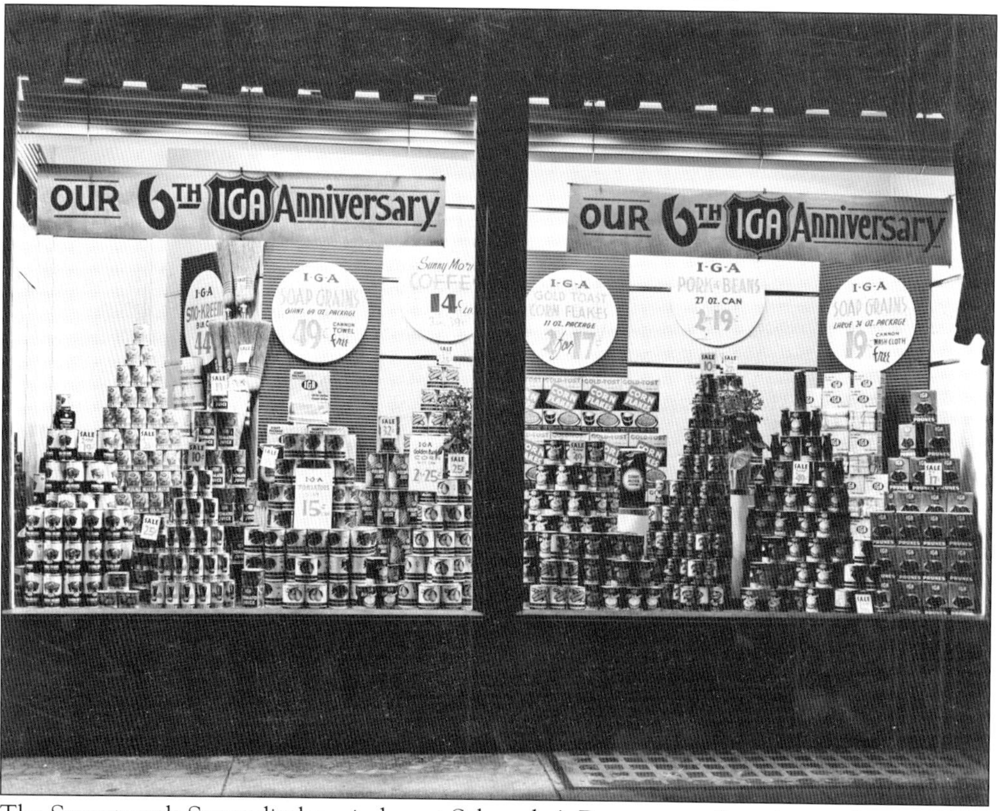

The Seventeenth Street display window at Schroeder's Department Store is seen here in 1932. Schroeder's was promoting the sixth anniversary of the Independent Grocers Alliance (IGA). The IGA was founded in 1926, bringing together independent grocers across the United States to ensure that the trusted, family-owned local grocery store remained strong in the face of growing chain competition. (Courtesy of Paul J. Braun and the Schroeder Brothers Company)

This overview is of the early morning hours before all the attendees visit Schroeder's Home Show. Every department was on display for the entire city of Two Rivers to see. (Courtesy of Vassar Studio and the Schroeder Brothers Company)

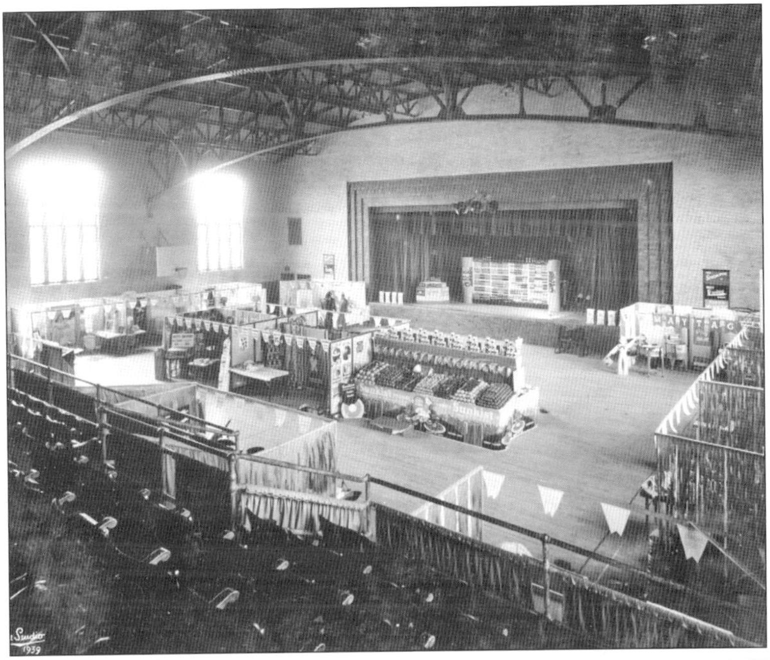

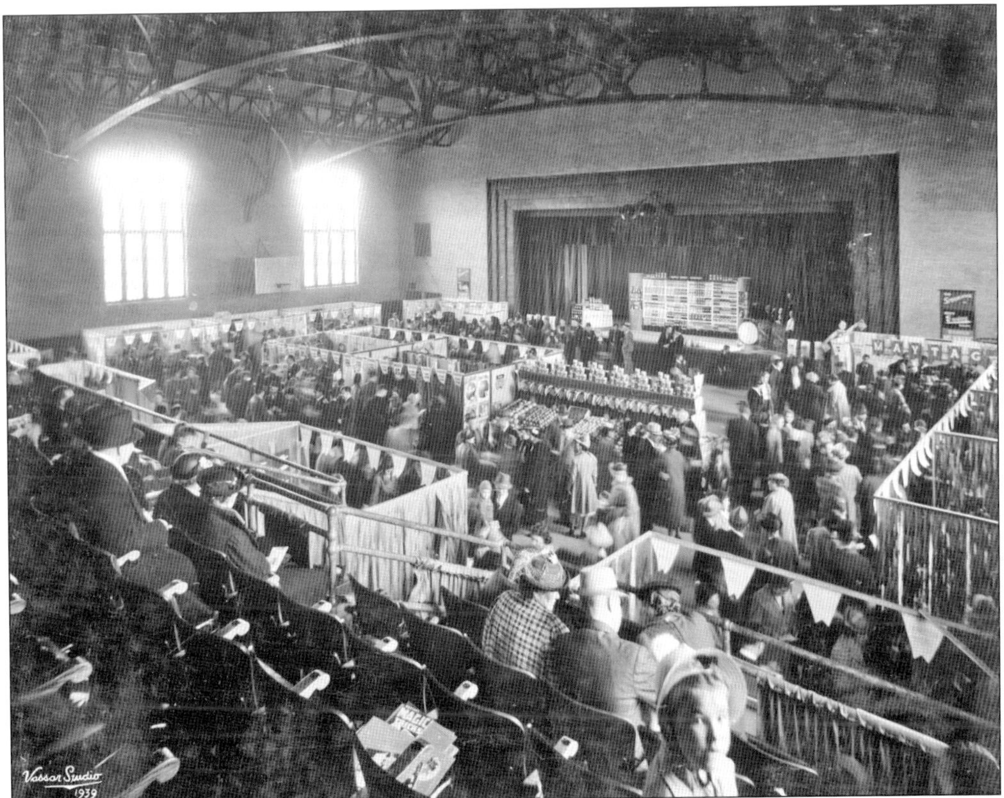

Everyone was welcome to see what Schroeder's Department Store had to offer at the Home Show. Displays were set up in the gymnasium of the J.E. Hamilton Community House. (Courtesy of Vassar Studio and the Schroeder Brothers Company.)

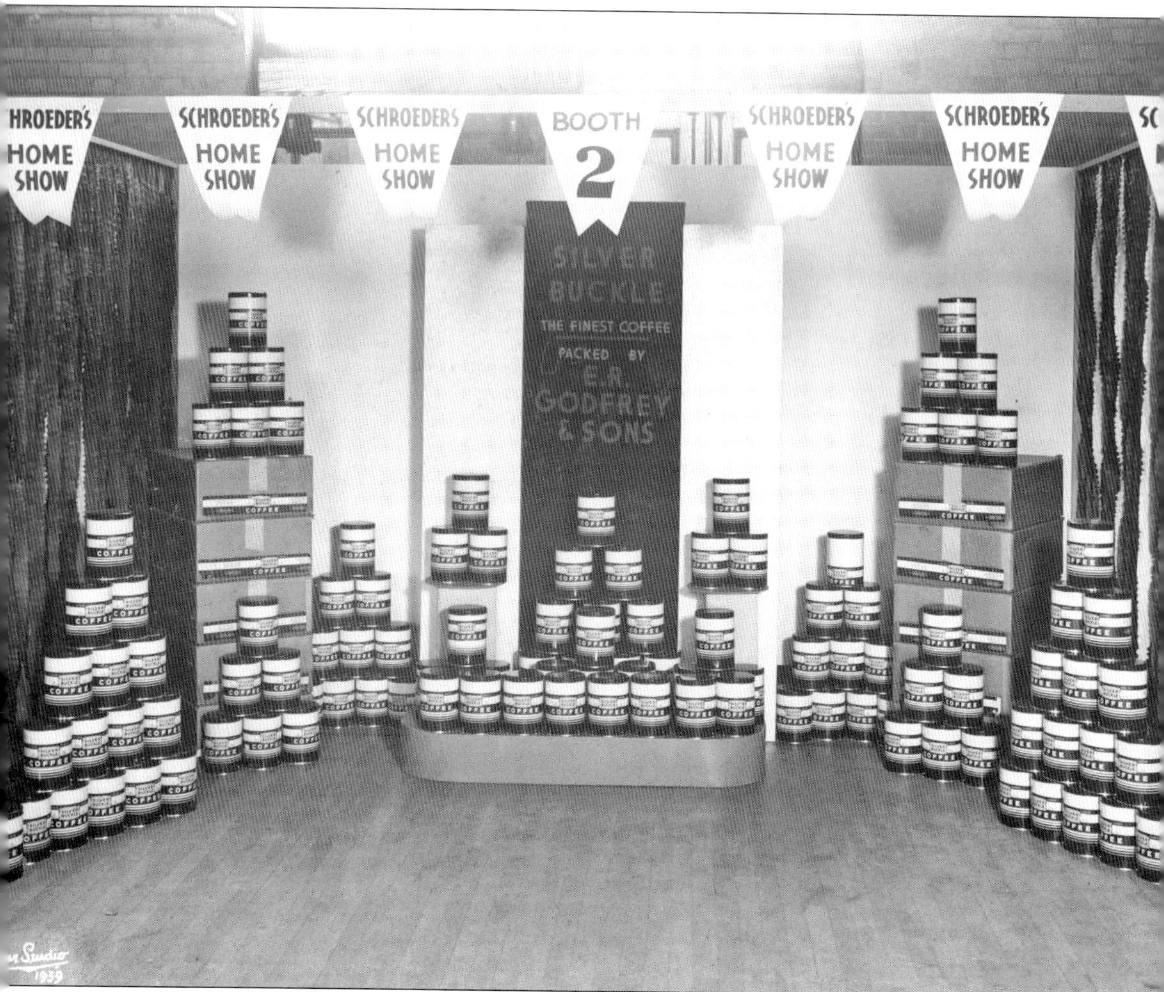

Silver Buckle Coffee was an item sold at the Schroeder's grocery department. The E.R. Godfrey & Sons company was based in Milwaukee and belonged to the independent grocer alliance to help promote the independent retailer. (Courtesy of Vassar Studio and the Schroeder Brothers Company.)

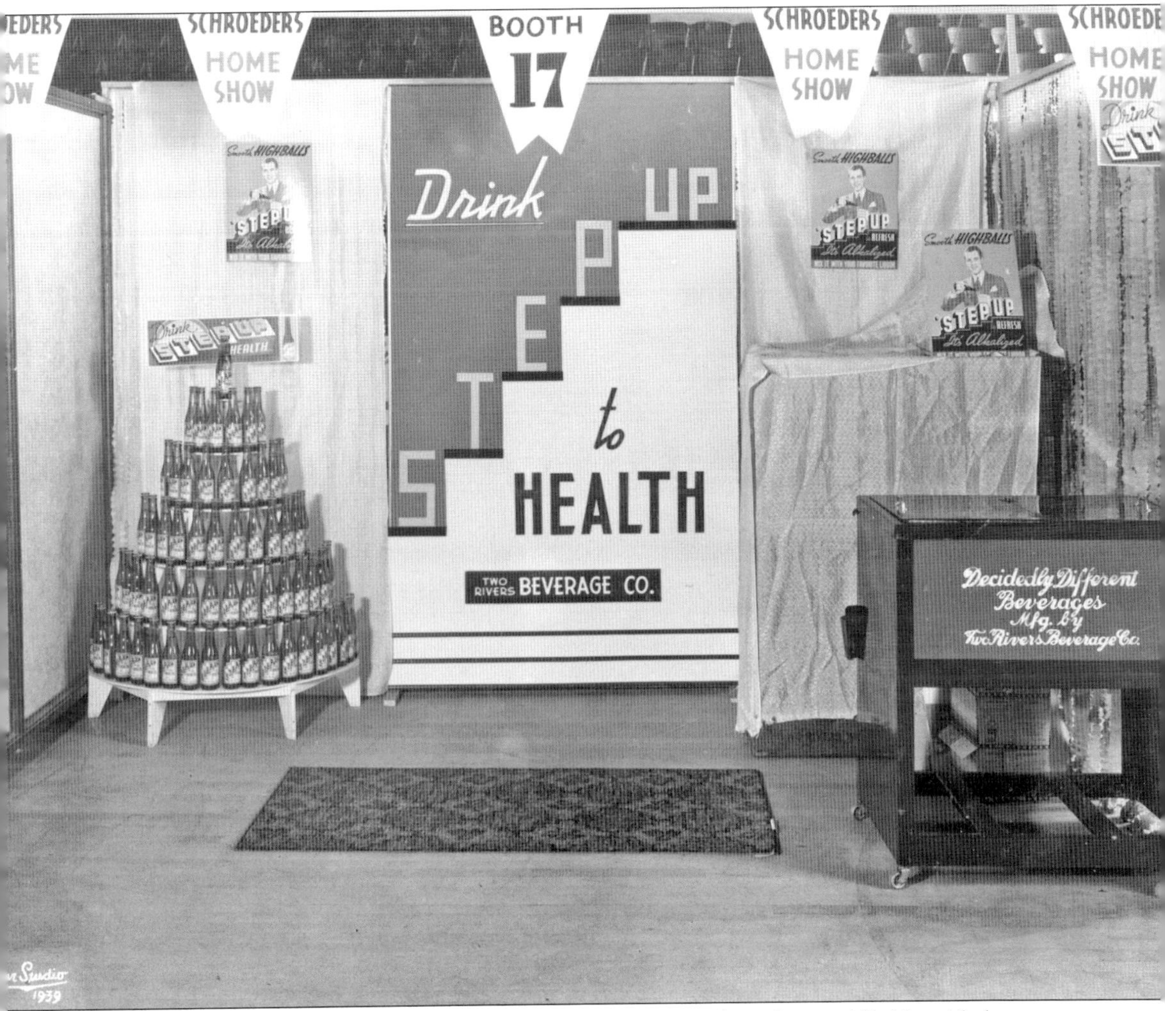

The Two Rivers Beverage Company was known for making White Cap and Bobbie Ale beers as well as Step Up, an alkalized drink. The Two Rivers Beverage Company was located on Adams Street in Two Rivers. (Courtesy of Vassar Studio and the Schroeder Brothers Company.)

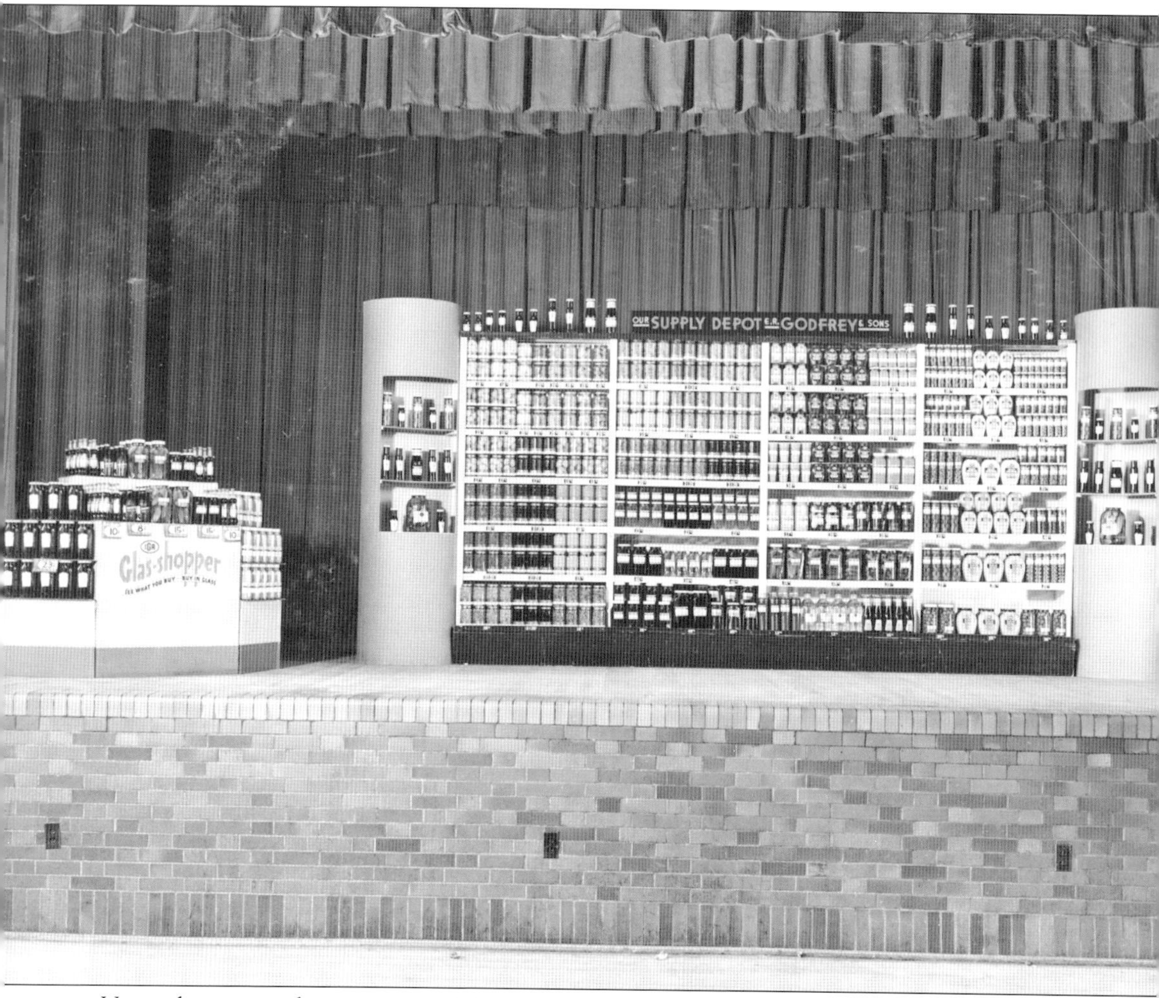

Up on the stage in the gymnasium, Glas-shopper, another creation from the company E.R. Godfrey & Sons based in Milwaukee, Wisconsin, is on display. They used the catchy phrase, "See what you buy, buy in glass." (Courtesy of Vassar Studio and the Schroeder Brothers Company.)

Thinshell Cookies offered many varieties of cookies and crackers. The Thinshell Product Company was based out of Chicago, Illinois. (Courtesy of Vassar Studio and the Schroeder Brothers Company.)

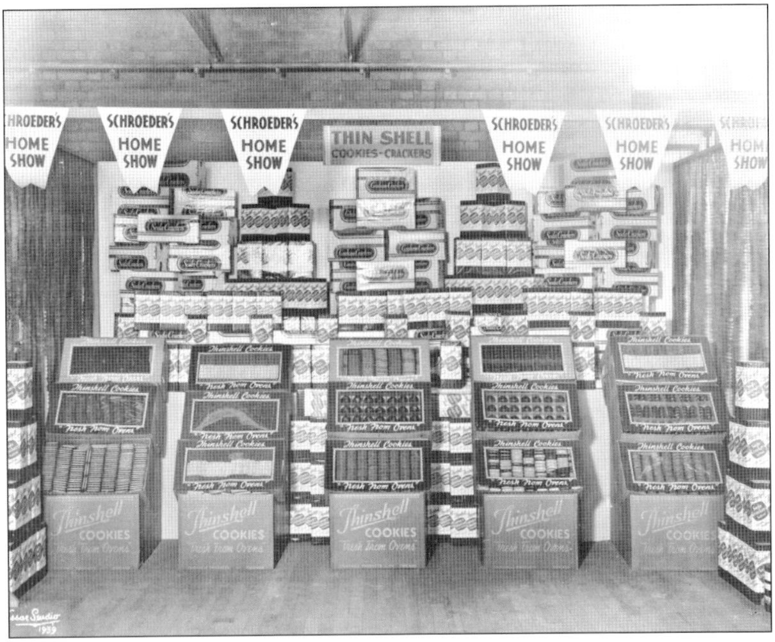

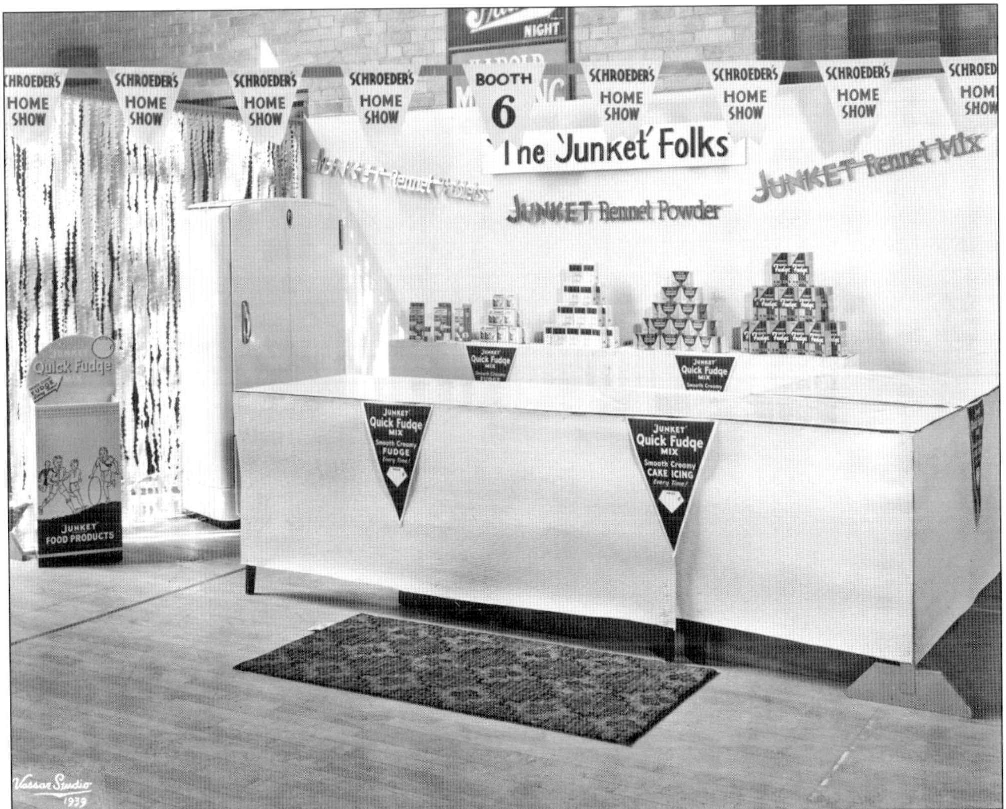

The Junket Quick Fudge Mix was a popular mix in 1939. The Schroeder's grocery department sold the fudge mix to help moms easily frost cakes and make creamy fudge. (Courtesy of Vassar Studio and the Schroeder Brothers Company.)

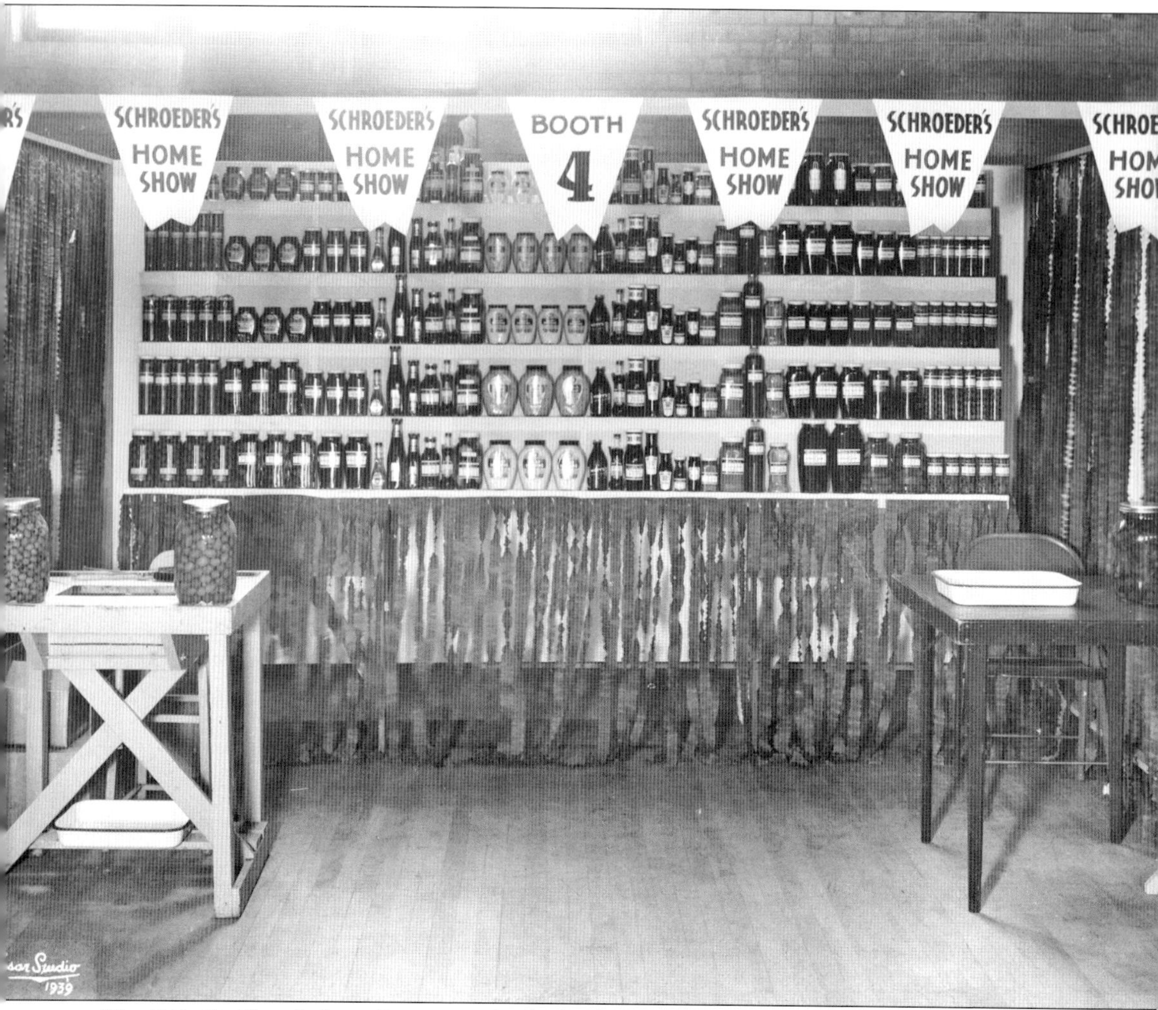

The E.R. Godfrey & Sons Company also had a display on the floor of the gymnasium. They had olives and preserves to mustard and salad dressing. (Courtesy of Vassar Studio and the Schroeder Brothers Company.)

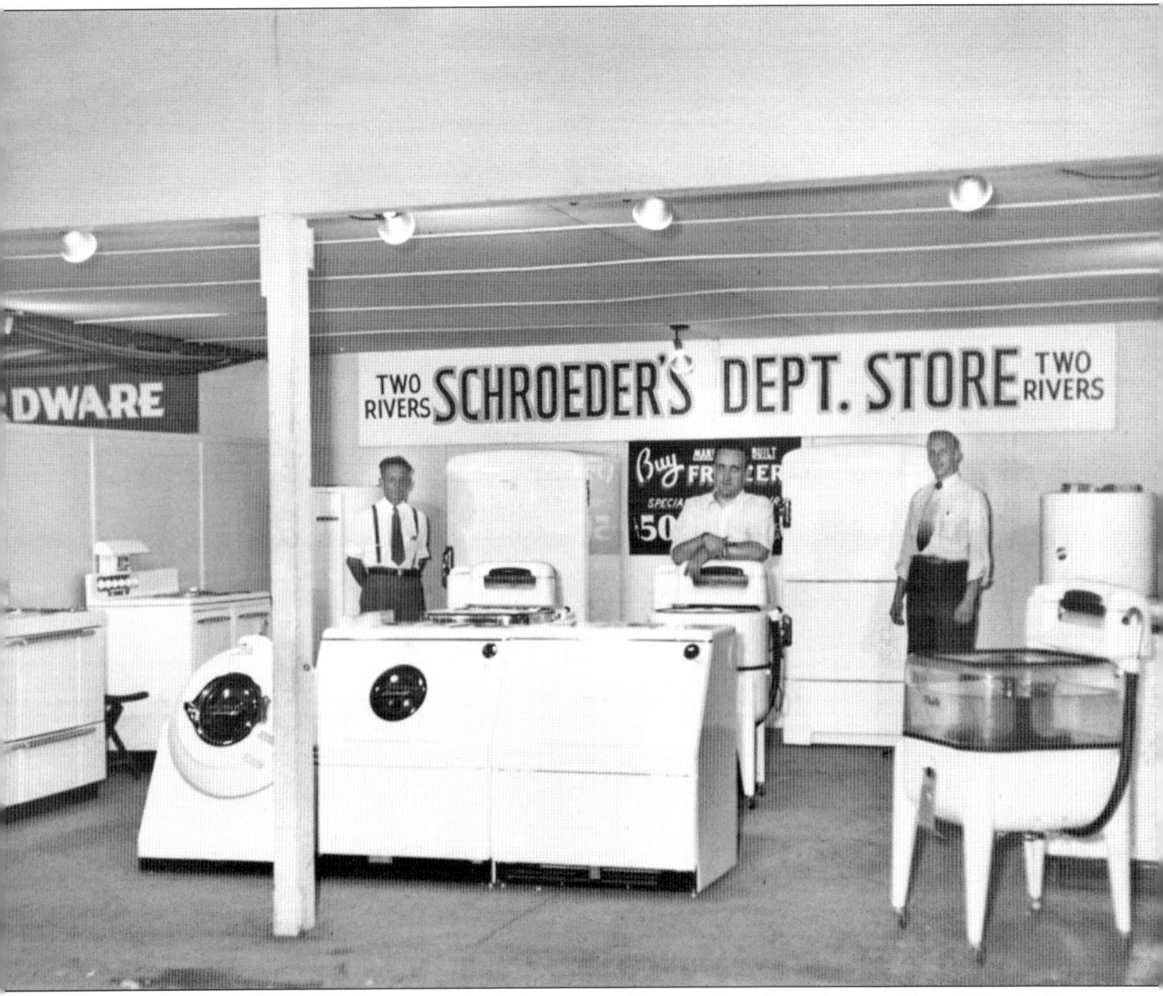

Schroeder's appliance display was at the Manitowoc County Fair from August 25 to 28 in 1949. The new and modern appliances of the day are on display, including Maytag and Westinghouse washers and dryers. Schroeder's delivered and installed all appliances and even offered service to fix machines. In the booth are manager Joseph Ruelle (far right) salesperson Dick Allie (center) and an unidentified person. (Courtesy of Schroeder's Department Store.)

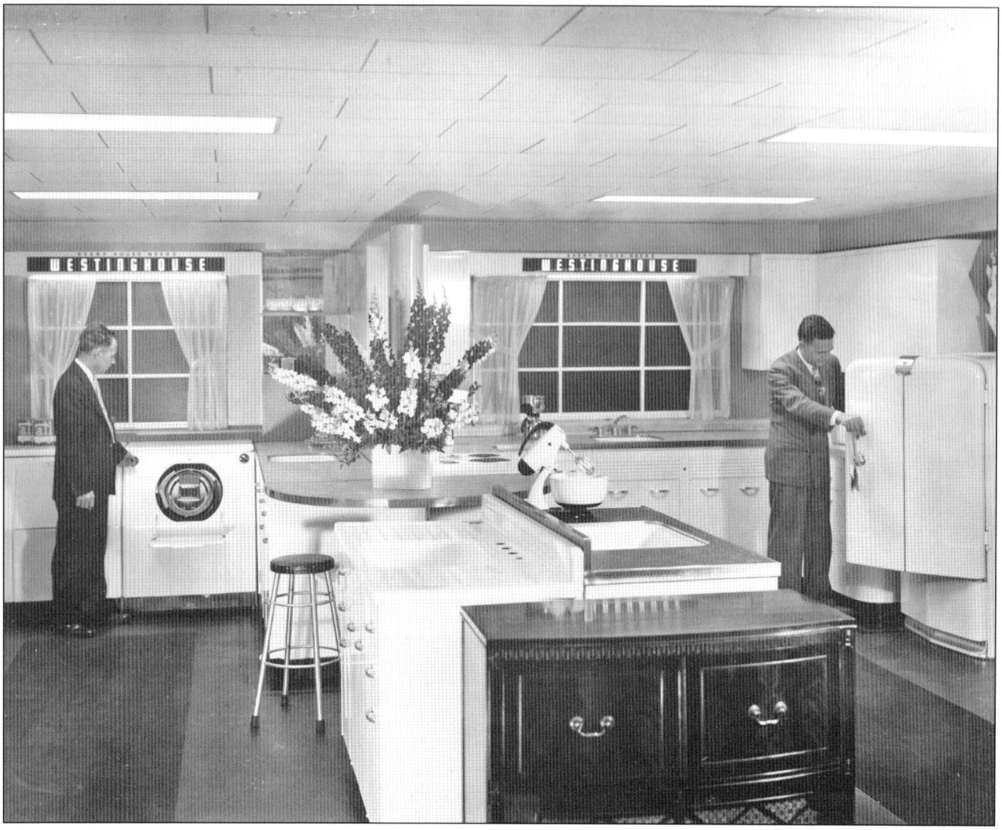

The newly renovated appliance department featured modern appliances. Schroeder's carried large items like washers and dryers and small appliances like mixers, coffeemakers, and radios. This photograph features appliance department manager Joseph Ruelle (left) and Schroeder's owner Gary Schroeder. (Courtesy of Schroeder's Department Store.)

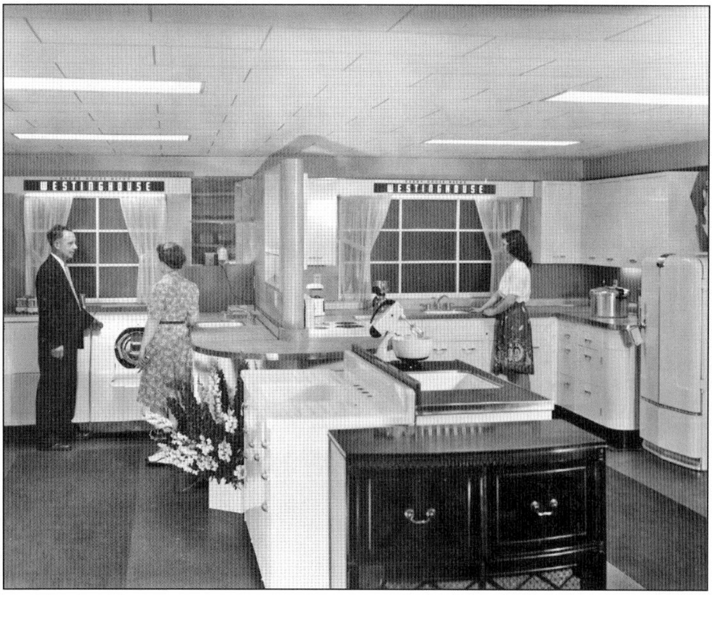

Two customers shop in the newly renovated appliance department. Manager Joseph Ruelle (far left) answers questions about a new front-load washer by Westinghouse. (Courtesy of Schroeder's Department Store.)

Maytag's ringer washers were the featured appliance at the Schroeder's Home Show in 1939. Maytag boasted they would save people money and time cleaning clothes. (Courtesy of Vassar Studio and the Schroeder Brothers Company.)

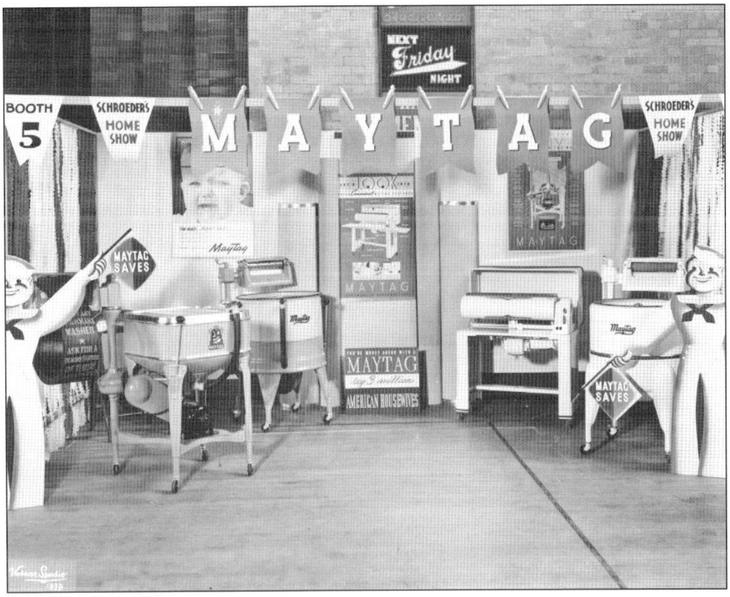

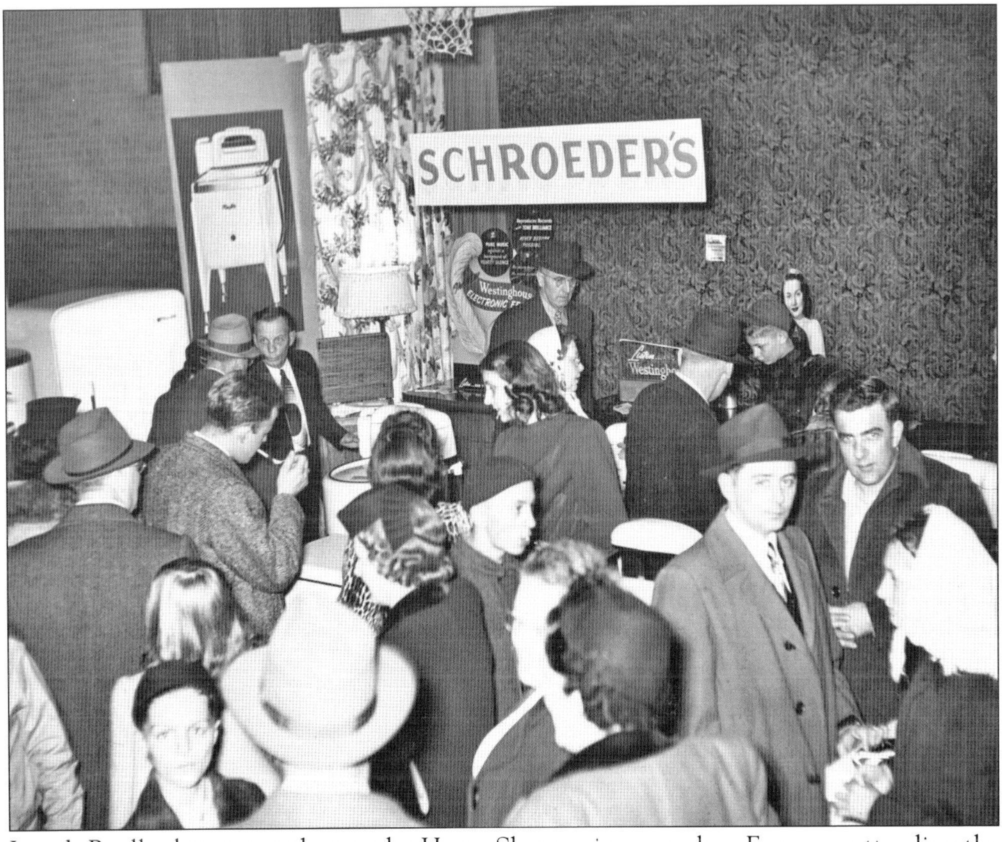

Joseph Ruelle shows attendees at the Home Show a ringer washer. Everyone attending the Schroeder Home Show at the J.E. Hamilton Community House could see daily demonstrations and try the products out for themselves. (Courtesy of Ariens Photo Service and the Schroeder Brothers Company.)

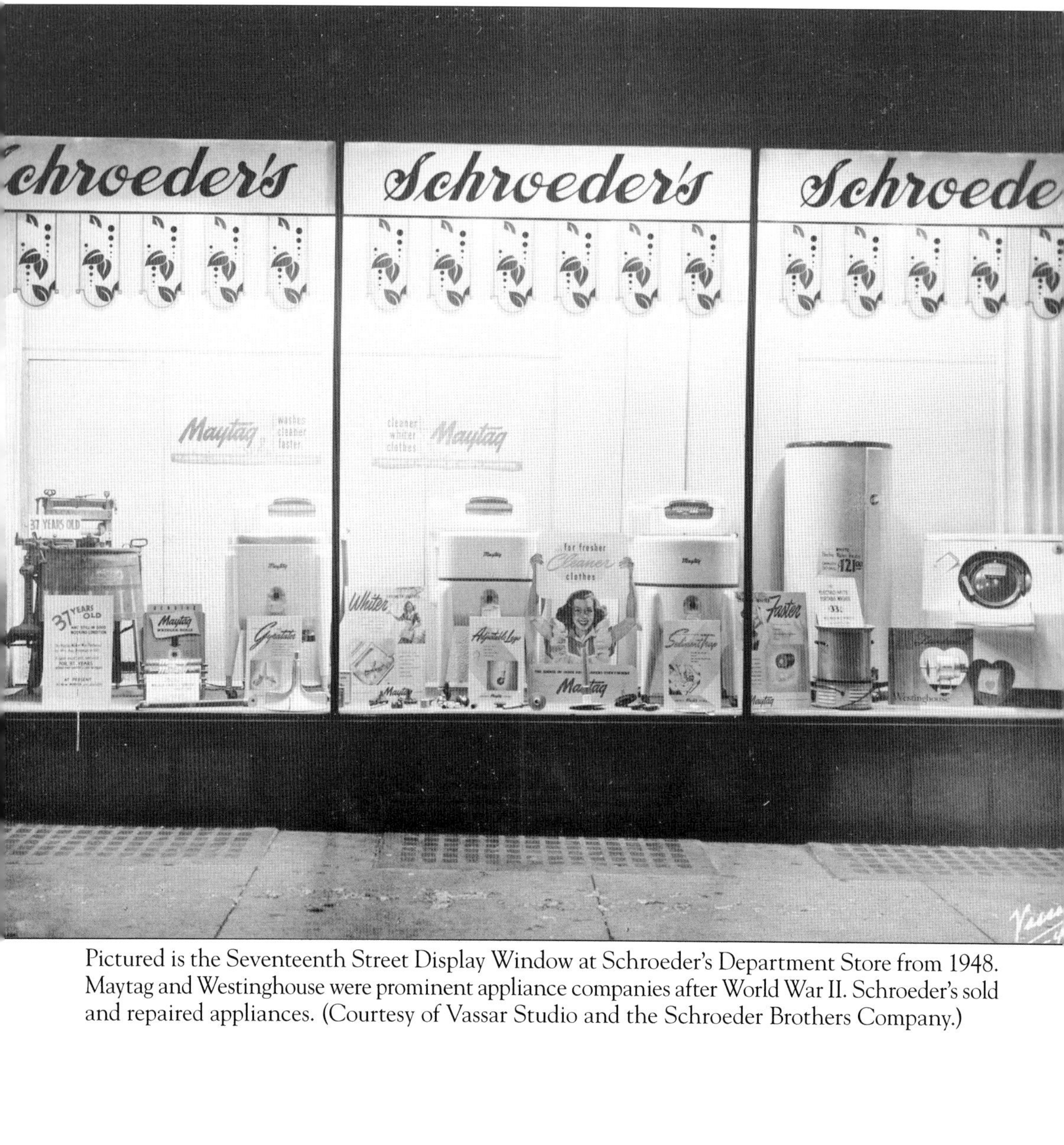

Pictured is the Seventeenth Street Display Window at Schroeder's Department Store from 1948. Maytag and Westinghouse were prominent appliance companies after World War II. Schroeder's sold and repaired appliances. (Courtesy of Vassar Studio and the Schroeder Brothers Company.)

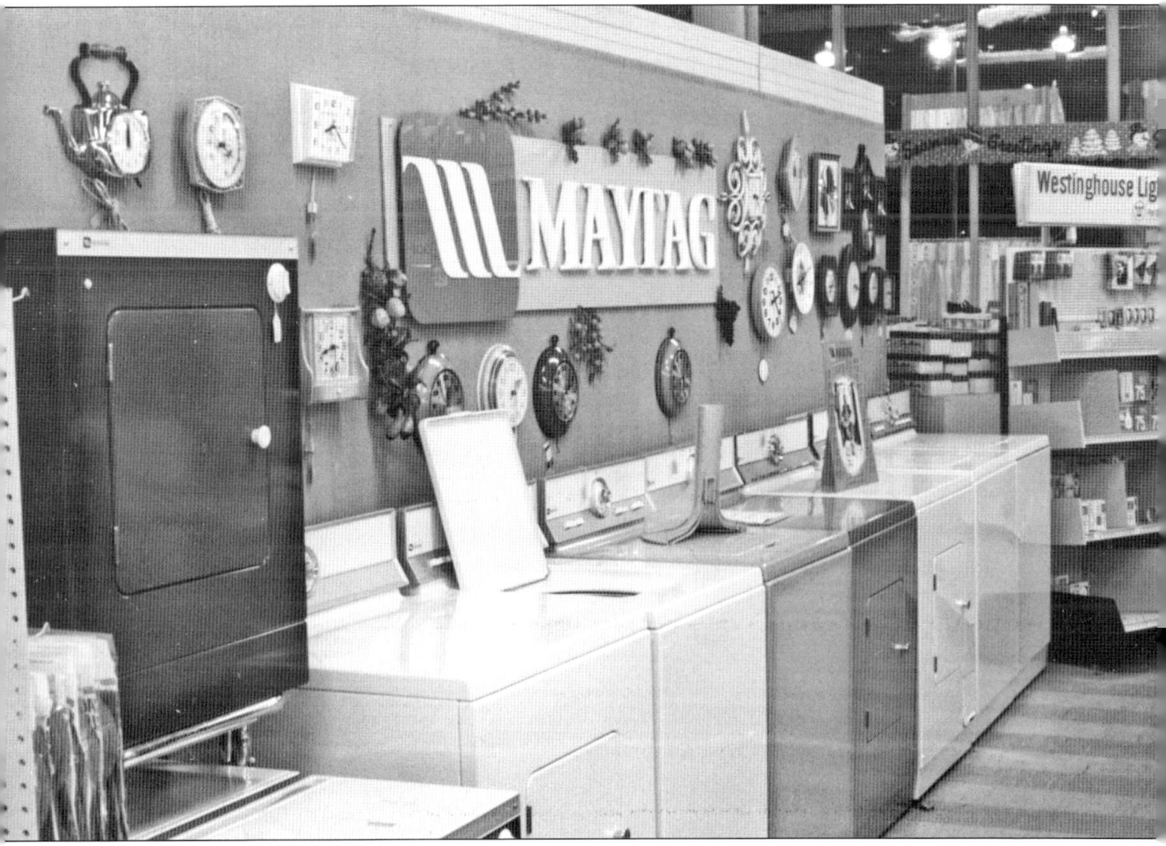

In 1971, the appliance department was still located at the back of the Schroeder's store. Maytag and Westinghouse were the appliance of choice in 1971. The appliance department suffered losses almost since the day it was brought into Schroeder's, and in 2000 John and Tim finally sold all the inventory and closed that area down. The minutes of the Schroeder's board meetings recorded the directors talking about the struggling sales for almost 55 years. (Courtesy of John Schroeder.)

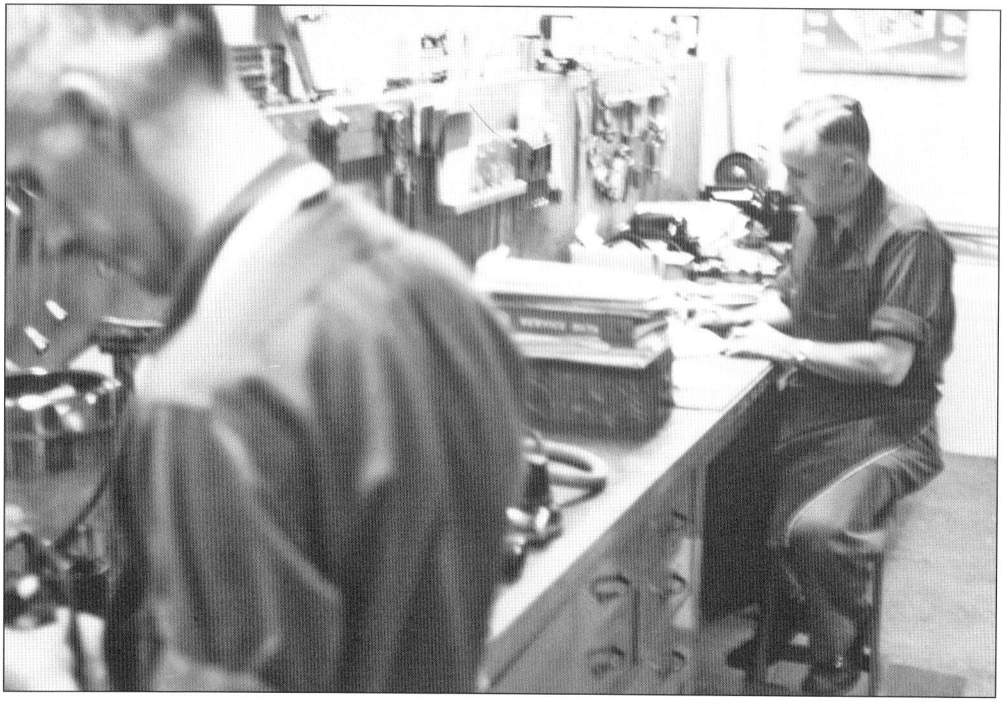

The Wachtel boys are pictured at work in their workshop at Schroeder's. Hilary (left) and Leo Wachtel (right) fixed anything and everything mechanical for Schroeder's Department Store. They serviced all of the appliances if a customer ever had a problem. (Courtesy of Julie Schroeder.)

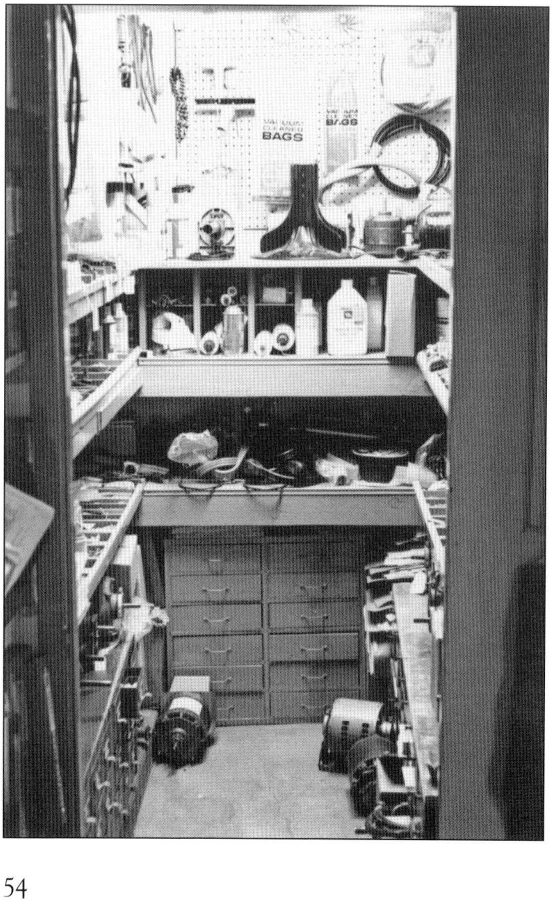

Pictured is the Wachtel boys' storage closet adjacent to their workspace next to the appliance department in the lower level of Schroeder's Department Store. Hilary and Leo could fix anything, and they had a storage space for every tool that would help them accomplish that goal. (Courtesy of John Schroeder.)

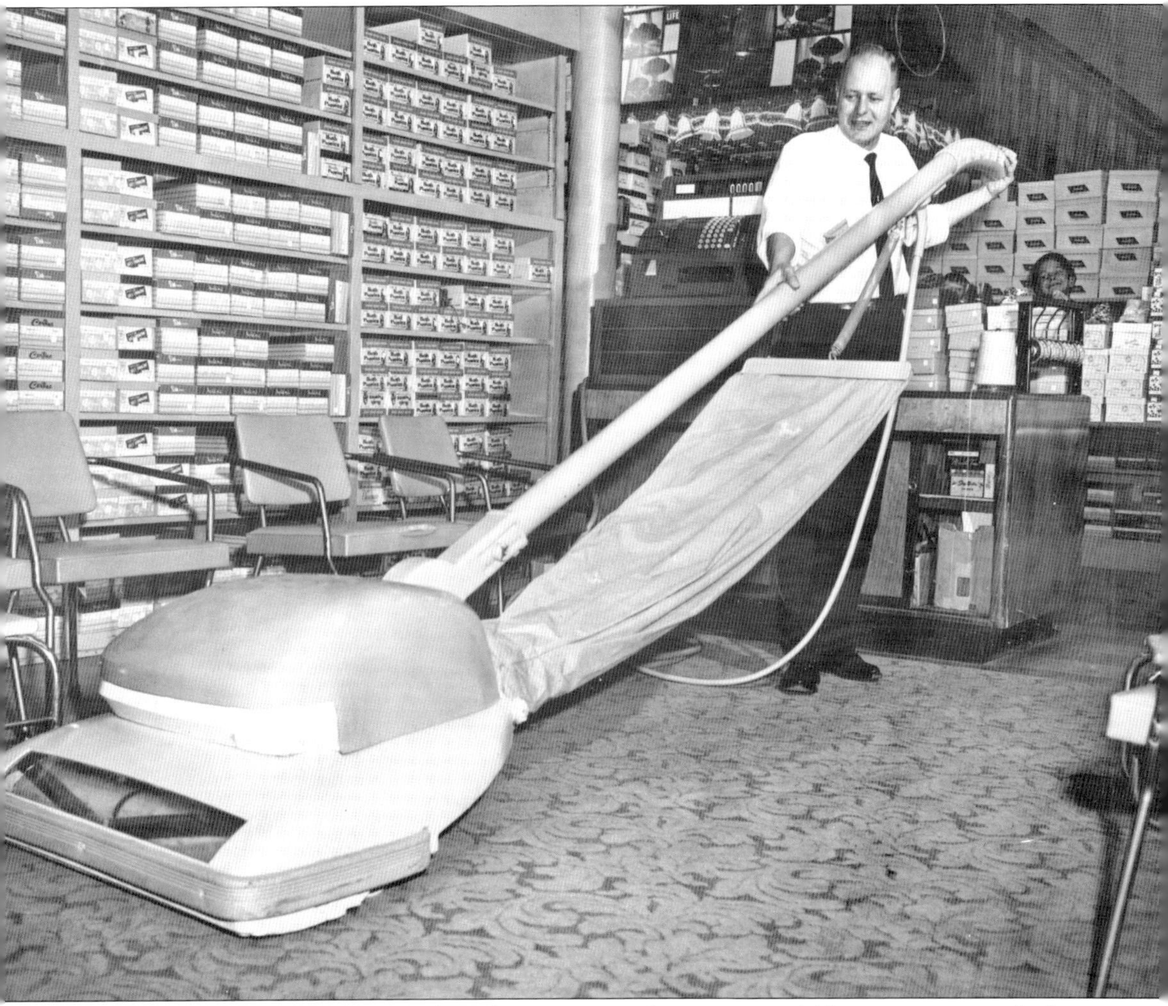

Dick Froeming cleans the men's shoe department with an oversized Hoover vacuum, which was featured in Schroeder's newspaper ads during the 1970s. (Courtesy of the Schroeder Brothers Company.)

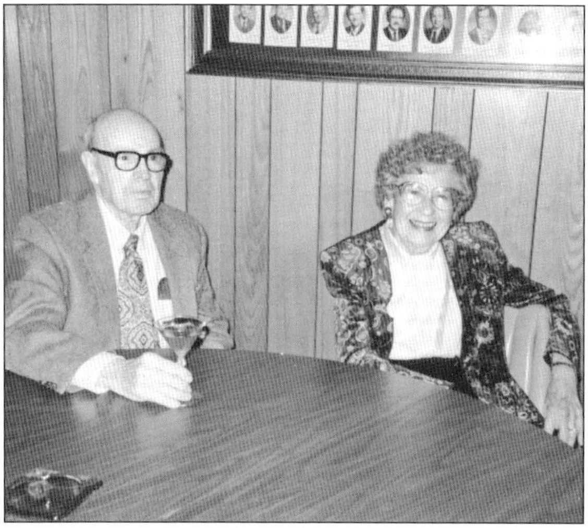

Hilary Schroeder started mending clothing while he worked in the men's clothing department in the 1920s. He had a little room tucked behind the men's shoe department in the basement. The alterations department slowly started expanding after the 1950s, and more space was needed. Alterations' new home was paired with the women's ready-to-wear department on the second floor. In the 1970s, Schroeder's introduced custom window treatments and blinds in addition to prepackaged window treatments. Pictured are Hilary (left) and Agnes Schroeder. (Courtesy of Schroeder's Department Store.)

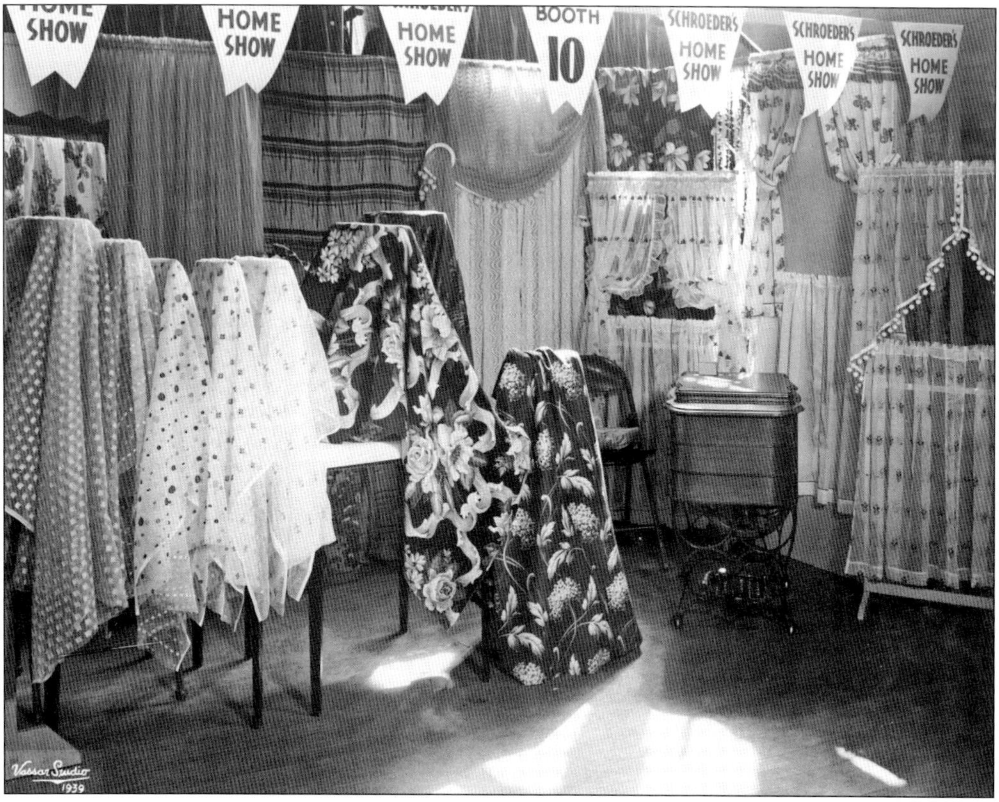

The fabric and window treatments were not left out of the Home Show in the Community House in 1939. Bolts of shear fabric are on display and premade, prepackaged draperies are on display for housewives to inspect. A treadle sewing machine sits on display also. Creating custom window treatments was a very time-consuming task that included measuring, making, and installing draperies and blinds. In 2010, Theresa and A.J. chose to close the department. The Schroeder's alterations department still exists today and flourishes. The employees mend simple zippers to tailoring suits. (Courtesy of Schroeder's Department Store.)

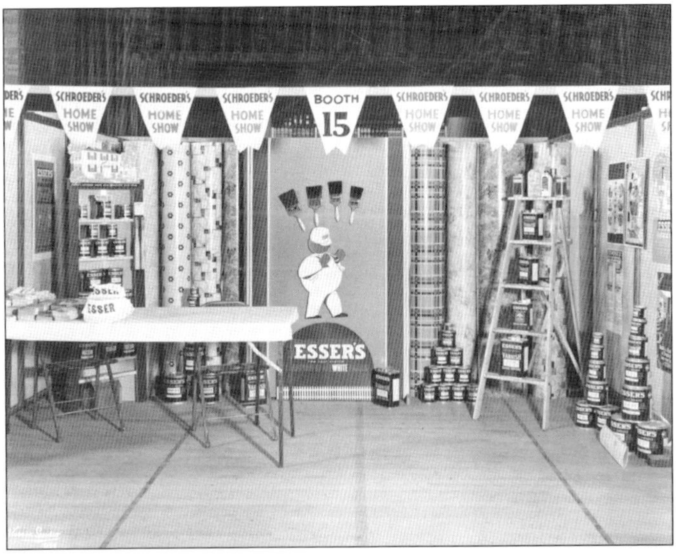

Booth 15 at the Home Show sponsored solely by Schroeder's featured paint by Esser, flooring by Royal, and Western window shades. The T.C. Esser Company was created by Theodore Clemens Esser. Esser Paints was based out of Milwaukee, Wisconsin. (Courtesy of Vassar Studio and the Schroeder Brothers Company.)

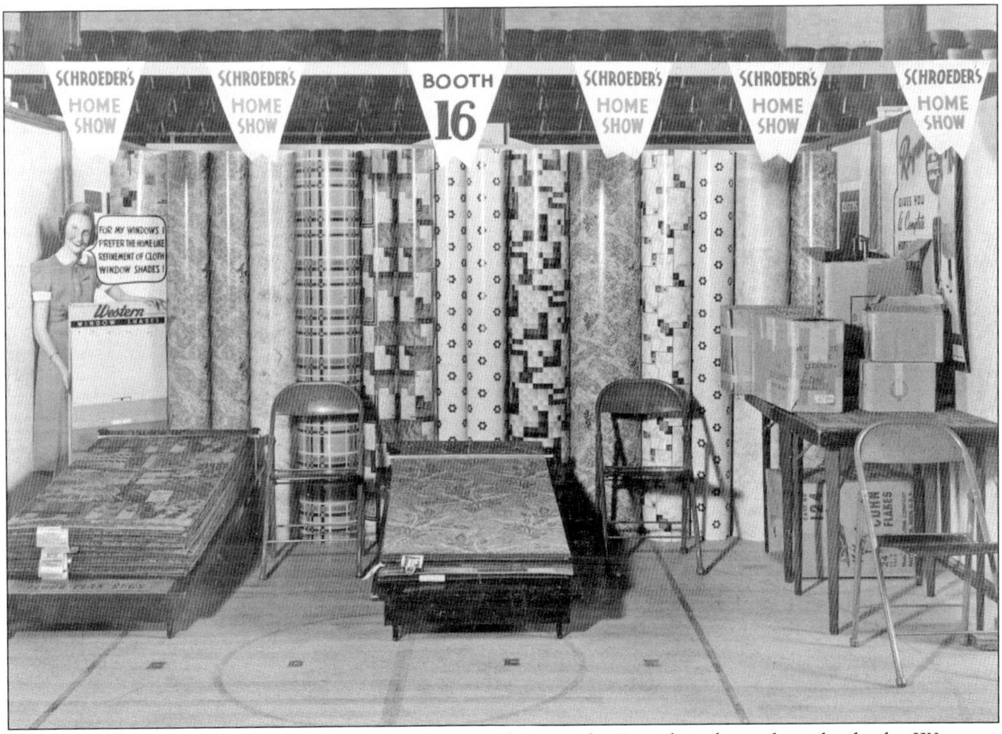

In this booth, Schroeder's was able to showcase flooring by Royal and window shades by Western Window Shades. While many people of 1935 had fabric curtains decorating their windows, roller shades kept out the bright summer sun. The Western window shades of 1935 were sold at Schroeder's Department Store. Laminate flooring was sold at Schroeder's for just a brief time. Little was ever documented about the flooring and hardware departments at Schroeder's. The departments were created after the bank moved out in 1935. Shortly after getting into the flooring and hardware business, Schroeder's decided to close the departments and help Suettinger Hardware, a business adjacent to the Schroeder Building, get into paints and hardware. (Courtesy of Vassar Studio and the Schroeder Brothers Company.)

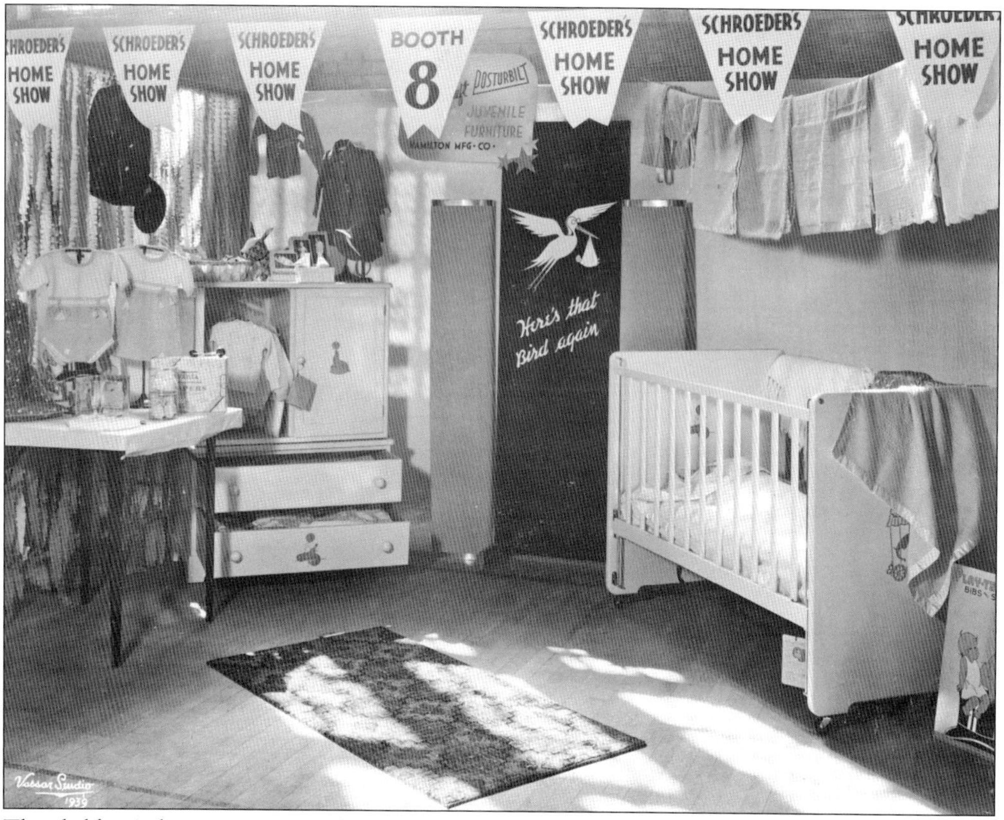

The children's department was a fun area in the Schroeder Home Show. Quality juvenile furniture was made locally at the Hamilton Manufacturing Company, located just one block away from Schroeder's on Jefferson Street. An armoire, dresser, and crib are on display with advertising for the Play-Tex brand for bibs and shirts. (Courtesy of Schroeder's Department Store.)

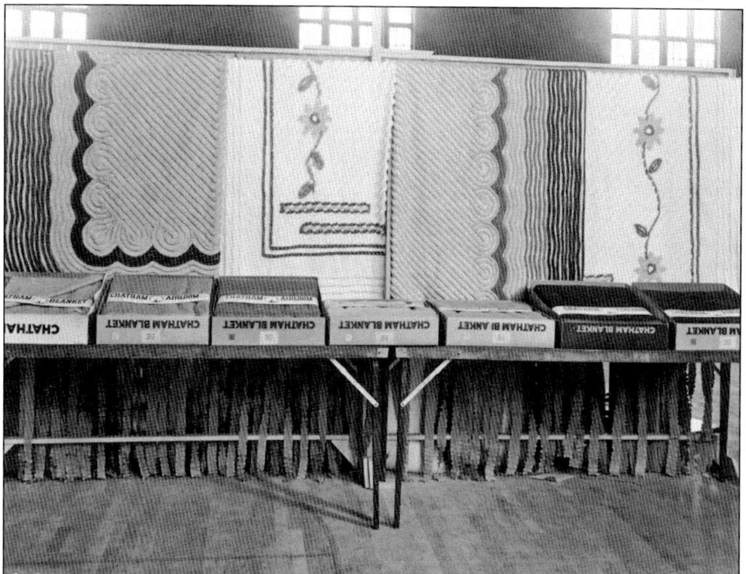

Blankets by Chatham were made at the Elkin Woolen Mills in Elkin, North Carolina. The Elkin Woolen Mill made more than a million wool blankets for the US Military during World War I and World War II. (Courtesy of Vassar Studio and the Schroeder's Department Store.)

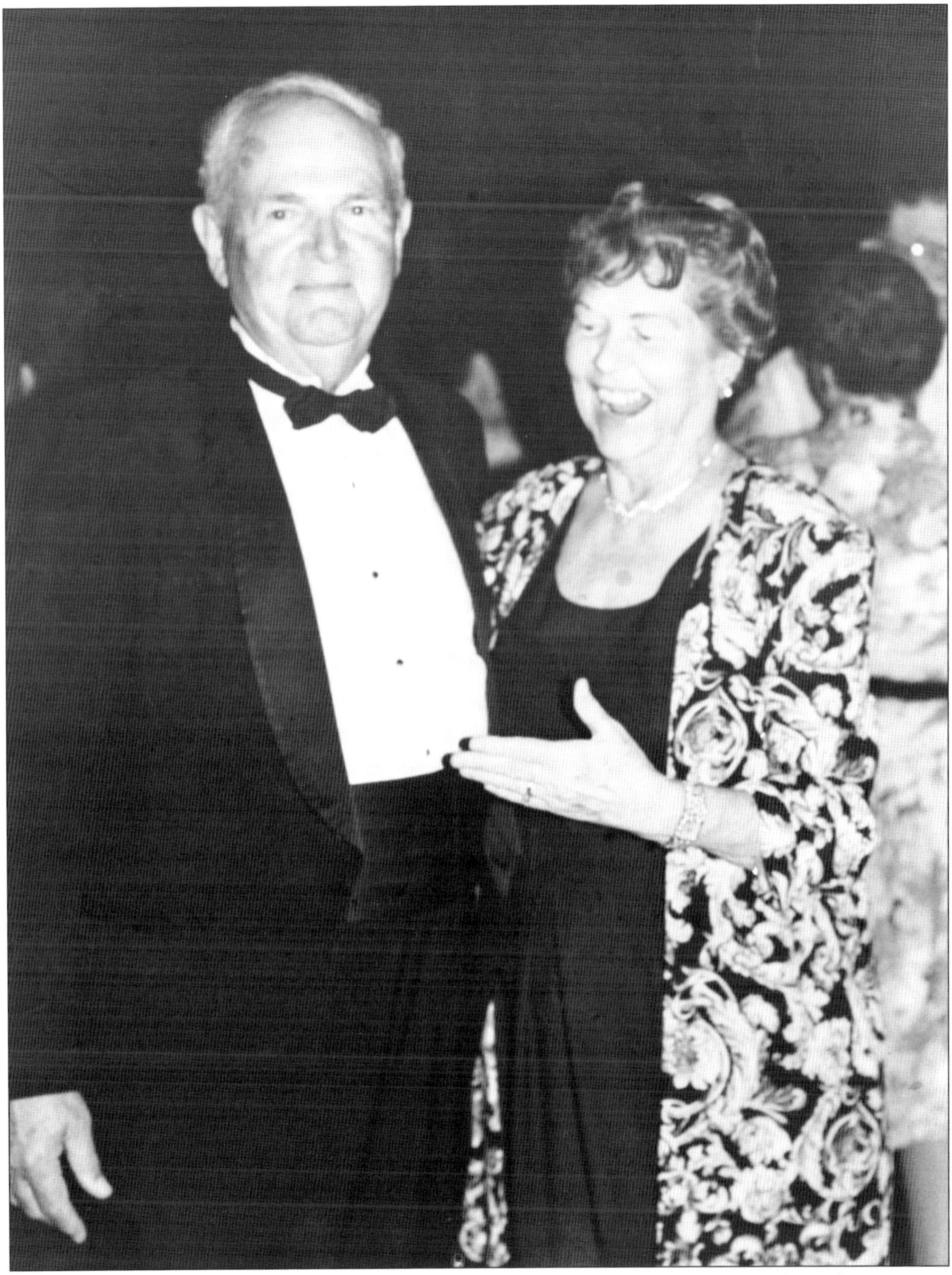

The northwest corner of the Schroeder Building was home to the children's clothing department, affectionately known as "Grandma's Corner." Famous clothing brands like London Fog, Oshkosh B'Gosh, and Carters were all sold in the children's department. Schroeder's closed the children's department in 1994 due to sluggish sales and Walmart opening a store in Manitowoc, Wisconsin. It was at Connie Schroeder's suggestion at a board meeting that the store open a coffeehouse in the quaint corner of the Schroeder Building. Gary and Connie are pictured here at the Centennial Ball on September 4, 1991. (Courtesy of Schroeder's Department Store.)

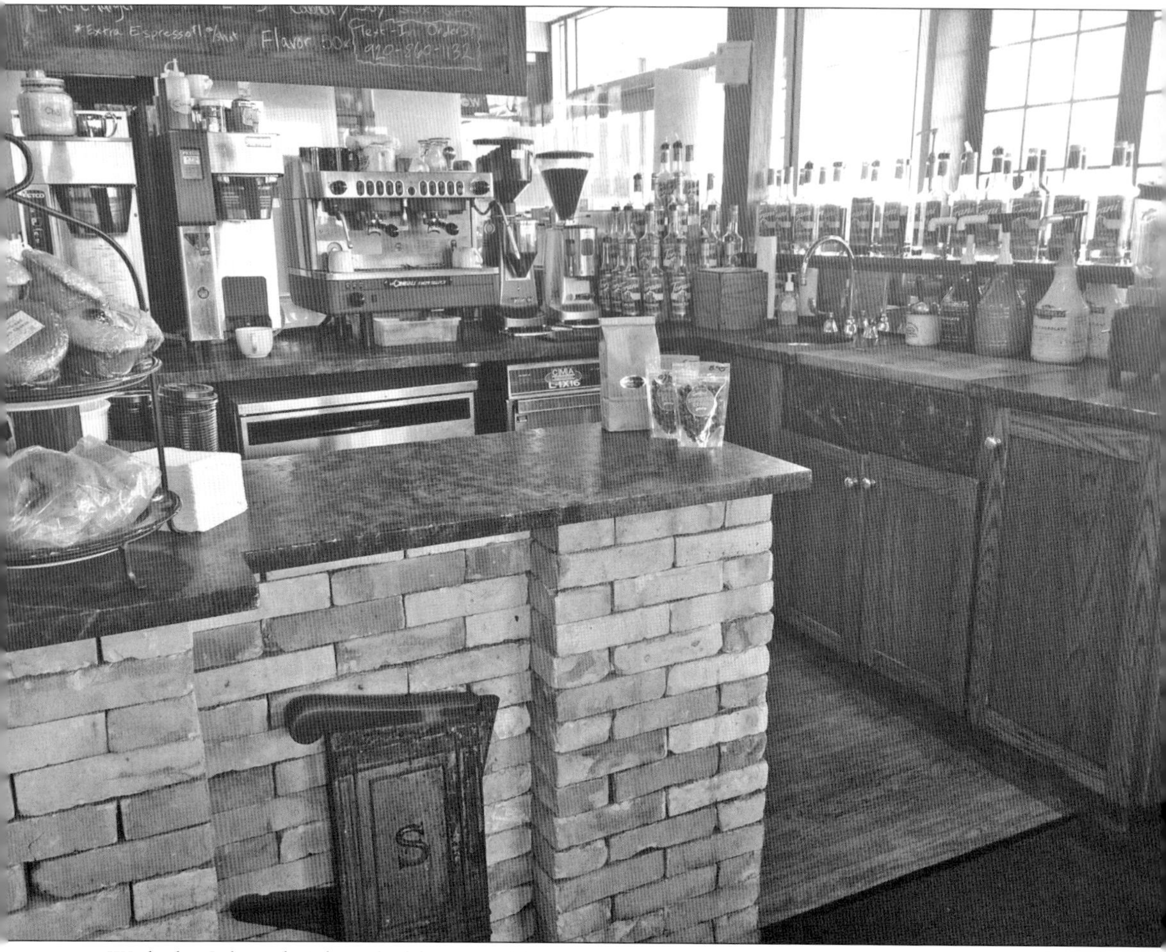

With the Schroeder's board of directors' blessing, construction of the Red Bank Coffeehouse began to take place in 1996. The corner was where the Two Rivers Savings Bank started, and it was named in honor of the bank. Demolition of the display windows on Washington and Seventeenth Streets made way for more seating. Wood pillars and beams were created to make the area cozier. The Red Bank Coffeehouse opened its doors in November 1997 and started a new chapter in the Schroeder history books. By the 11th anniversary, the Red Bank Coffeehouse needed to expand to offer larger seating and counter space. In the spring of 2008, another remodeling was completed to accommodate the thriving department. (Courtesy of Schroeder's Department Store.)

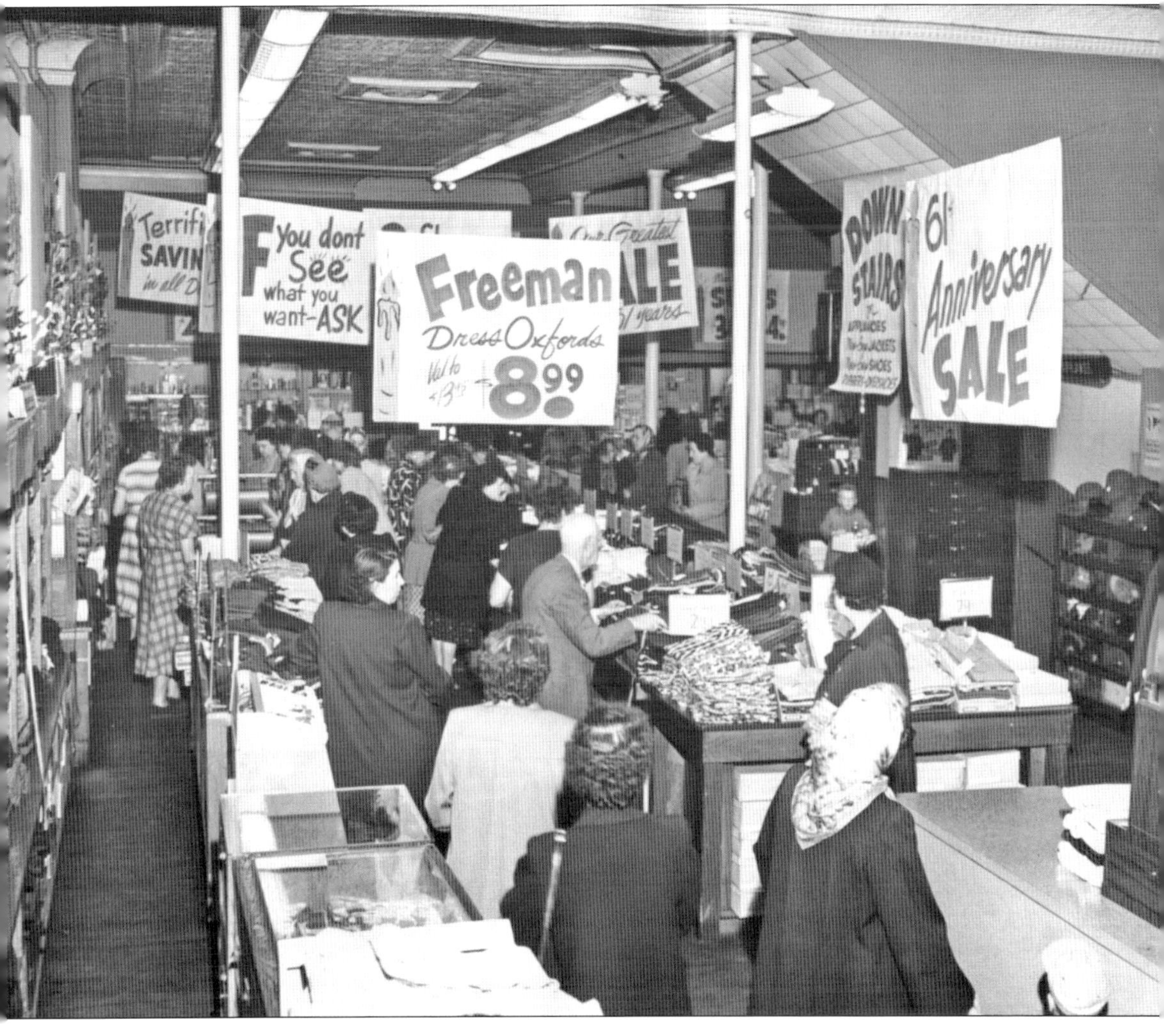

The view is from the balcony at the 61st anniversary sale in October 1952. Freeman oxfords were on sale for only $8.99, and the store was packed with customers looking to bring home some great deals. The men's and women's footwear departments have moved around the store and have received many different facelifts since the beginning. The shoe departments were always joined, and slowly, with the increase of different styles and functions of footwear, the departments needed to be separated. (Courtesy of Schroeder's Department Store.)

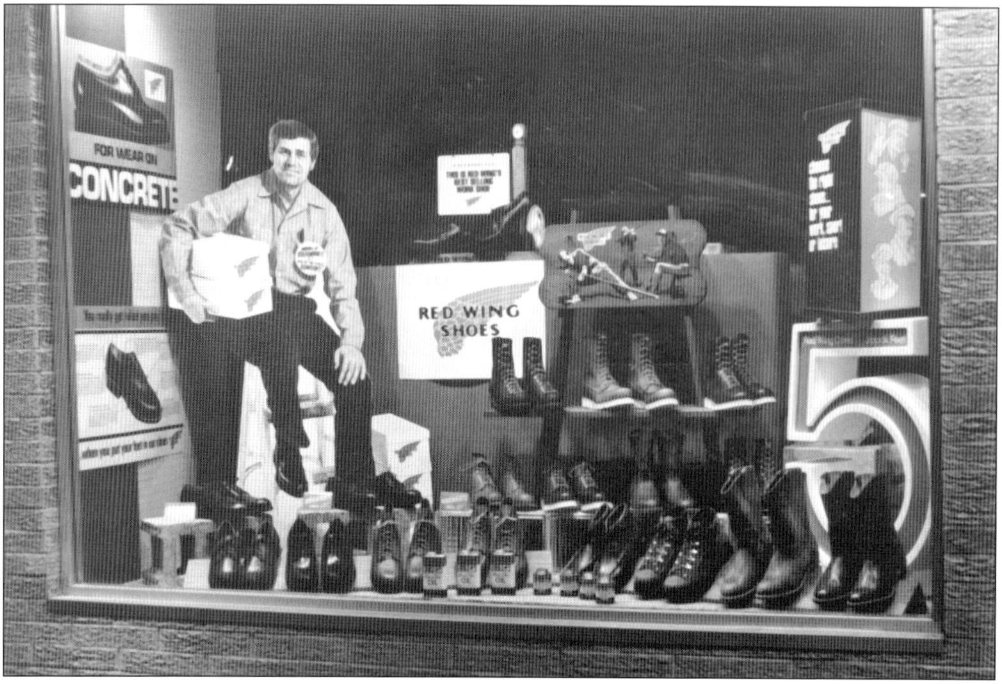

Schroeder's Department Store was an exclusive dealer in Red Wing shoes and boots in 1971. John Schroeder designed this window displaying all the current Red Wing models sold in the men's shoe department. This window faced Seventeenth Street. In the late 1980s, a large remodeling took place in the lower-level men's footwear department. (Courtesy of John Schroeder.)

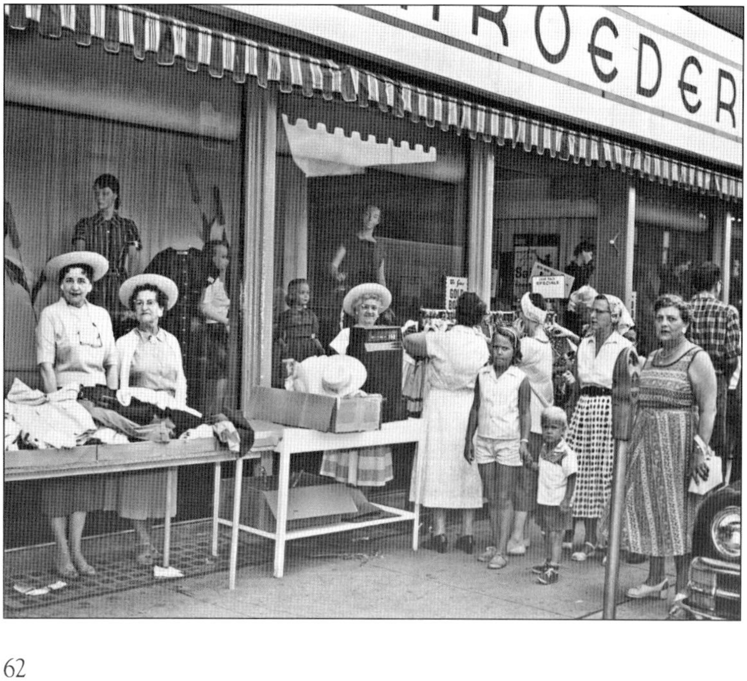

The annual sidewalk sale in downtown Two Rivers was always held in August. This image captures the employees ready to wait on customers. The awning was rolled out as the sun started to make its way over the building. (Courtesy of Schroeder's Department Store.)

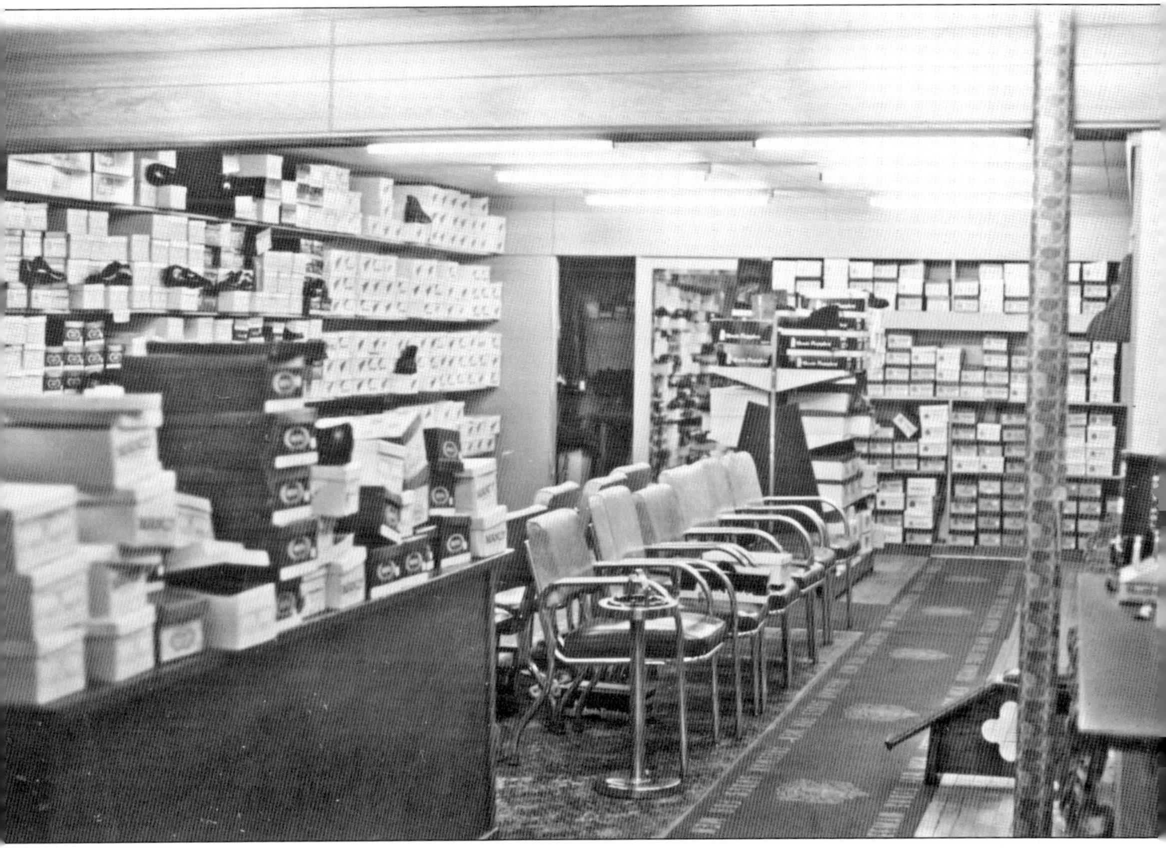

This view from the men's shoe checkout counter overlooks the department in 1970. Shoe boxes were all arranged on shelves, and employees helped customers with measuring their feet and helping them with the footwear purchase. (Courtesy of John Schroeder.)

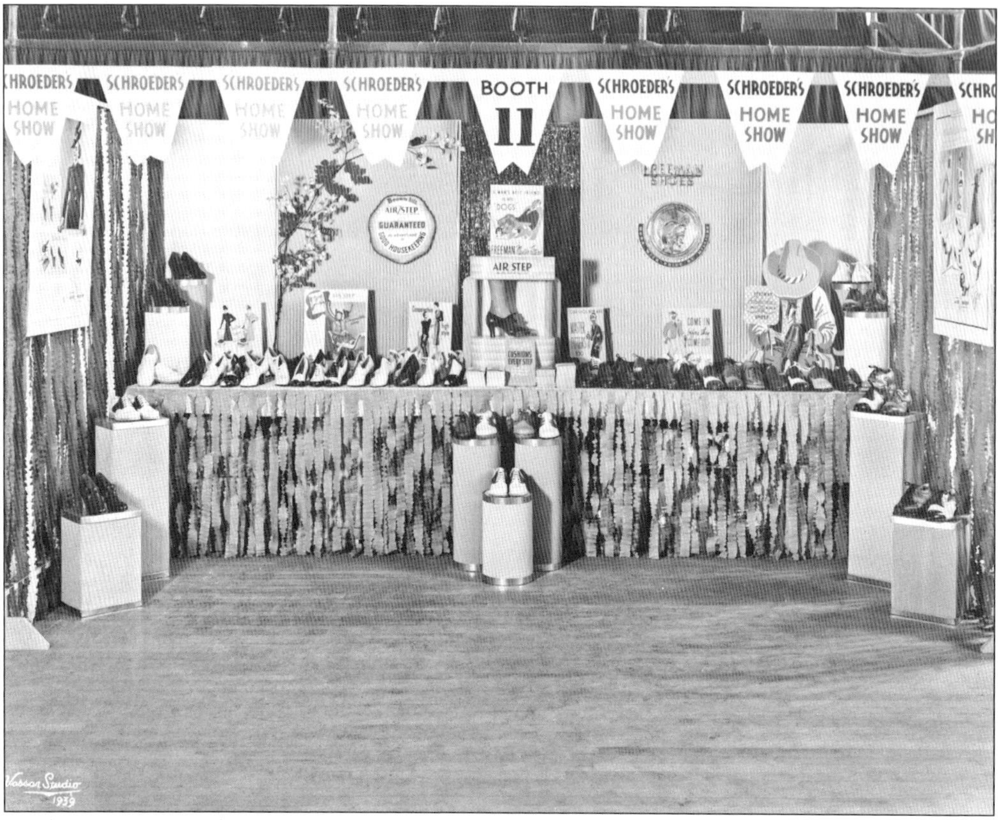

At the 1939 Home Show, held at the J.E. Hamilton Community House, a large display of men's and women's footwear was on display for the citizens of Two Rivers. Freeman Shoes offered many fashionable footwear options for men in 1939, and Air Step shoes for women also offered a magic sole for cushioning with every step. (Courtesy of Vassar Studio and the Schroeder Brothers Company.)

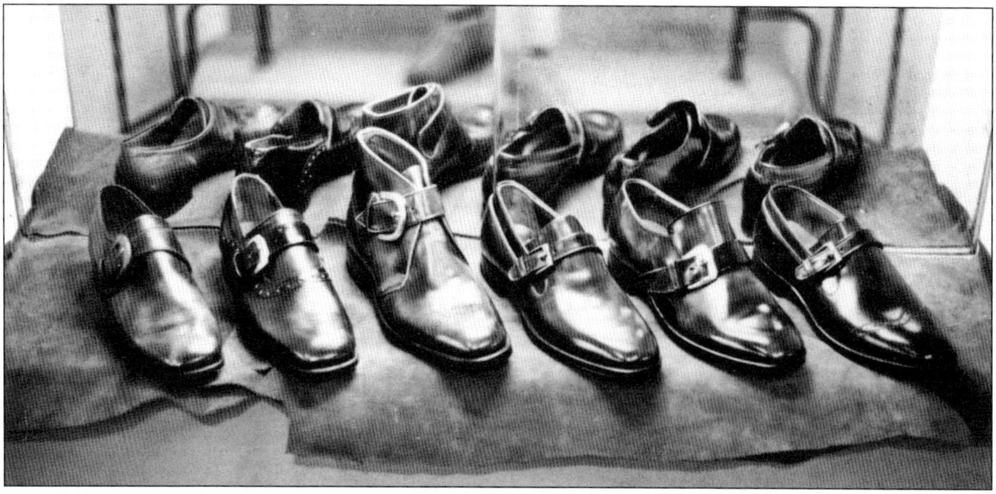

New fall Freeman shoes for men are lined up so John Schroeder, son of Gary Schroeder, can take a photograph for a newspaper ad. In 1970, John created the shoe ads for Schroeder's Department Store. (Courtesy of John Schroeder.)

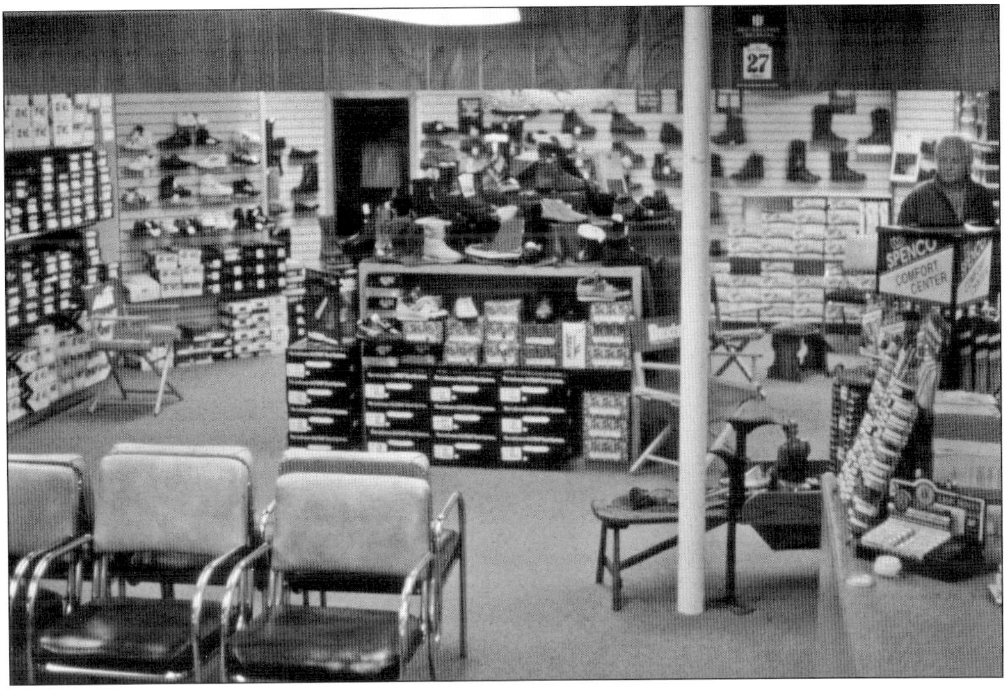

This photograph shows the newly renovated men's shoe department. The large bookcases on the right of the photograph are gone, and in its place is a new slatwall. No longer do the employees just grab the shoe boxes; the shoes are showcased, and employees find what the customer sees in front of them. While Schroeder's respected the way retail was changing, John still made sure to continue offering the customer knowledgeable service, with measuring the customers' feet and taking care of them for the entire sale. (Courtesy of Schroeder's Department Store.)

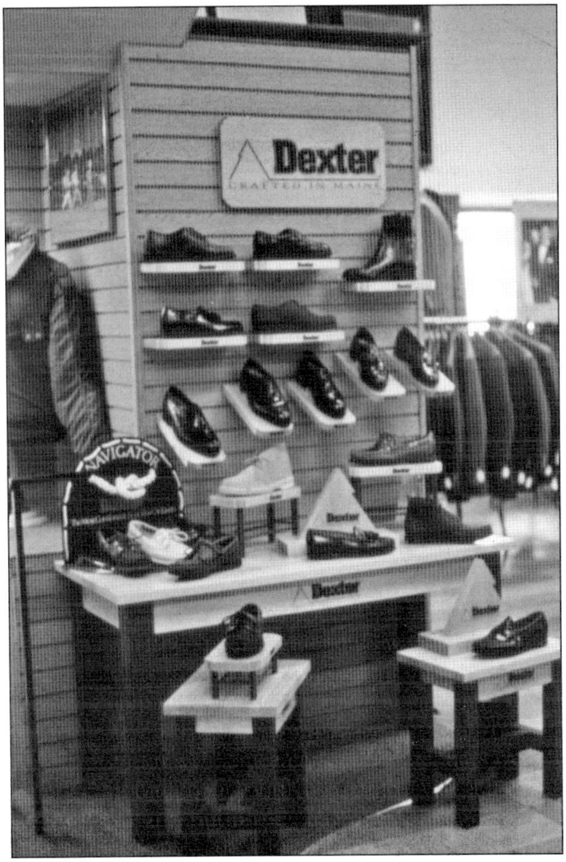

Seen here is a display at the top of the stairs heading down to the men's shoes and outerwear department. Dexter Shoe Company was a favorite brand of Schroeder's. It featured many men's and women's styles, and all the shoes were made in Dexter, Maine. (Courtesy of Schroeder's Department Store.)

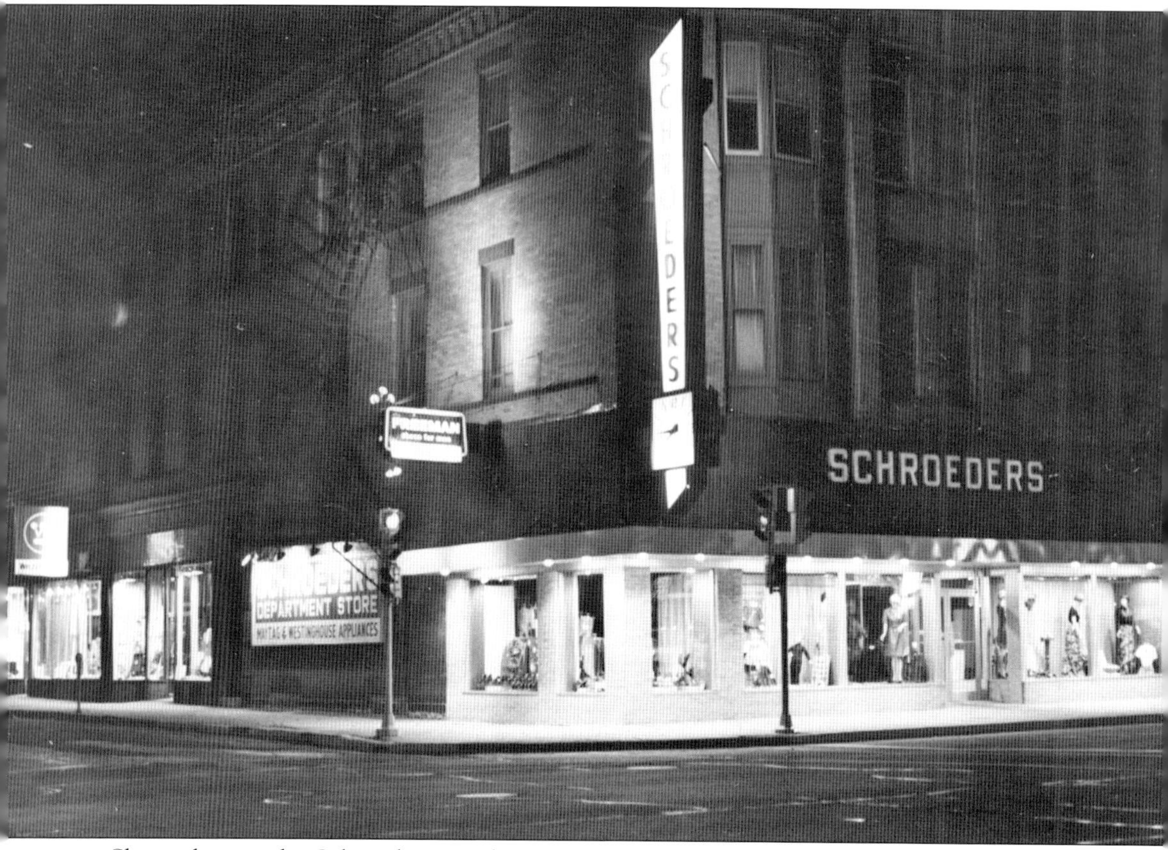

Shown here is the Schroeder store lit up at night in 1971. This was before the Seventeenth Street side of the building was covered up due to the energy crisis in the late 1970s. (Courtesy of John Schroeder.)

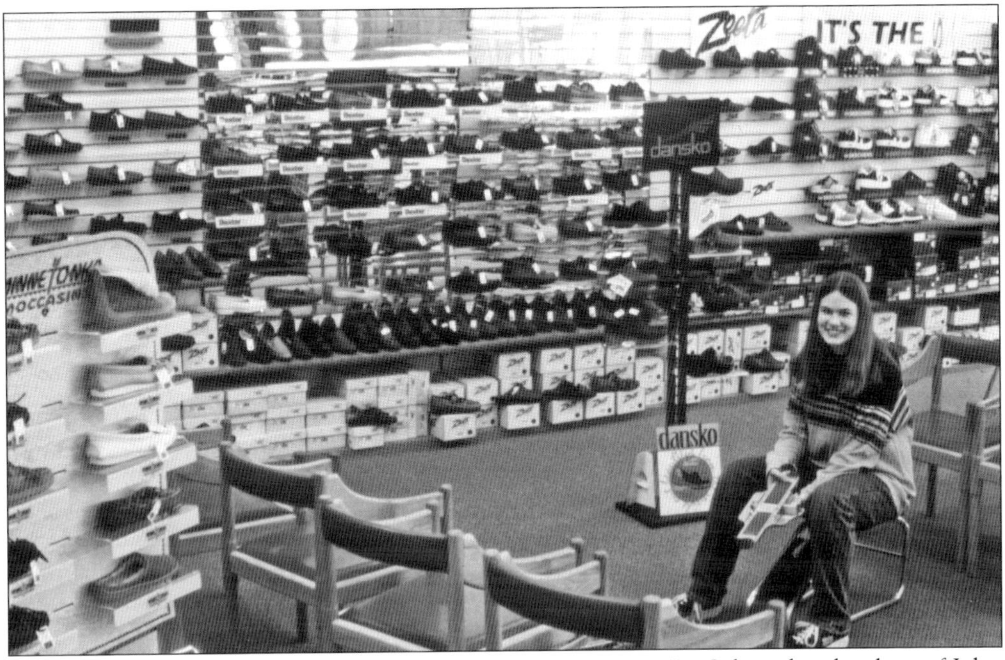

In May 1999, Schroeder's was fully stocked to help customers. Liz Schroeder, daughter of John Schroeder, waits on the fitting stool to help a customer. Just like in the beginning, Schroeder's employees take the time to measure the customers' feet and fit them with shoes. (Courtesy of Schroeder's Department Store.)

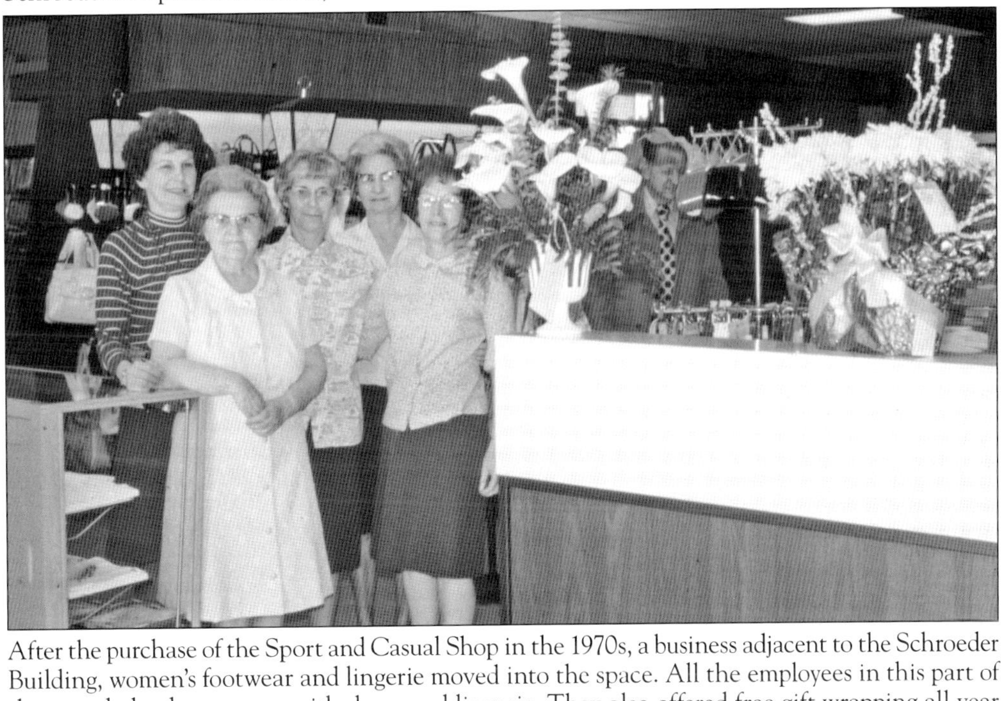

After the purchase of the Sport and Casual Shop in the 1970s, a business adjacent to the Schroeder Building, women's footwear and lingerie moved into the space. All the employees in this part of the store helped customers with shoes and lingerie. They also offered free gift wrapping all year round. Pictured from left to right are Joyce Ducat, Cele Durocher, Bea Naidl, Louise Bravit, and Lucile Peshek. (Courtesy of Schroeder's Department Store.)

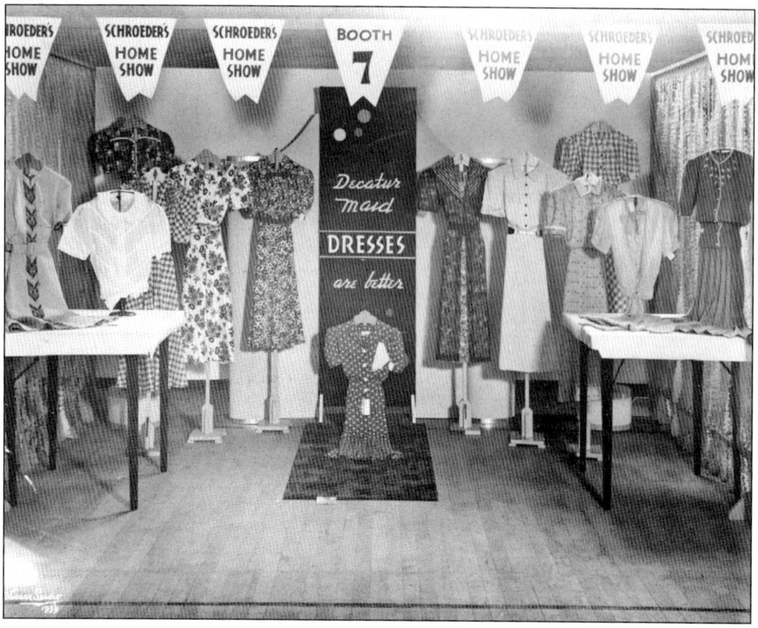

The women's ready-to-wear department had a booth at the Schroeder's Home Show. They featured Decatur dresses and separates. The ready-to-wear women's clothing department was located on the second floor of Schroeder's. (Courtesy of Vassar Studio and the Schroeder Brothers Company.)

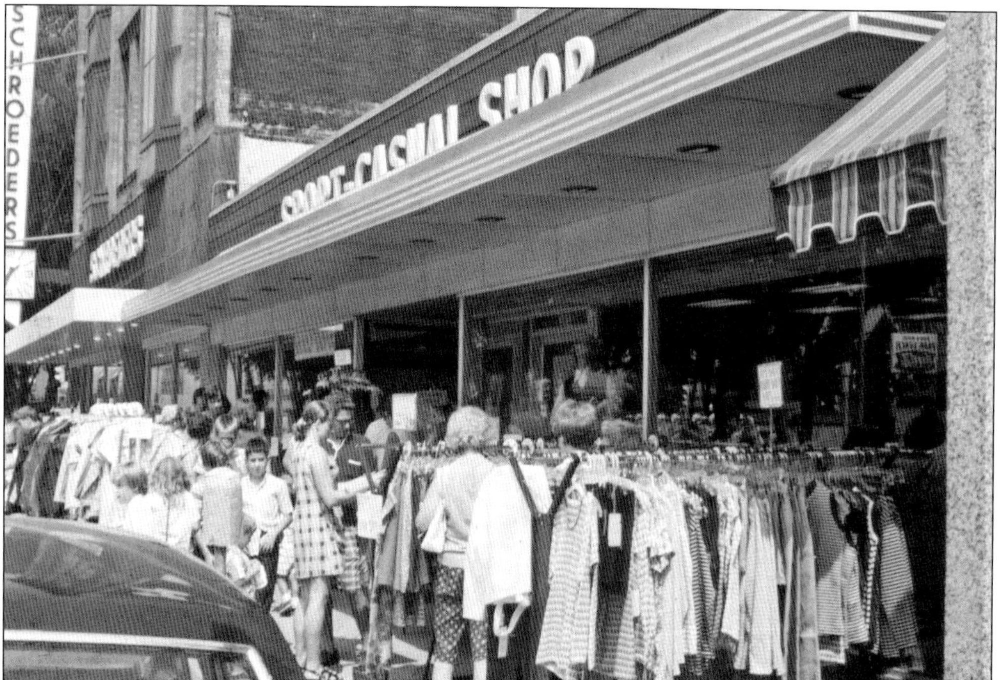

This image was captured during the Maxwell Street Day Sale in August 1970. Clearance sales could be found everywhere in the city of Two Rivers during this event. In addition to sales at local businesses, local clubs sold food in Central Park, and a ping pong ball drop took place in the afternoon. (Courtesy of John Schroeder.)

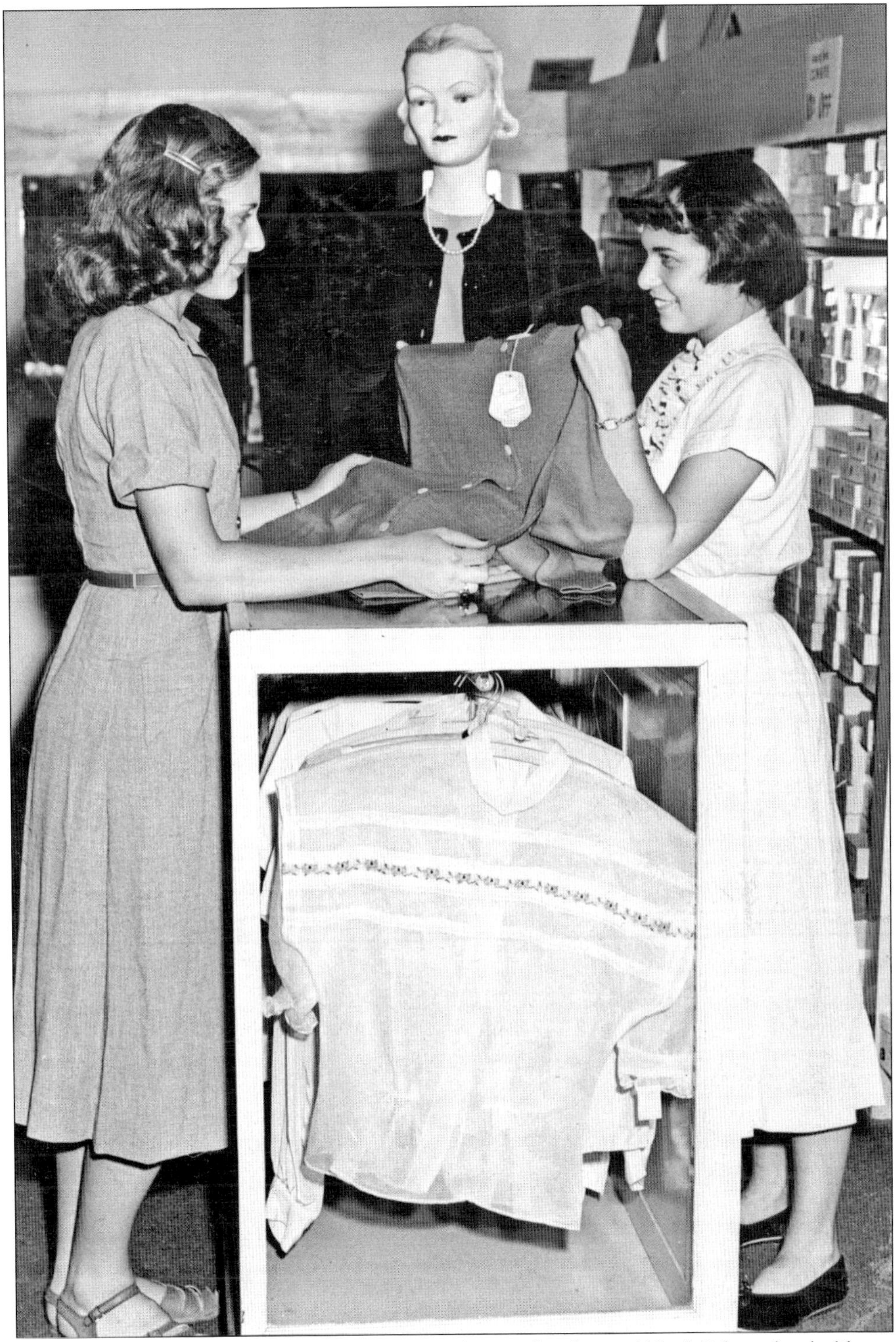

Pictured here on the right, Betty Schroeder Schnorr, daughter of Neal Schroeder, holds up a cardigan sweater with a coworker. Many family members have worked at Schroeder's over the years. (Courtesy of Schroeder's Department Store.)

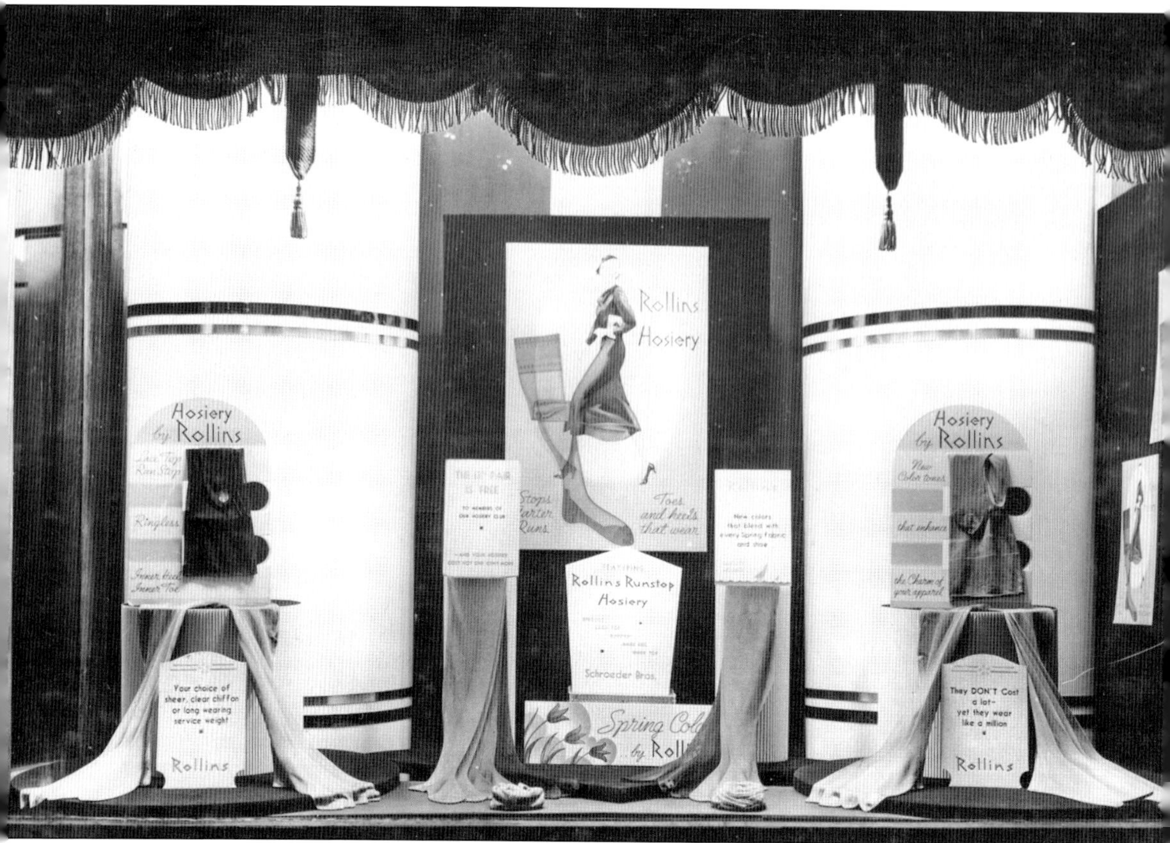

Window displays were a great way to showcase the items for sale inside Schroeder's. In this window facing Washington Street, Rollins Hosiery is featured. These hosiery options for ladies were sold in the women's department in slender boxes. (Courtesy of Schroeder's Department Store.)

Gregory "Gunner" Schroeder works outside at the 1971 Maxwell Street Day Sale. Gunner worked with his dad, Gary, and brother John in the men's shoe department before heading back to college. (Courtesy of John Schroeder.)

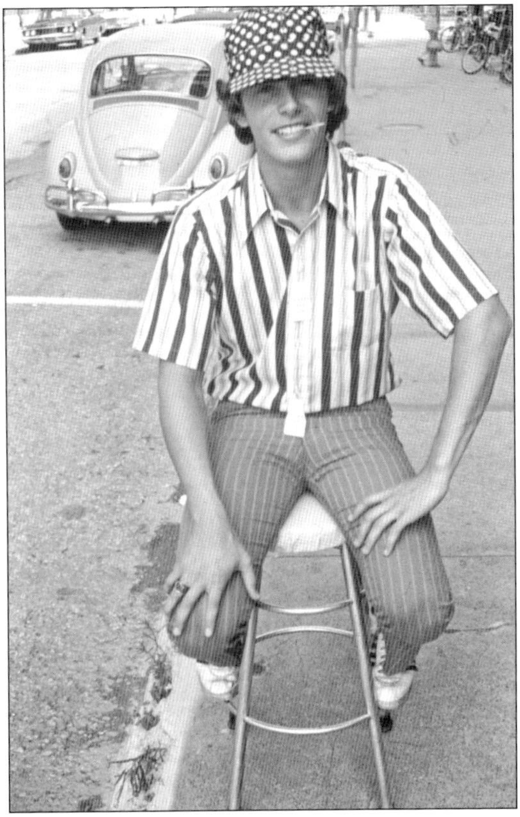

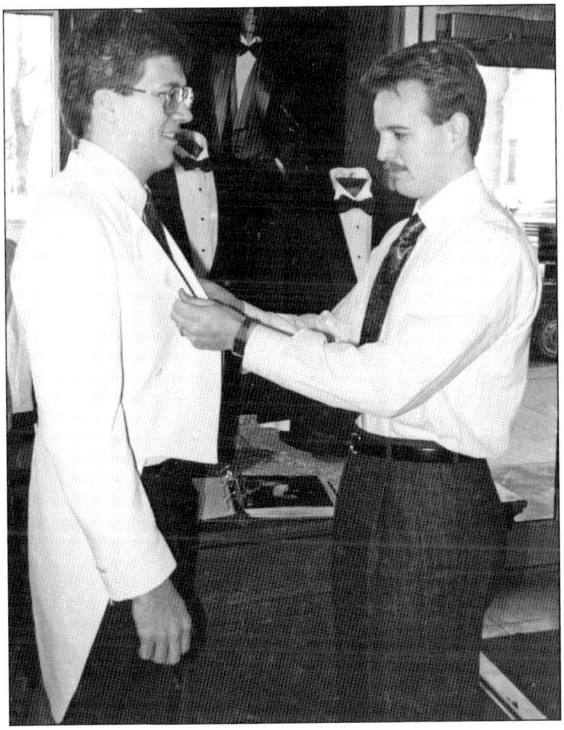

Lowell Johnson is being fitted in a tuxedo by Don Klingseisen in the men's apparel department. Even today, couples with upcoming nuptials can rent tuxedos or suits at Schroeder's Department Store. This photograph was used in newspaper advertising in the 1980s. (Courtesy of Schroeder's Department Store.)

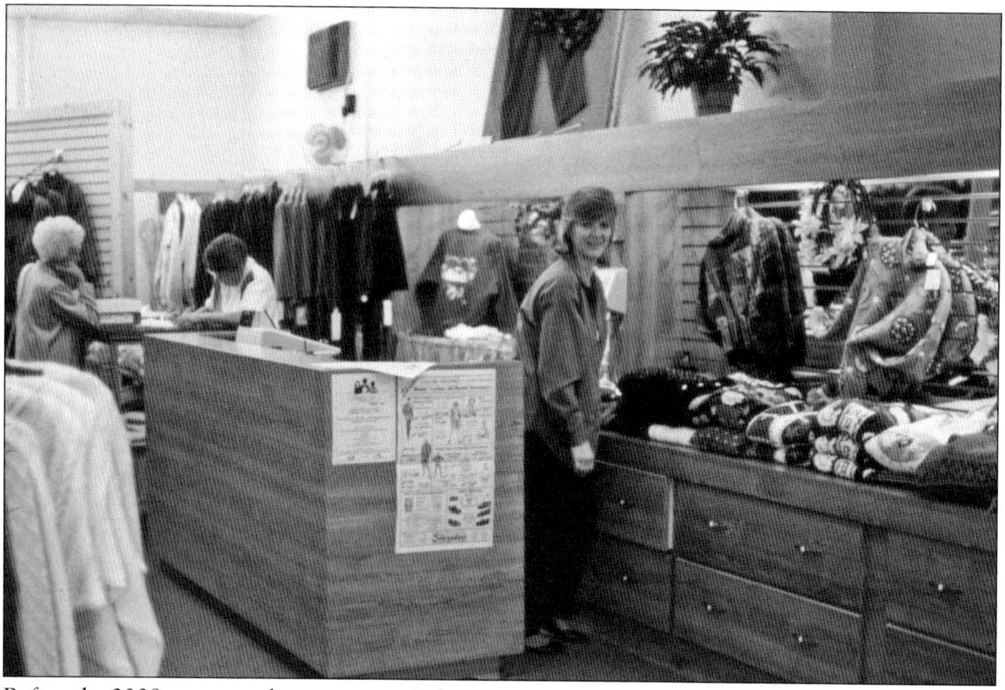

Before the 2008 move combining women's departments on the first floor, several employees worked in the women's dress department. In 2008, the women's department on first floor was expanded so the then-current managers, John and Tim, could combine the second-floor women's dress department with the first-floor casual women's department. This move made women's clothing more accessible to everyone traveling through to visit the coffeehouse. This photograph was taken during the 100th anniversary sale in 1991. (Courtesy of Schroeder's Department Store.)

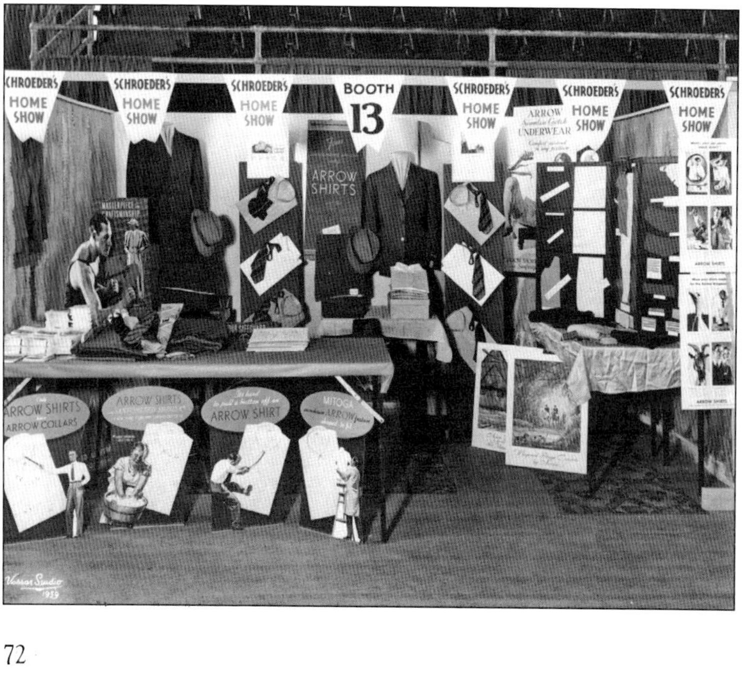

Booth 13 features a prominent Arrow shirt display for the attendees at the Home Show. Stylish suits and hats make for a very classic display. (Courtesy of Vassar Studio and the Schroeder Brothers Company.)

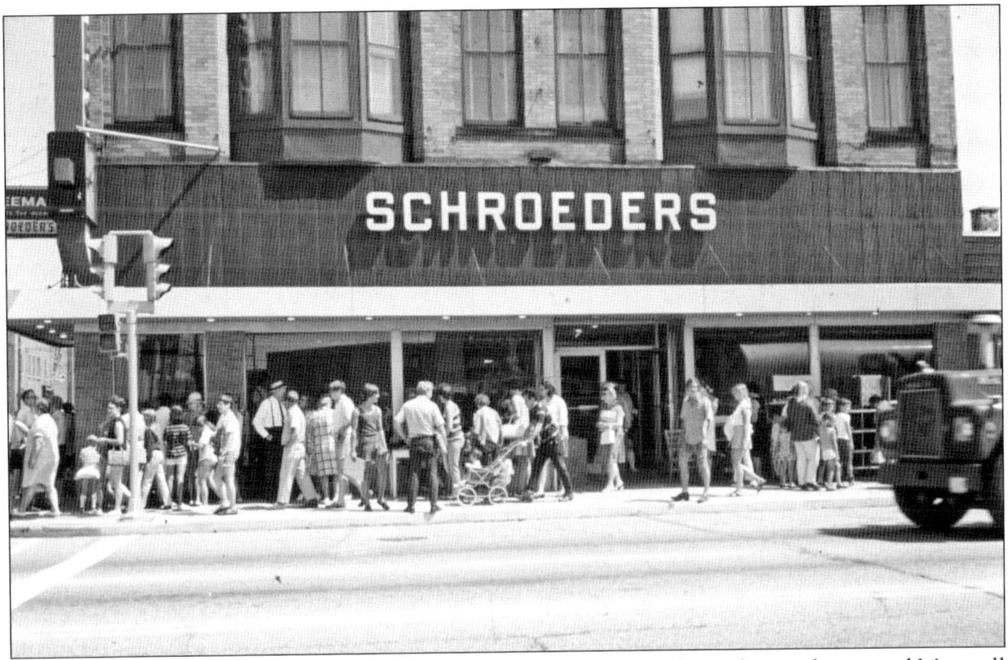

Seen here is a view of the crowds outside Schroeder's Department Store during the annual Maxwell Street Day Sale in August 1971. Crowds gathered in the afternoon, waiting for the helicopter to drop ping pong balls. (Courtesy of John Schroeder.)

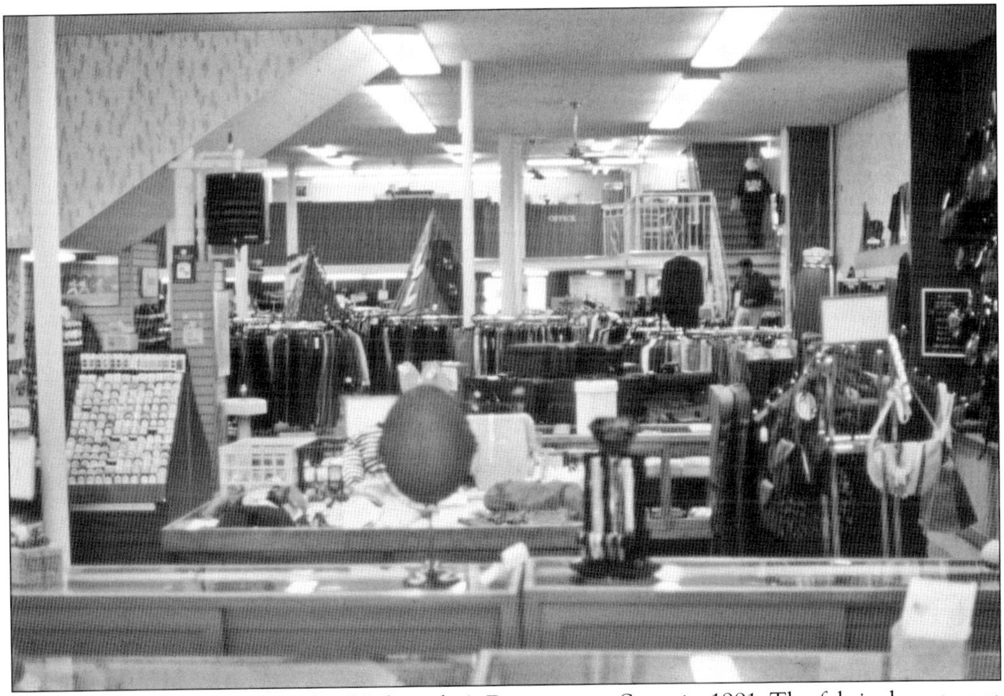

This is an interior photograph of Schroeder's Department Store in 1991. The fabric department was located to the left of the image; a thread display can be seen. Men's clothing takes up the entire body of the first floor. (Courtesy of the Schroeder Brothers Company.)

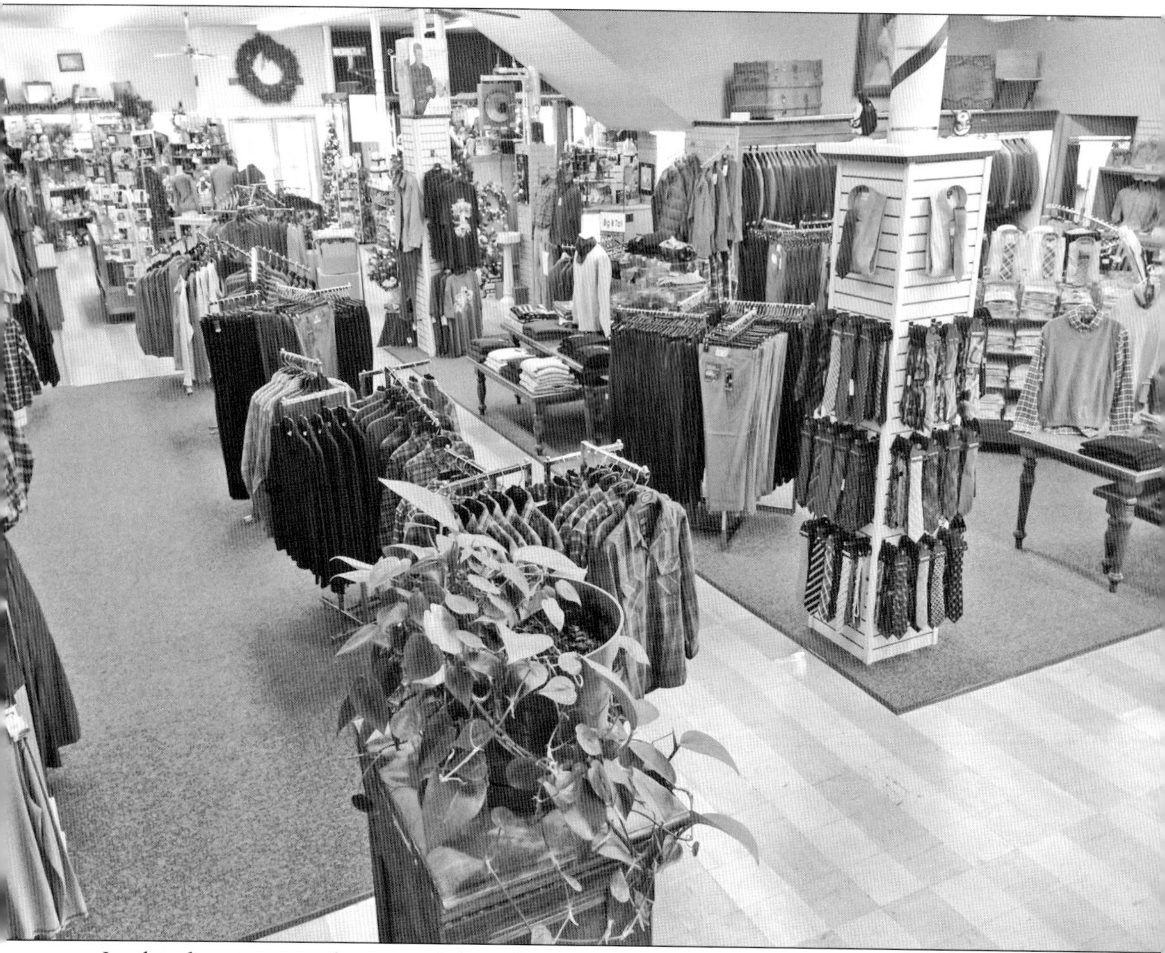

In this favorite view for many Schroeder's customers, one can see the entire store from the balcony and the office area. In 2014, A.J. and Theresa moved the men's shoes and outerwear to the very east part of the first floor. A few remodeling changes took place to make the space feel more inviting, but in the course of a few weeks, the move was complete. Now, walking into the rear entrance of Schroeder's, one will see the men's shoe department. The original men's chairs and fitting stools, along with the trusty Brannock devices, are all ready for employees to help customers. (Courtesy of Schroeder's Department Store.)

Four

Great Depression Survival

Many businesses did not survive the stock market crash of 1929 or the Great Depression that followed. Struggles at the store lasted longer than the national average, but changes were made to make the future of Schroeder's possible. According to the minute books from Schroeders Brothers Company, Inc., many family members assumed roles at the business. The first-generation employees included Frank, Peter, and John. The second-generation employees included Neal (Joseph Schroeder), Hubert (John Schroeder), Hilary (Joseph Schroeder), Louis (John Schroeder), and Peter Beth (Katherine). In early 1929, founding brother Joseph passed away from typhoid fever. Throughout the 1930s, more Schroeder family members were brought into the business. Many Schroeder's were leaching off the store during the Great Depression. Frank stepped in and assumed the role of "ax-man" and fired most of the family members not pulling their weight. In addition to firing personnel, the Schroeder's needed to collect on large balances kept on account. Due to many shareholders not paying on their accounts, Neal presented a plan that would reduce capital stock and help pay off the account balances. One family took advantage of this exchange, but many did not pay on their accounts. Heated exchanges happened at almost every board meeting. Neal worked on fixing the financial situation by reducing expenses and having customers pay more money on the overdrawn accounts. Neal, Hubert, and Ray formed a committee to improve conditions on the sales floor. They traveled to Kaukana and Green Bay to visit other area stores and gain ideas on changes to be made. One successful trip helped form the fabric department. The Great Depression left families with little money to buy finished goods. It was cheaper to buy fabric and make the clothing themselves. Schroeder's installed a full fabric department along with patterns and notions. Until 1939, advertising for the store was done through the Rivoli firm; Neal went ahead and discontinued use of the service and made Raymond merchandise and advertising manager. The first and second generations made changes to put the business back on a secure business footing by calling in bad debts, cutting expenses, and adding business categories that would be more profitable. They cut employees and unnecessary grocery deliveries and reigned in advertising expenses. They added a fabric department, paint, and linoleum and expanded the grocery department. Schroeder's attributed their success on good leadership and great employees. The Schroeder model of success is knowledge of products, friendliness, and service.

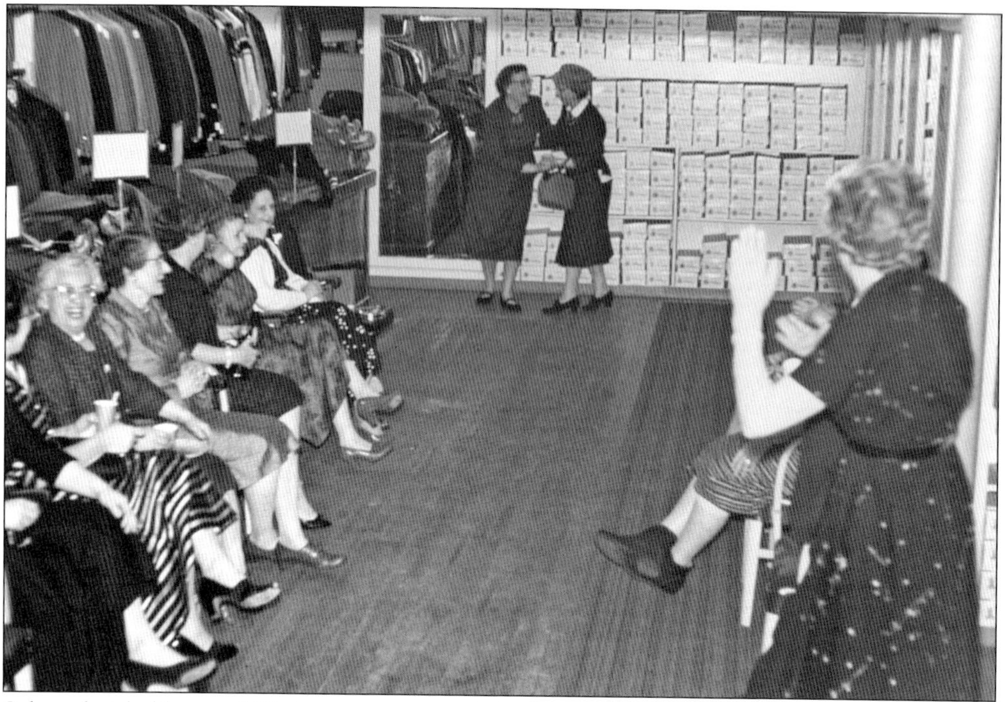

Schroeder's held annual Christmas parties and shopping nights for the employees. Owners would play music and serve food and beverages. Pictured here are the ladies of Schroeder's dancing and having a fun time. (Courtesy of Julie Schroeder.)

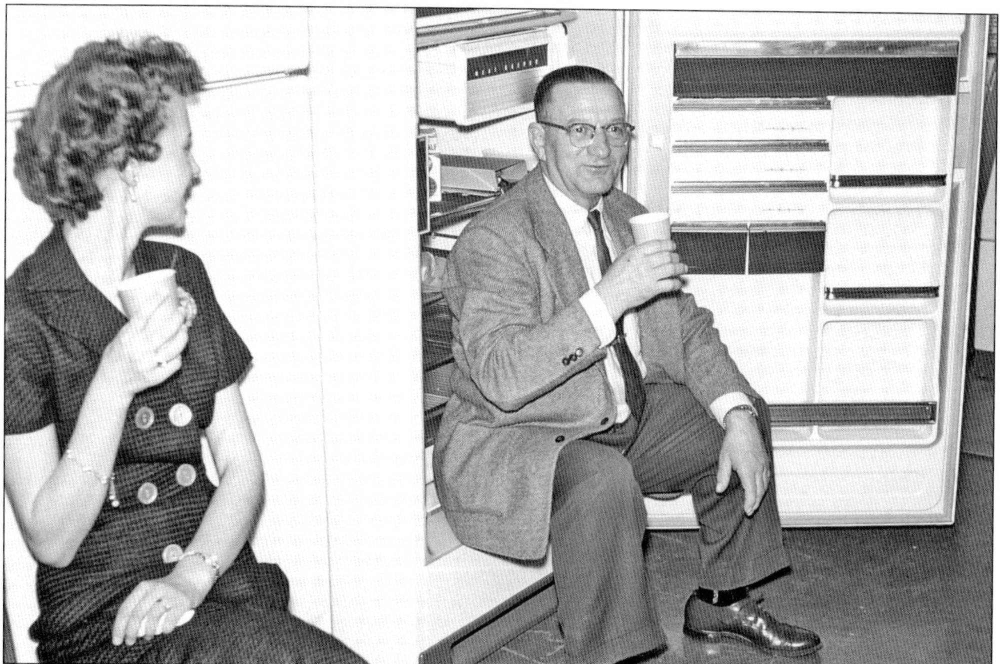

The employees found seating whereever they could. The men would sit and chat while the ladies danced and laughed. Here, one of the employees is resting in a Westinghouse refrigerator. (Courtesy of Julie Schroeder.)

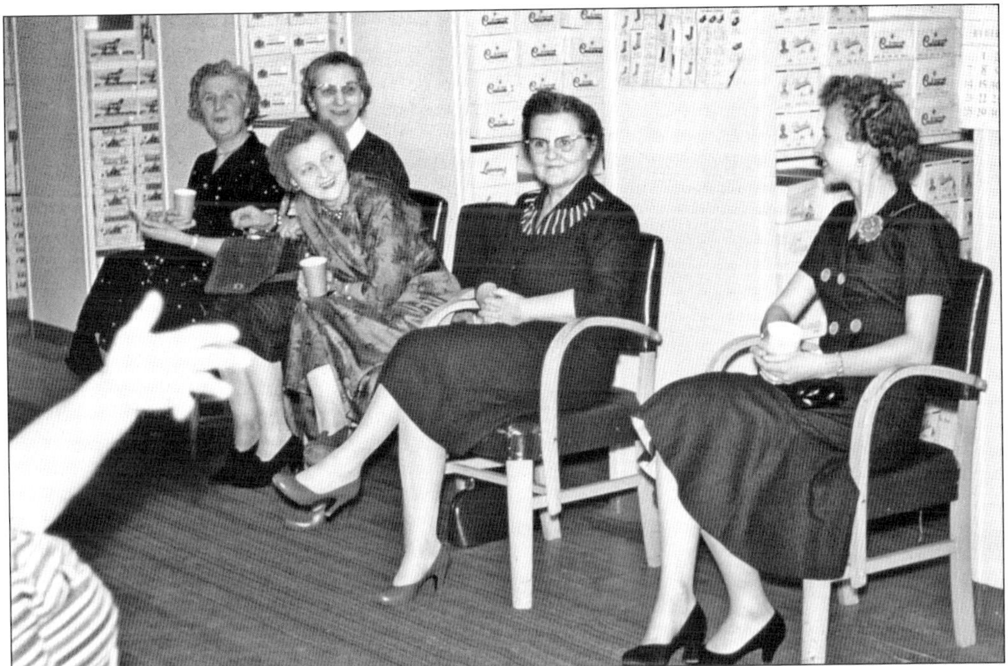

This is another view of the Christmas festivities as the ladies take a break from dancing. Behind them are the large bookcases used to hold the men's shoe boxes. This party was held in the basement of the Schroeder Building. Some of the ladies were employees, while others are spouses. (Courtesy of Julie Schroeder.)

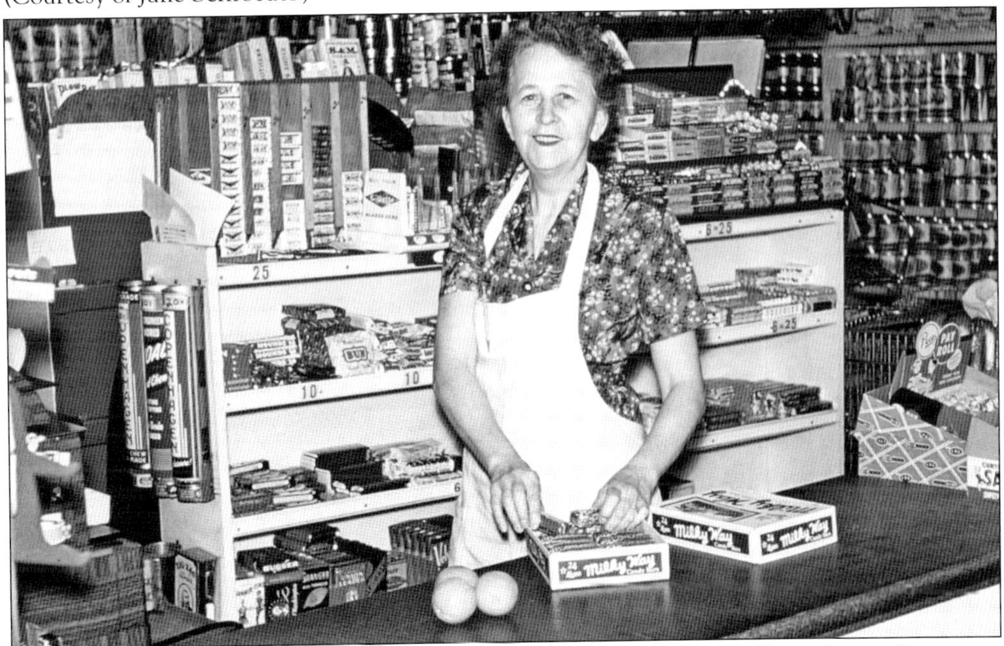

Margaret Arnemann worked in the grocery department. She was busy filling the candy counter in 1958 when this photograph was taken. The grocery department was located near the rear entrance of Schroeder's. The store was always closed on Sundays, and this is when Gary and Connie Schroeder would do their grocery shopping. (Courtesy of Julie Schroeder.)

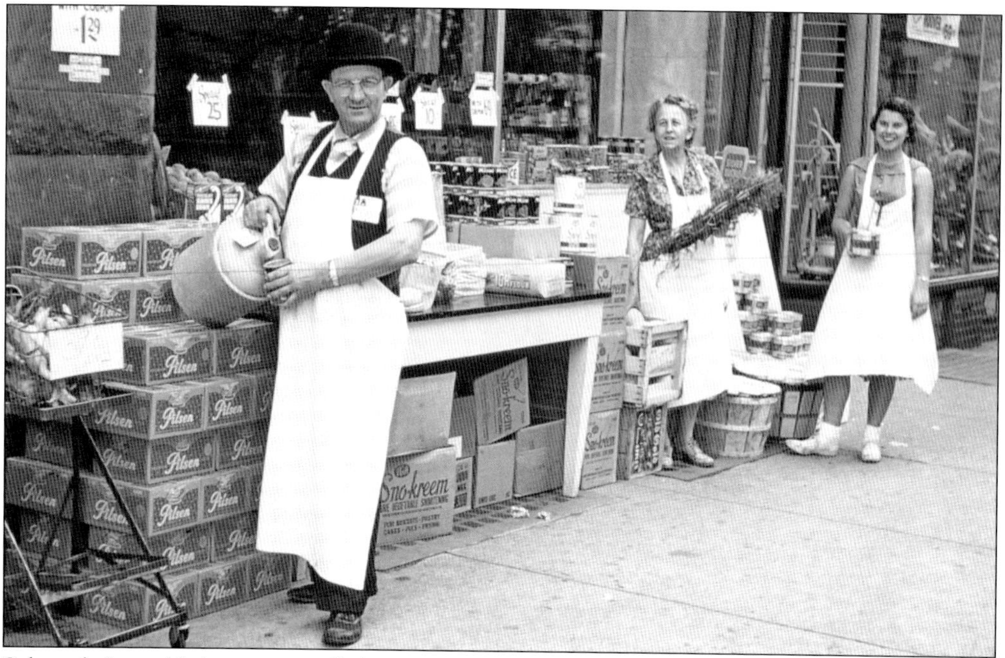

Schroeder's would always move all the grocery displays outside on nice days. Here, three employees set up shop for the day on Seventeenth Street. Customers would stroll up and down and stop at all the shops. The grocery department was in a steady decline in sales for nearly 20 years, and after 1960, Schroeder's finally closed the department. (Courtesy of Julie Schroeder.)

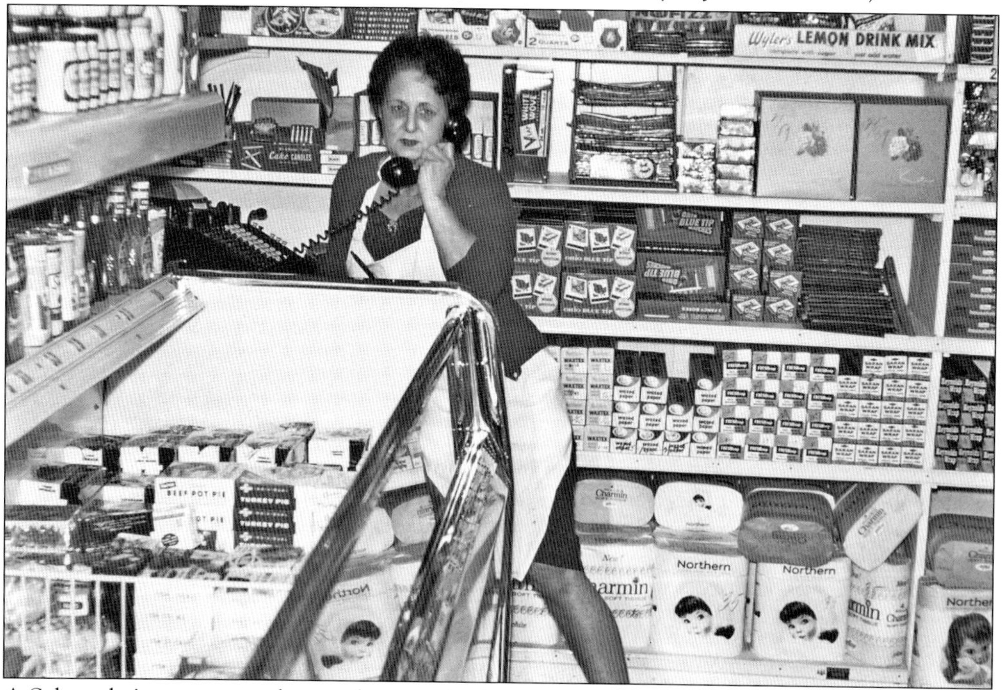

A Schroeder's grocery employee take an order from a customer over the phone. Schroeder's used every usable space for sales space. The phone and adding machine are tucked in a tiny space by the paper products. (Courtesy of Julie Schroeder.)

Five

Memorabilia

Schroeder's is a working museum. Theresa was working in the coffeehouse when a customer walked in with a younger person, saying, "This what stores looked like before Walmart." Theresa remembers thinking, "Am I working in a museum?" She laughs about it now, but it is true. Businesses do not operate the way Schroeder's operates anymore. The Schroeders know the customer walking in the door, they buy with that customer in mind, and they carry their packages out to their car for them, not because they have to, but because it is the right thing to do. Walking around Schroeder's, one will see items used years ago still being used today: the Brannock device and shoe horns in the shoe departments, the hemming device in alterations, and the simple measuring tape in men's clothing to assist in measuring guys for a new shirt or suit. Throughout the years at Schroeder's, many objects were given out to celebrate the different milestones. Gifts from Schroeder's, the Two Rivers Savings Bank, and the mill fill the artifacts case inside the Schroeder Building. While many articles were in the Schroeders' possession, customers have brought in various items as well.

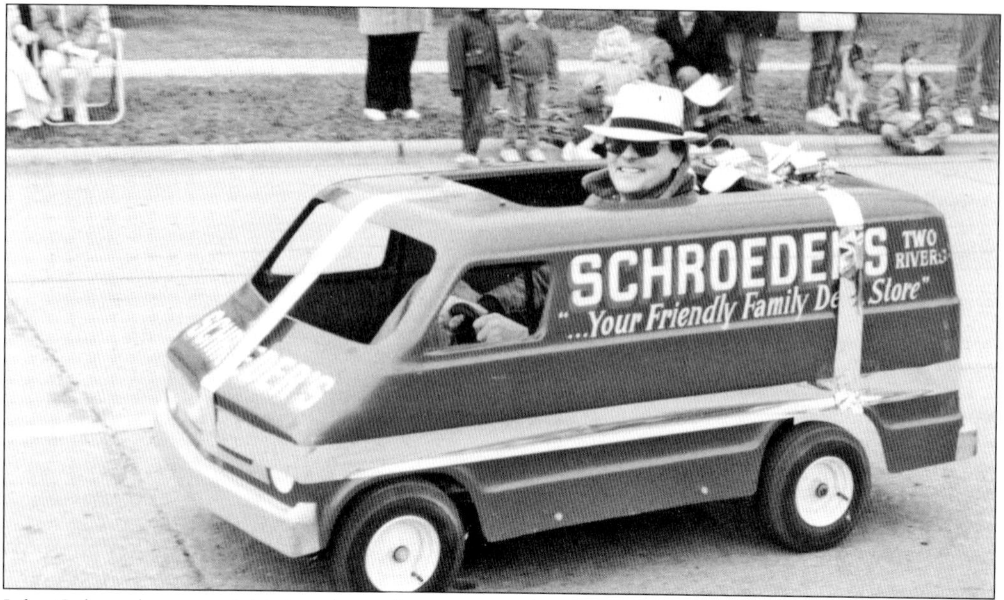

John Schroeder started driving the go-kart given to him by Wrangler as a free promotion in 1972. Every year, John would entertain people in the local Christmas and Snowfest parades. Bryan Ashenbrenner took over as driver in 2002, with John as maintenance crew. John was passing the baton to the next generation; as Bryan is A.J.'s husband, it was only fitting. The guys traveled to the Manitowoc holiday parades and had standing traditions every year. This is a photograph of John Schroeder tearing up the streets in the annual holiday parade. (Courtesy of the Schroeder Brothers Company.)

In 2004, there was a crash with the go-kart, and it went from blue to 1996 Viper Red. In Spring 2009, Connor Ashenbrenner was happy to pose with the Schroeder go-kart. His mother, A.J. Schroeder, used this photograph in newspaper advertising to promote Two Rivers t-shirts and sweatshirts for sale at the store. Bryan had the opportunity to buy another go-kart in 2014 for his son Connor Ashenbrenner, a fifth-generation Schroeder. (Courtesy of Schroeder's Department Store.)

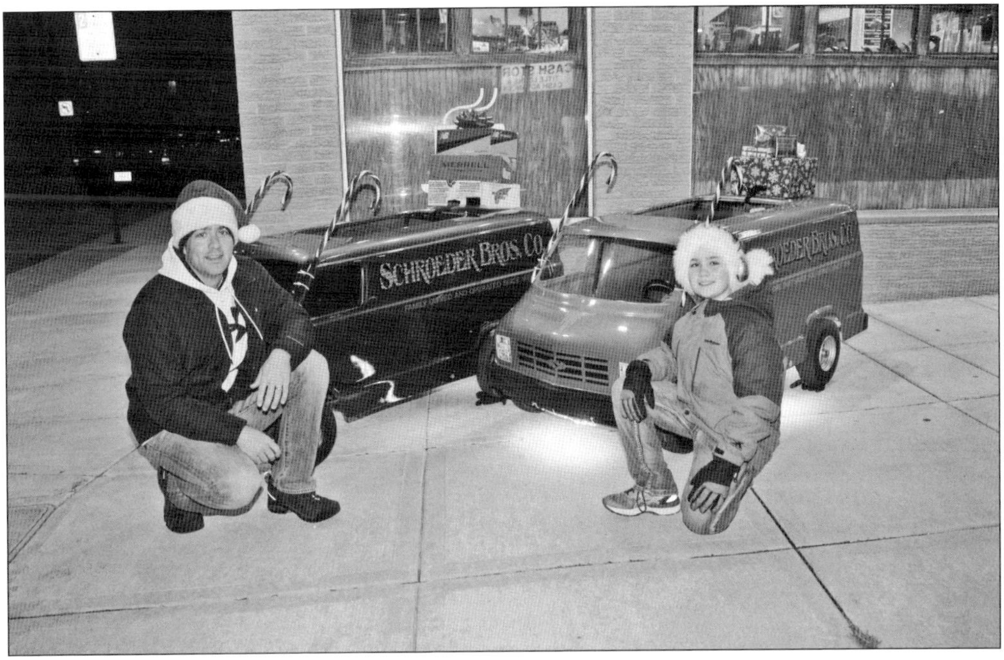

The fourth and fifth generation are now at the wheel of the famous Schroeder's go-karts. Bryan and Connor Ashenbrenner are the current drivers for the Schroeder's business. Pictured here from left to right, Bryan and Connor enjoy driving the go-karts during the holiday parades for Manitowoc and Two Rivers and the Fish Debry Parade in Two Rivers. (Courtesy of Rich Greenwood.)

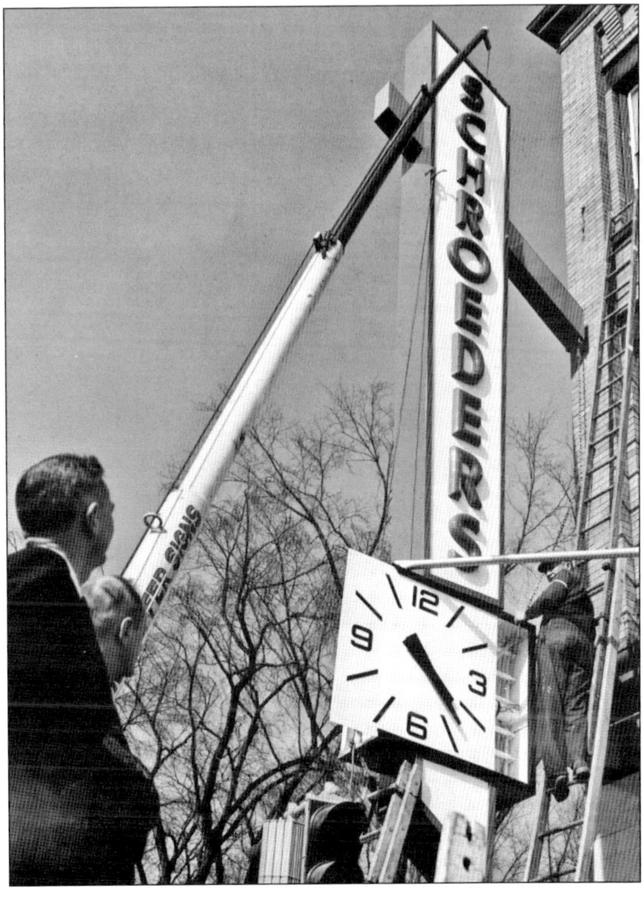

Schroeder's iconic store sign and clock can be seen when crossing the Washington Street Bridge while heading north on Washington Street. Gary, Neal, and Hilary Schroeder all had agreed to get the sign and clock installed on the building. In this photograph, Gary Schroeder watches from the sidewalk while the sign and clock face are put in place. (Courtesy of the Schroeder Brothers Company.)

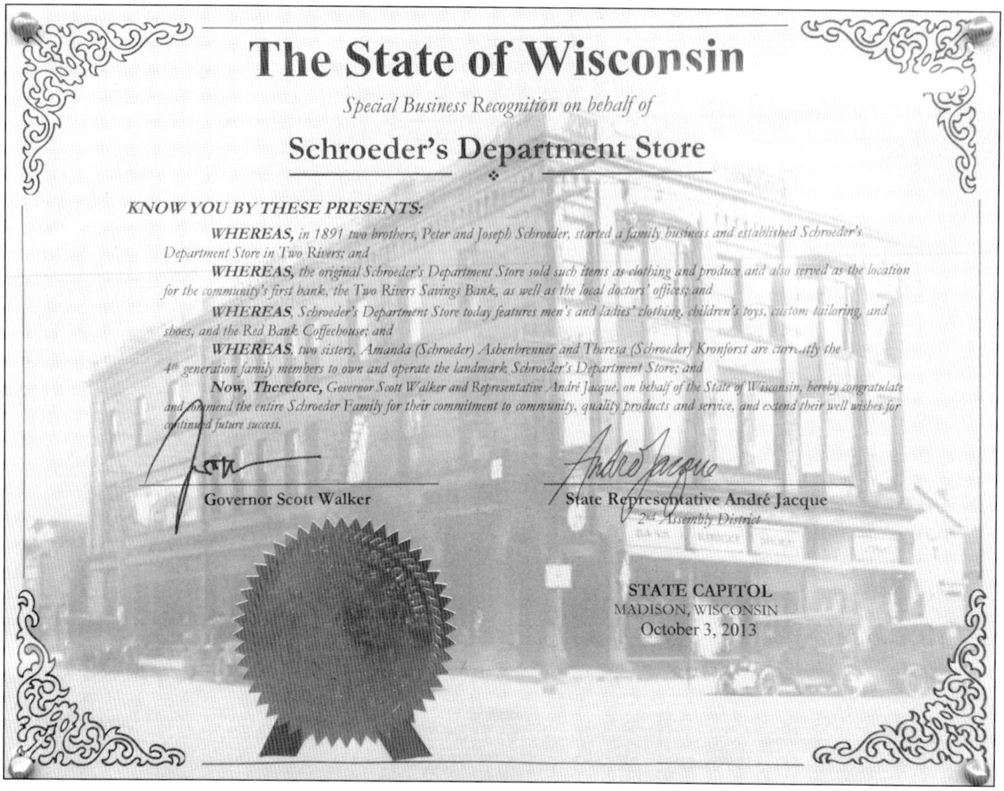

The State of Wisconsin

Special Business Recognition on behalf of

Schroeder's Department Store

KNOW YOU BY THESE PRESENTS:

WHEREAS, *in 1891 two brothers, Peter and Joseph Schroeder, started a family business and established Schroeder's Department Store in Two Rivers; and*

WHEREAS, *the original Schroeder's Department Store sold such items as clothing and produce and also served as the location for the community's first bank, the Two Rivers Savings Bank, as well as the local doctors' offices; and*

WHEREAS, *Schroeder's Department Store today features men's and ladies' clothing, children's toys, custom tailoring, and shoes, and the Red Bank Coffeehouse; and*

WHEREAS, *two sisters, Amanda (Schroeder) Ashenbrenner and Theresa (Schroeder) Kronforst are currently the 4th generation family members to own and operate the landmark Schroeder's Department Store; and*

Now, Therefore, *Governor Scott Walker and Representative André Jacque, on behalf of the State of Wisconsin, hereby congratulate and commend the entire Schroeder Family for their commitment to community, quality products and service, and extend their well wishes for continued future success.*

Governor Scott Walker

State Representative André Jacque
2nd Assembly District

STATE CAPITOL
MADISON, WISCONSIN
October 3, 2013

André Jacque, a 2013 Wisconsin state representative, honored A.J. and Theresa with plaques for special recognition regarding their commitment to keeping the business alive. (Courtesy of the Schroeder Brothers Company.)

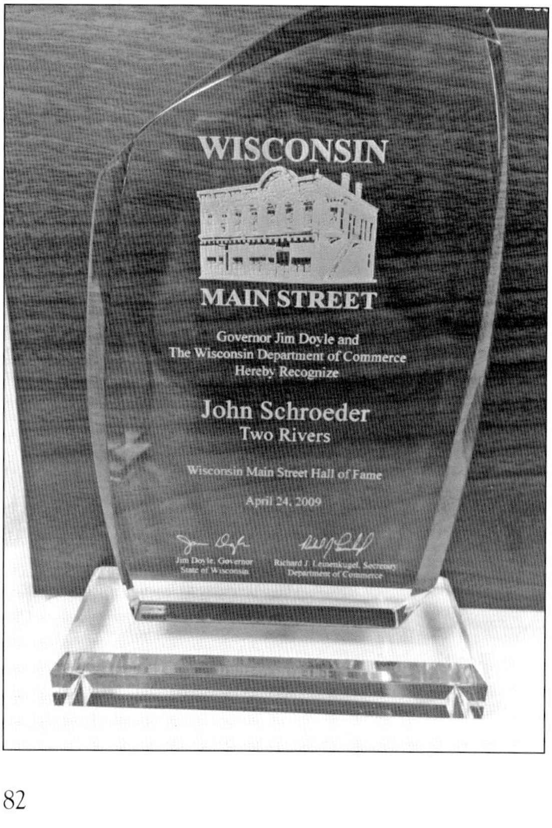

At the 2009 Wisconsin Main Street Awards banquet in Wausau, Wisconsin, John C. Schroeder was inducted into the Wisconsin Main Street Hall of Fame. John passed away December 22, 2008. (Courtesy of the Schroeder Brothers Company.)

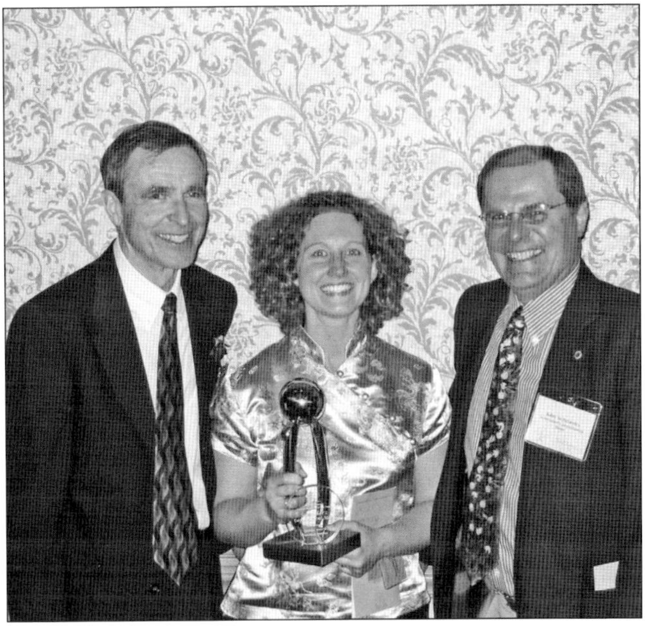

The Wisconsin Family Business of the Year Small Company Special Award Hometown Tradition was awarded to Schroeder's Department Store in 2004. Mike Molepske, son of Kay Schroeder (daughter of Neal Schroeder), was employed with Associated Bank. He nominated the Schroeder's store. Tim, Karen, Nancy, John, A.J., and Bryan all headed down to Madison with no expectations to win, but they did. Pictured from left to right are Tim Schroeder, A.J. (Schroeder) Ashenbrenner, and John Schroeder. (Courtesy of the Schroeder Brothers Company.)

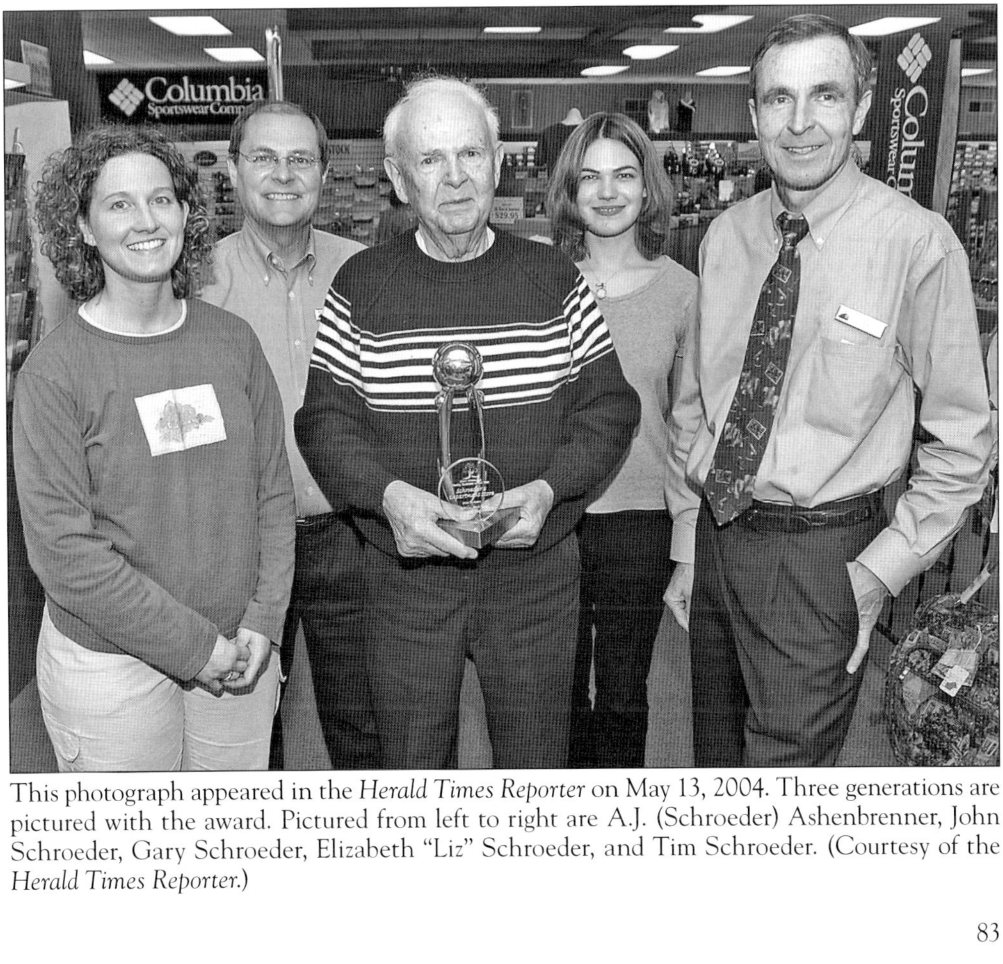

This photograph appeared in the *Herald Times Reporter* on May 13, 2004. Three generations are pictured with the award. Pictured from left to right are A.J. (Schroeder) Ashenbrenner, John Schroeder, Gary Schroeder, Elizabeth "Liz" Schroeder, and Tim Schroeder. (Courtesy of the *Herald Times Reporter*.)

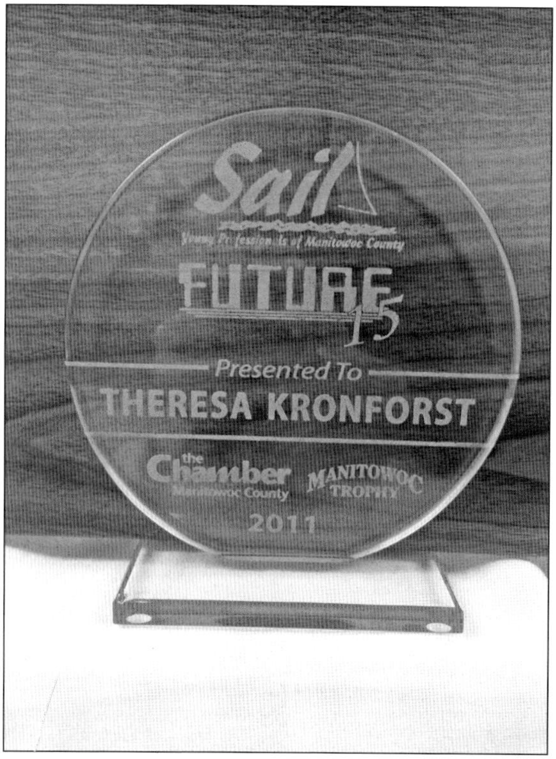

Theresa Kronforst was awarded the Future 15 award from the Manitowoc County Chamber of Commerce. The Future 15 honors business owners 40 years old and younger in Manitowoc County. (Courtesy of Schroeder's Department Store.)

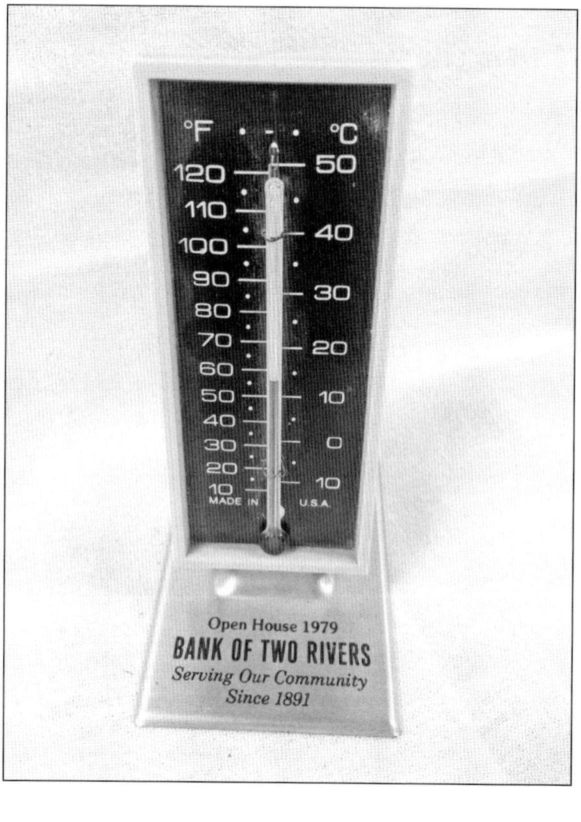

This thermometer was given to loyal customers that banked with Two Rivers Savings Bank, located in the northwest corner of the building. (Courtesy of the Schroeder Brothers Company.)

A dime bank given to children to save money was a common gift to encourage children to save every penny—or in this case, dime. (Courtesy of the Schroeder Brothers Company.)

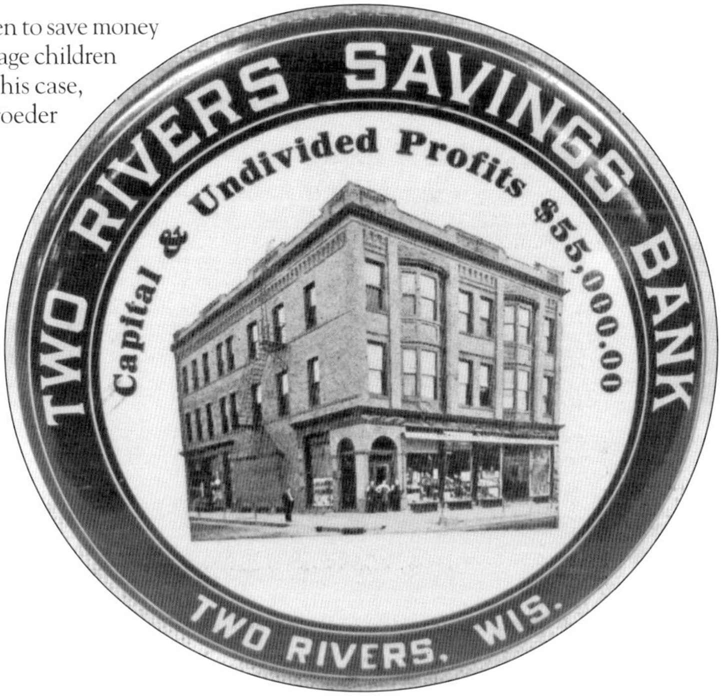

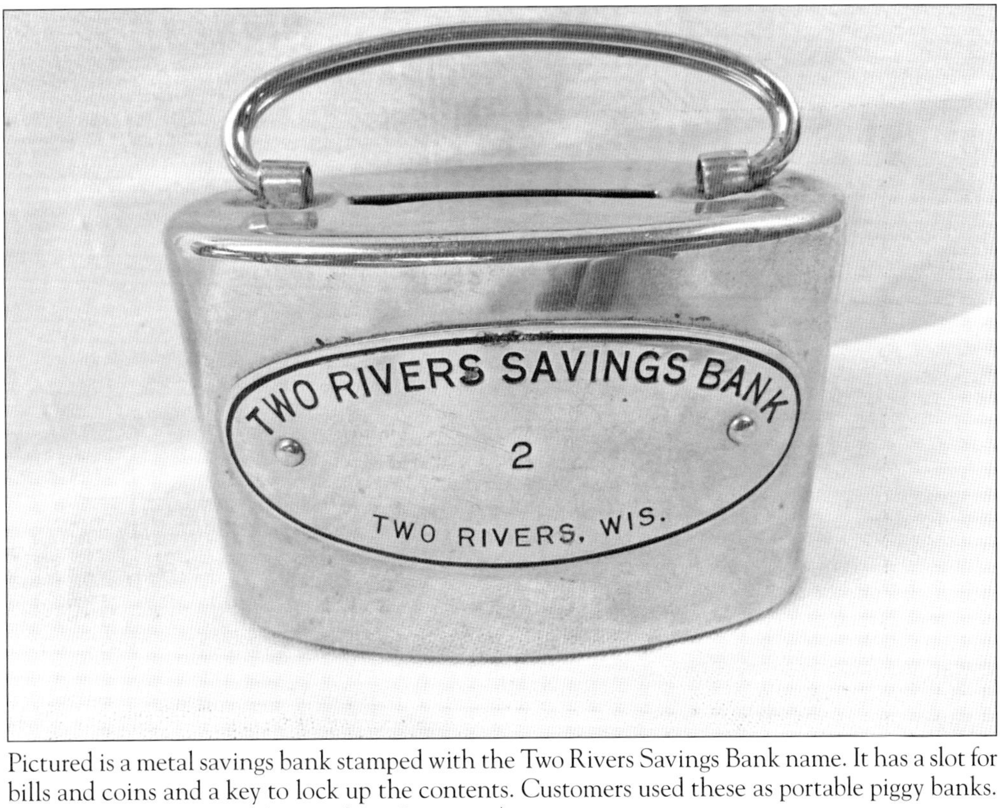

Pictured is a metal savings bank stamped with the Two Rivers Savings Bank name. It has a slot for bills and coins and a key to lock up the contents. Customers used these as portable piggy banks. (Courtesy of the Schroeder Brothers Company.)

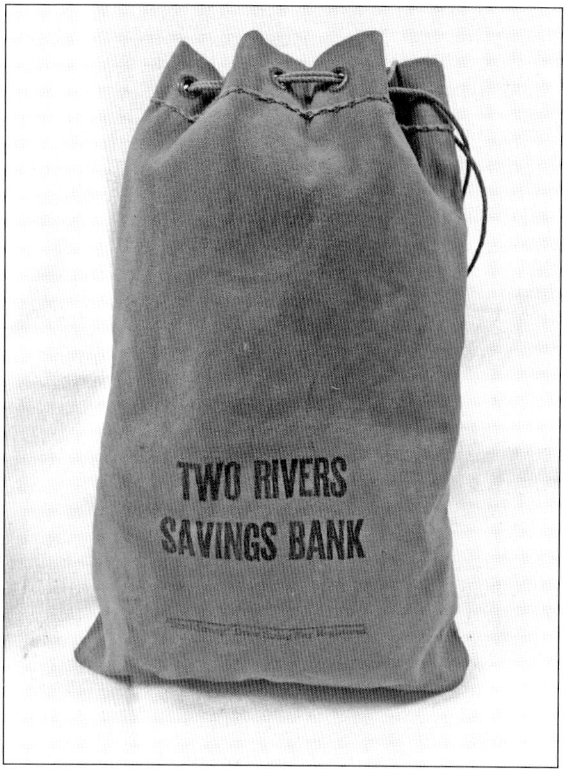

The Two Rivers Savings Bank bags were found while cleaning the Schroeder's office. Mostly used to carry change and notes, the bags were tied simply at the top. (Courtesy of the Schroeder Brothers Company.)

Dustpans were given as gifts from the Schroeder Mill in 1948. The pans were very useful gifts to the many farmer patrons that supported the mill. Schroeder's has three dustpans in their possession: one with a handle and two without. (Courtesy of the Schroeder Brothers Company.)

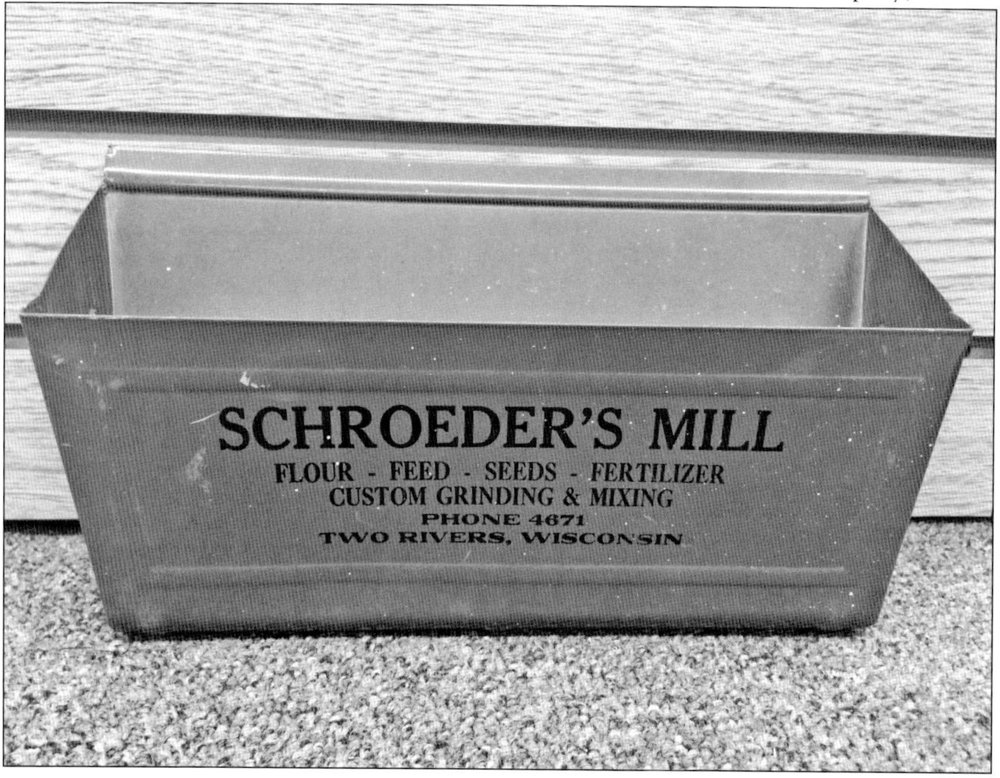

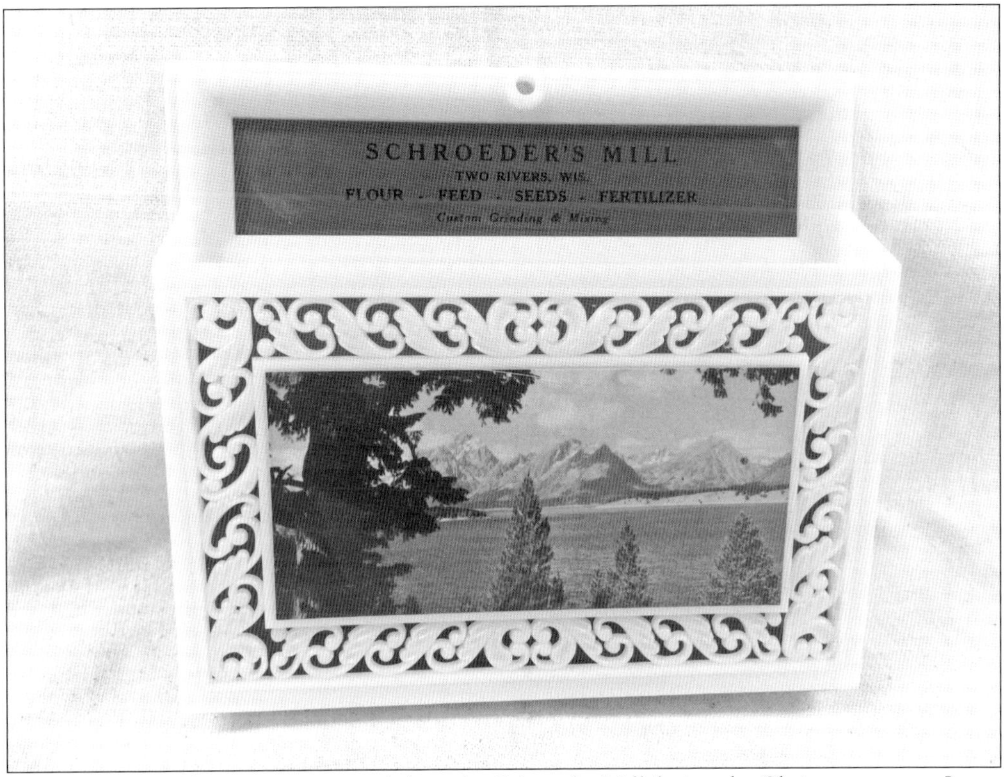

This envelope holder was given as a gift from the Schroeder Mill during the Christmas season. It was used to promote the products at the mill and reminded customers of the custom grinding and mixing. The mill housed a special mixer for molasses. (Courtesy of the Schroeder Brothers Company.)

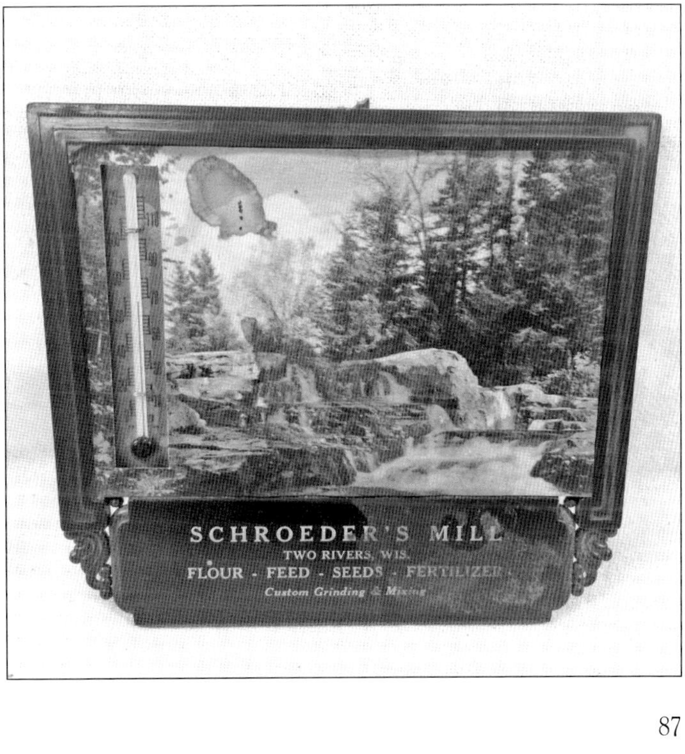

This thermometer was another Christmas gift from the Schroeder Mill to its customers. This thermometer was brought in from a farmstead just north of Two Rivers. It features a scene similar to the falls near Maribel Caves, near Maribel, Wisconsin. (Courtesy of the Schroeder Brothers Company.)

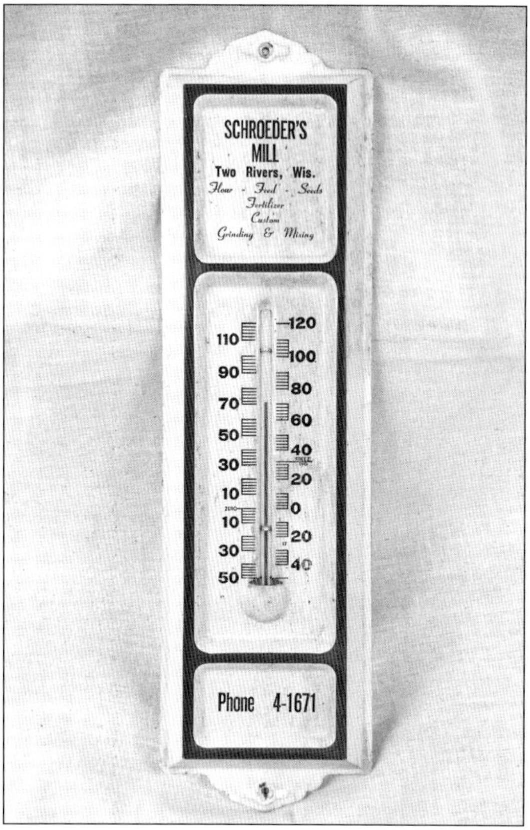

A metal thermometer was given to farmers of the community that were loyal customers to the mill. The Schroeder Mill added their phone number: 4-1671. (Courtesy of the Schroeder Brothers Company.)

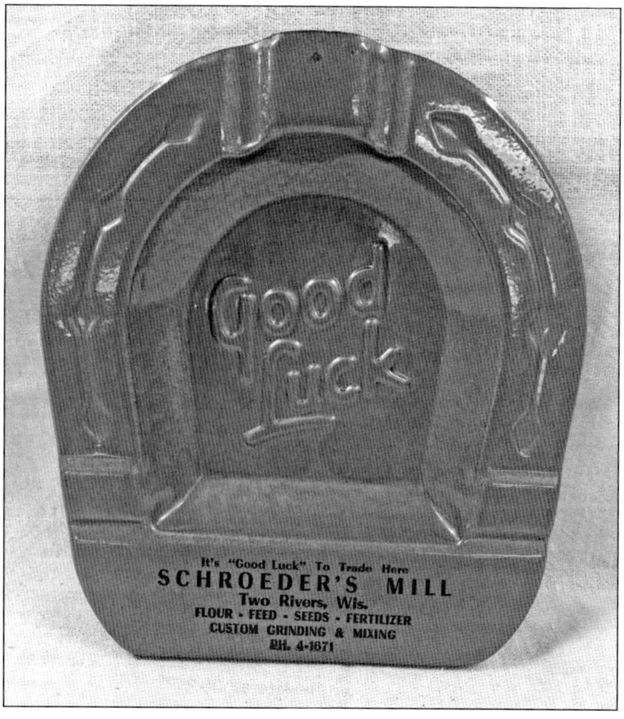

This ashtray is in the shape of a horseshoe, stating that it's "Good Luck to Shop Here." These metal ashtrays were given away to help advertise the Schroeder Mill. (Courtesy of the Schroeder Brothers Company.)

Schroeder's recovered this October 7, 1893, statement to a customer for goods taken out on credit. The customer was the Hamilton Manufacturing Company, located one block from Schroeder's on Jefferson Street in Two Rivers. The amount owed to the store was $17.83. (Courtesy of the Schroeder Brothers Company.)

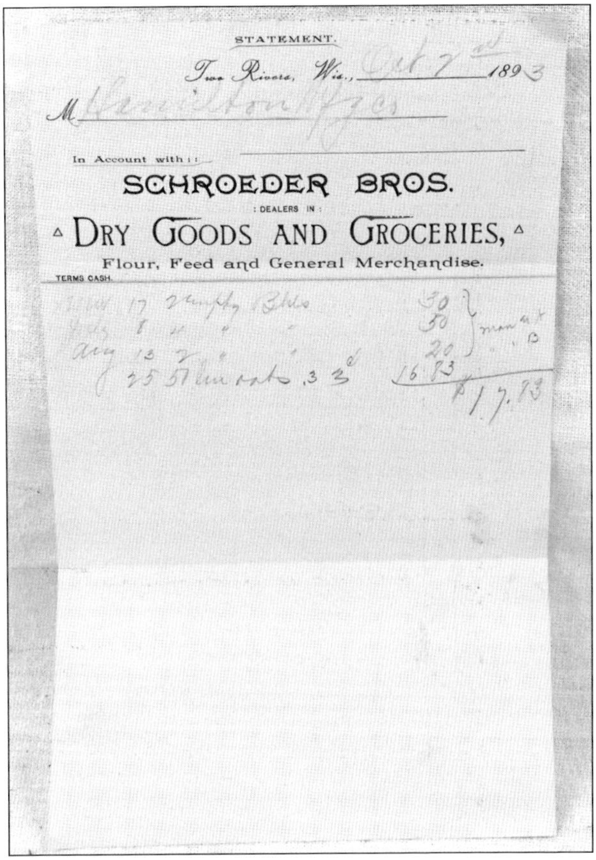
STATEMENT.

Two Rivers, Wis., Oct 7th 1893

M

In Account with ::

SCHROEDER BROS.

: DEALERS IN :

DRY GOODS AND GROCERIES,

Flour, Feed and General Merchandise.

TERMS CASH.

$17.83

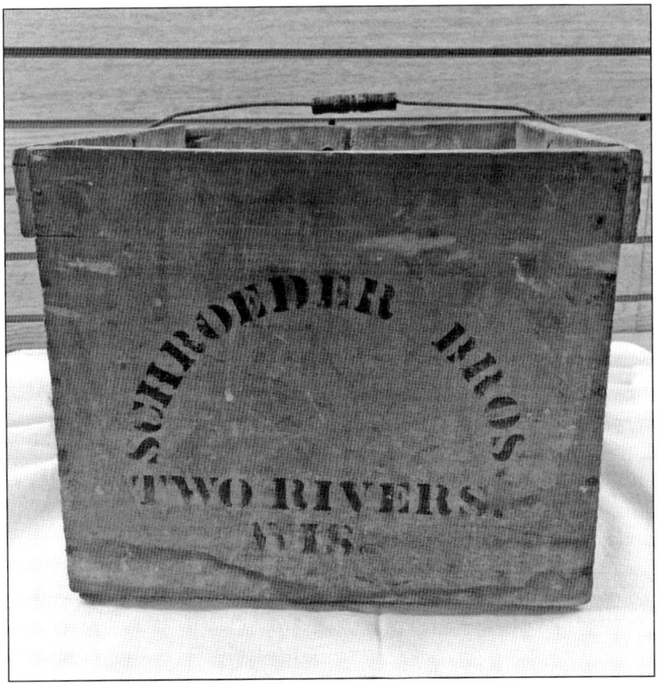

Liz Schroeder, daughter of John Schroeder, bought this egg crate and donated it to the Schroeder artifacts area. Farmers would fill the crate with fresh eggs and bring it to Schroeder's grocery department. The store would then give that farmer credit on account. (Courtesy of Schroeder's Department Store.)

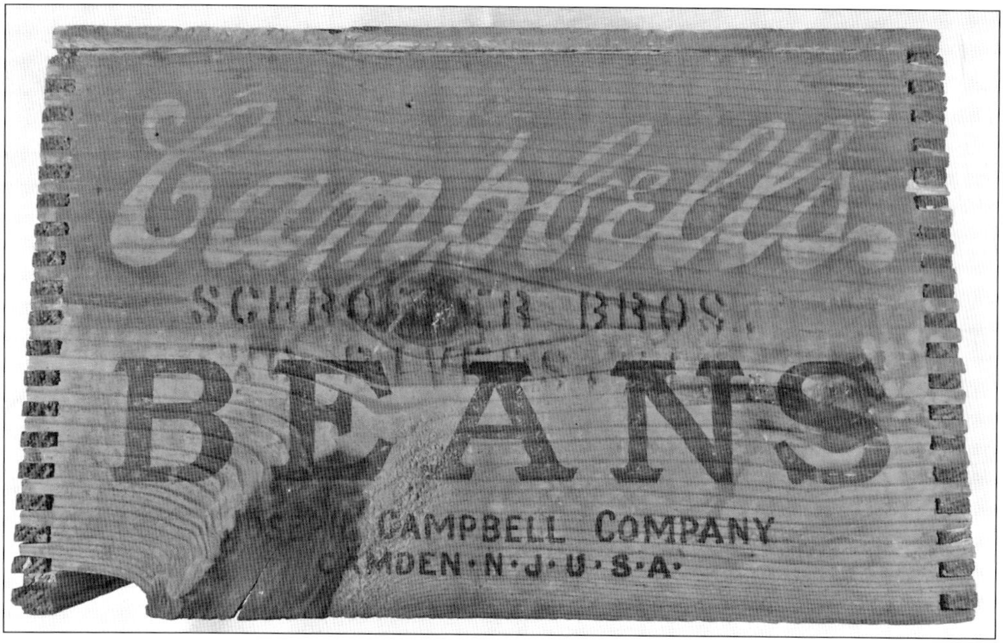

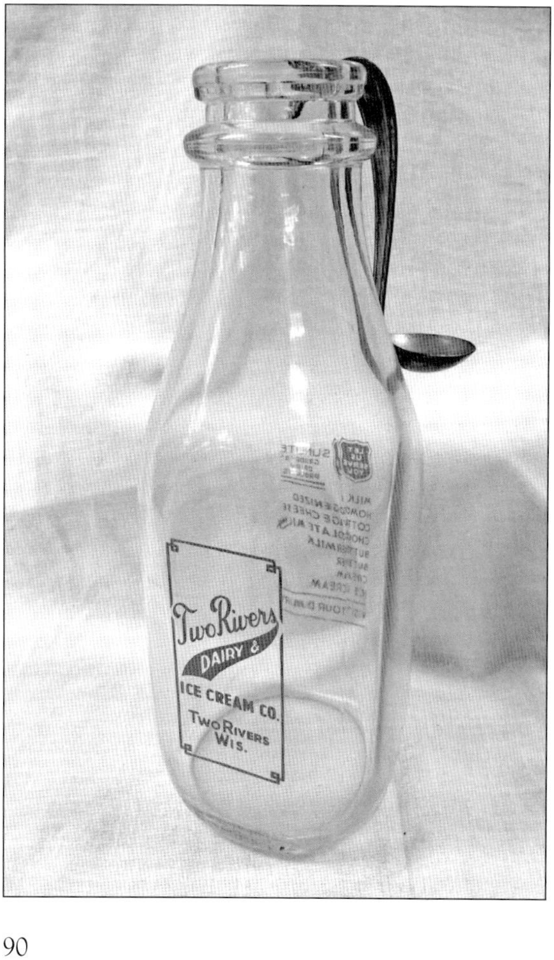

A customer found this Campbell's Soup crate broken apart in an attic, fixed it, and donated it to the Schroeder's display area. Food companies shipped everything in wooden boxes with the business name stamped on the crate. These goods were shipped in on railcars, and Schroeder's would hitch up the trailer to one of their horses to pick up the goods at the train station. (Courtesy of Schroeder's Department Store.)

This glass milk jar with a fat skimmer was donated by Julie Schroeder, daughter of Gary Schroeder. Before the age of plastics, milk was delivered directly to a customer's home. The empty bottles would be placed in a special cabinet outside for the milkman to pick up. (Courtesy of Schroeder's Department Store.)

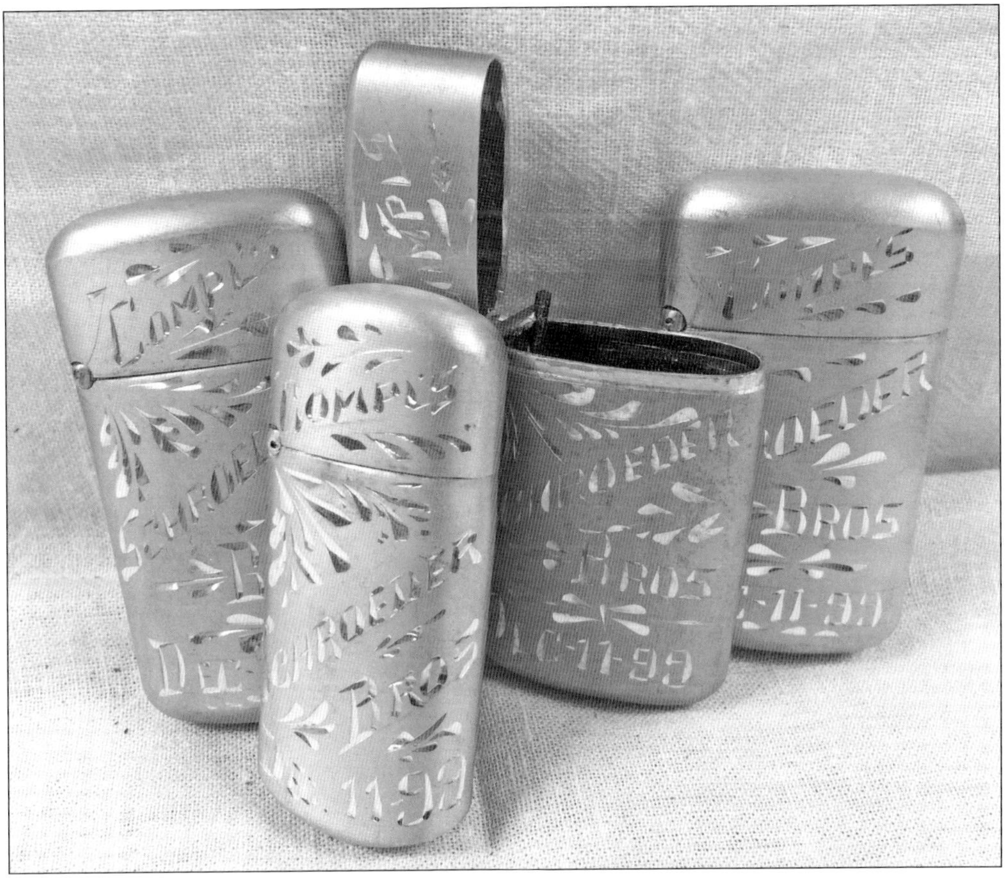

These four lighters are etched for the Schroeder Brothers Company and dated December 11, 1899. There are two different styles of lighters: one is narrow, and the others are a bit wider. They are each labeled with a brand, Compl's, on the upper portion of lighter. (Courtesy of Schroeder's Department Store.)

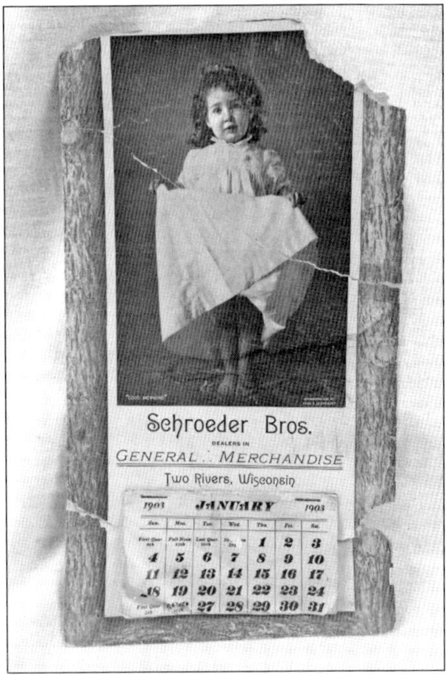

This 1903 wall calendar, found in a file cabinet, was a tear-away calendar with a photograph at the top. Over the years, Schroeder's has handed out calendars for the upcoming year. (Courtesy of Schroeder's Department Store.)

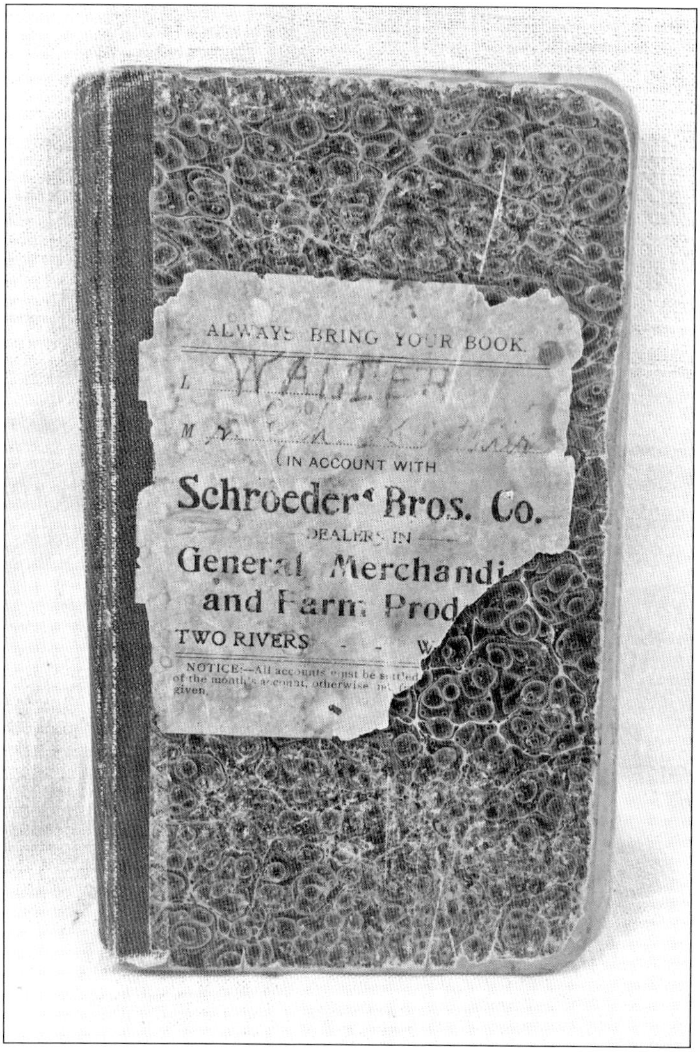

This ledger book was given to Schroeder's from a customer. It was meant for an accounting book to keep track of purchases and items on account for farmers. "Walter" used it to jot down very old recipes. One simple recipe listed was how to make sour milk. (Courtesy of Schroeder's Department Store.)

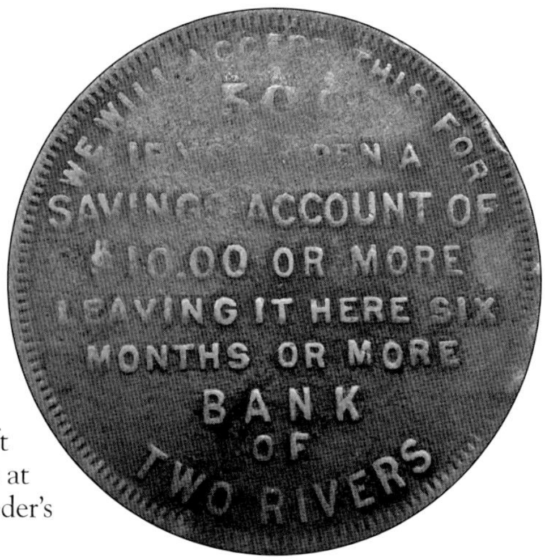

John Konop, Dean Konop's great-uncle, donated this coin to Schroeder's artifacts display. Coins were given to customers who deposited $10 and left the money at the bank for more than six months at the Two Rivers Savings Bank. (Courtesy of Schroeder's Department Store.)

In 1941, the 50th anniversary gift was a crockery bowl stamped with "Schroeder's 50th Anniversary" inside the bowl. The maker of the bowls is unknown. At the time, Schroeder's had a housewares department selling crockery. A total of 2,000 pieces were made and given away. (Courtesy of Schroeder's Department Store.)

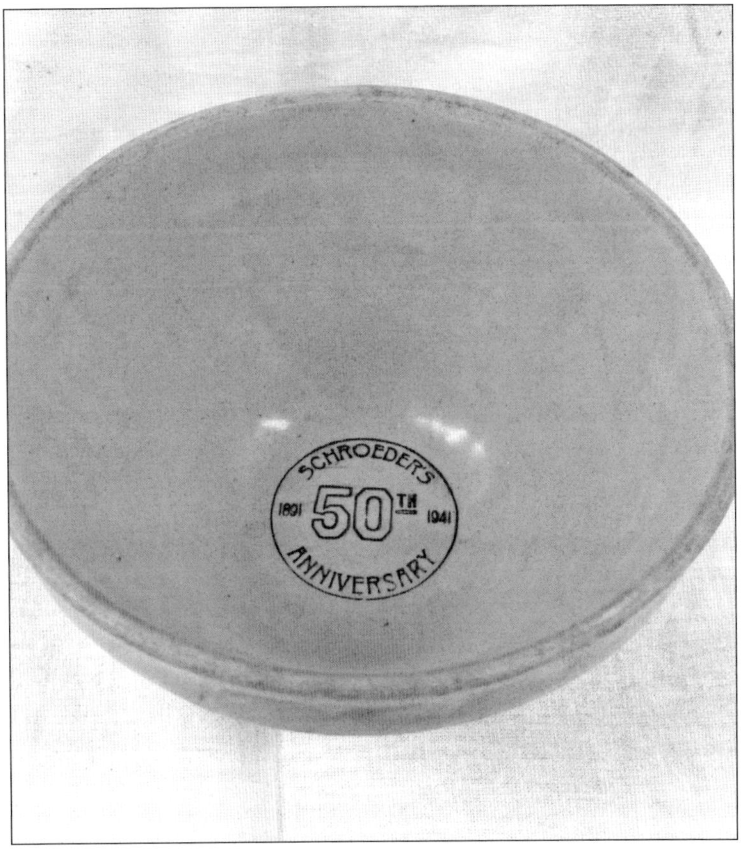

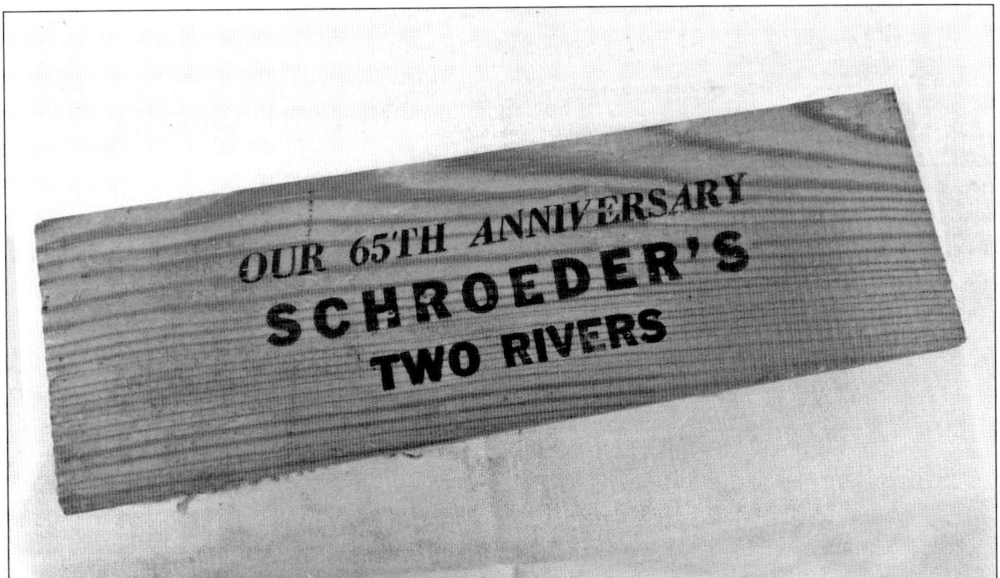

In 1956, the 65th anniversary gift was a shoe shine brush. Back in the 1950s every man, woman, and child shined their shoes and this gift was a great promotional tool for Schroeder's. Schroeder's still sells shoe shine brushes and polish. (Courtesy of Schroeder's Department Store.)

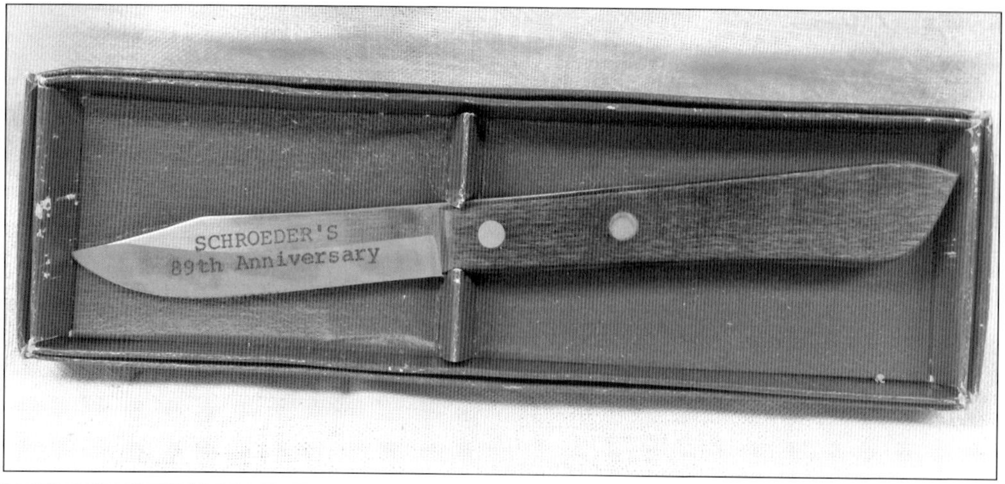

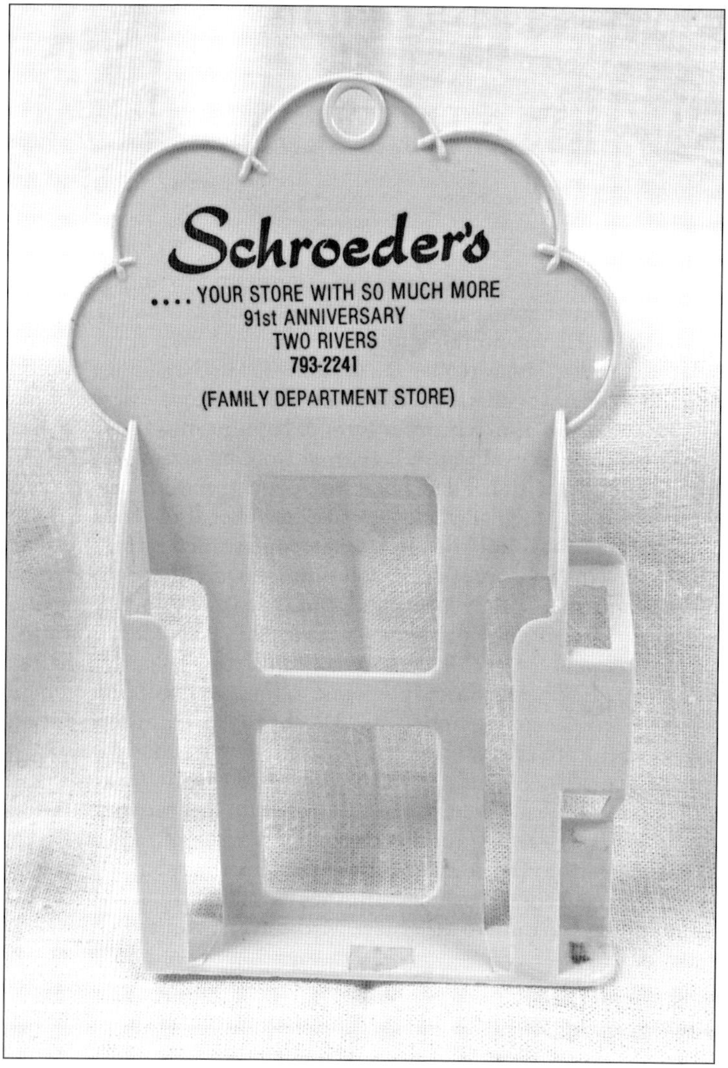

In 1980, Schroeder's 89th anniversary gift was a paring knife with wood handle. Few knives survived customer use, and this knife was found tucked away in a filing cabinet drawer at Schroeder's in the office. (Courtesy of Schroeder's Department Store.)

Pictured is the 91st anniversary notepad holder from 1982. These gifts handed out in celebration of another year in business were often found hanging on a wall in a garage or kitchen. It was a place to have a notebook and pen handy for the occasional note a customer had to jot down. (Courtesy of Schroeder's Department Store.)

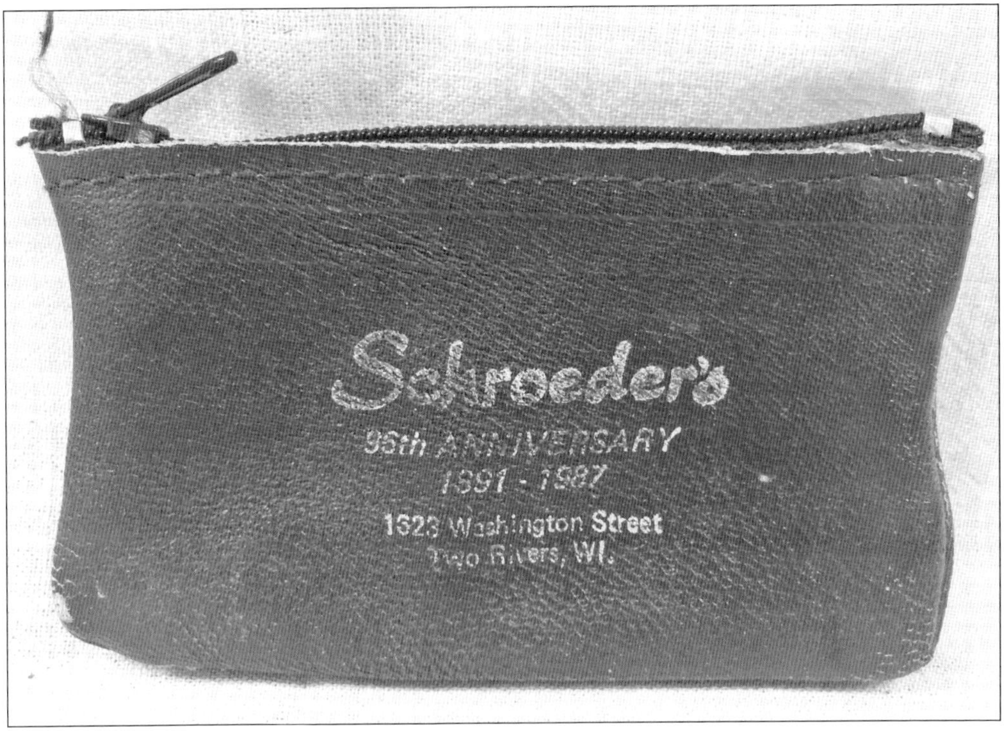

Pictured is the 95th anniversary gift coin purse from 1986. If a coin purse like this one is ever found, it is pretty beat up from being used so often. Leather coin purses were handed out to the first 100 customers for the 95th anniversary sale in October 1986. (Courtesy of Schroeder's Department Store.)

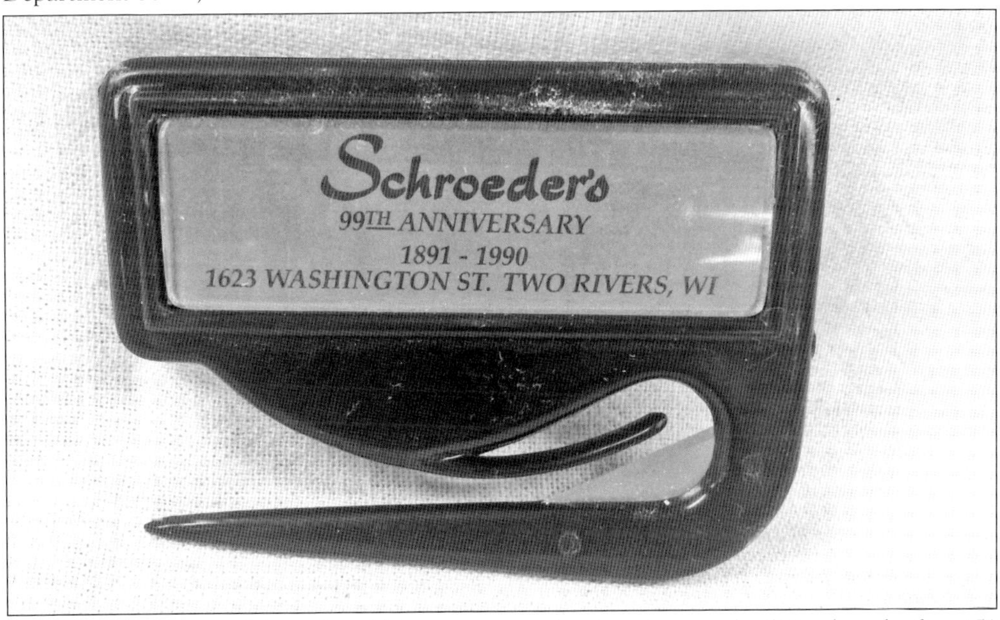

In 1990, Schroeder's celebrated its 99th anniversary. During the month of October, the first 150 customers received letter opener with the Schroeder logo and address. (Courtesy of Schroeder's Department Store.)

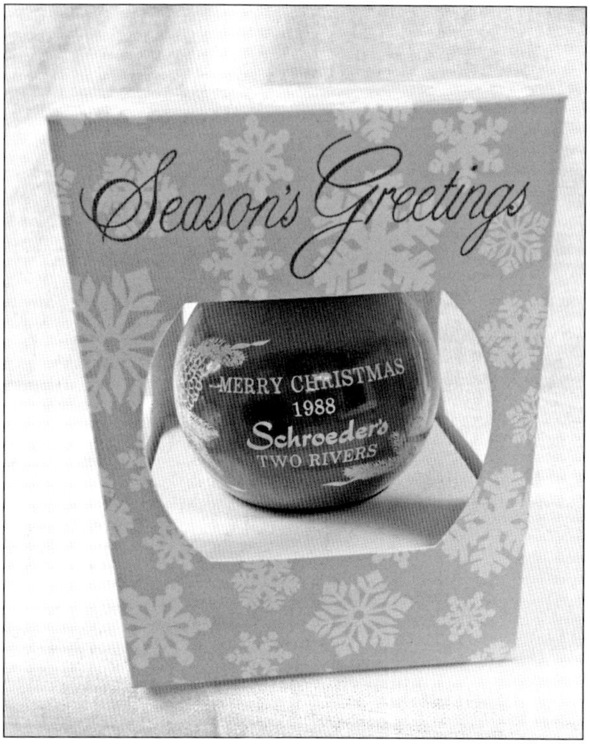

Merry Christmas ornaments were given to customers at Thanksgiving in 1988. The green thread-wrapped ornaments were a way to say thank you to customers for the patronage, and to keep the Schroeder name in front of people reminding them to shop at the downtown department store. (Courtesy of Schroeder's Department Store.)

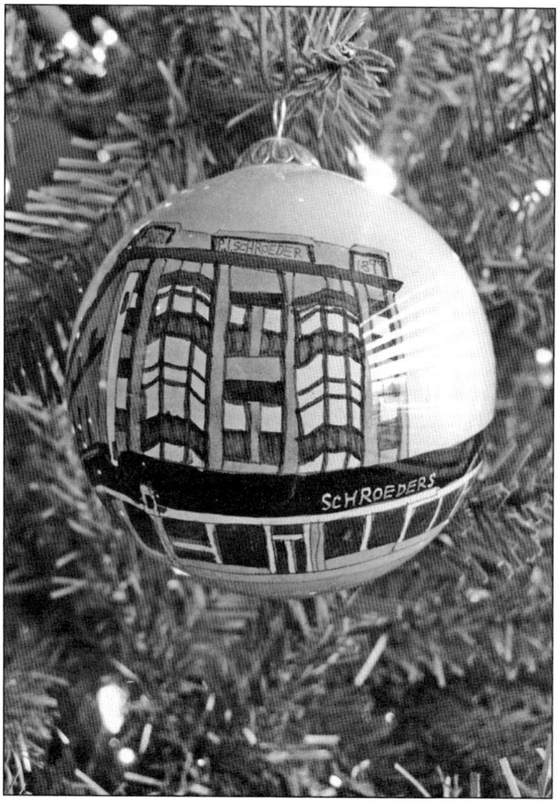

These glass ornaments are all hand painted from the inside. A talented artist received a photograph of Schroeder's and proceeded to hand paint each ornament on the inside. Schroeder's had 144 ornaments for sale. Other designs included Two River City Hall and Rawley Point Lighthouse at Point Beach. (Courtesy of Schroeder's Department Store.)

Pictured is the 100th anniversary coffee mug from 1991. The year 1991 was a year of celebration. The Schroeder store celebrated early in 1991 with a free gift for customers. It is unclear how many mugs were given out during the March 1991 sale to kick off the 100th anniversary. (Courtesy of Schroeder's Department Store.)

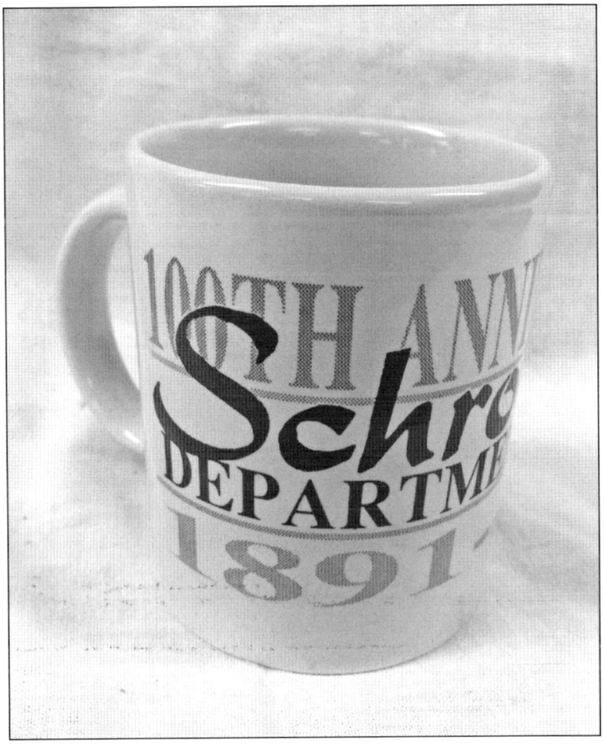

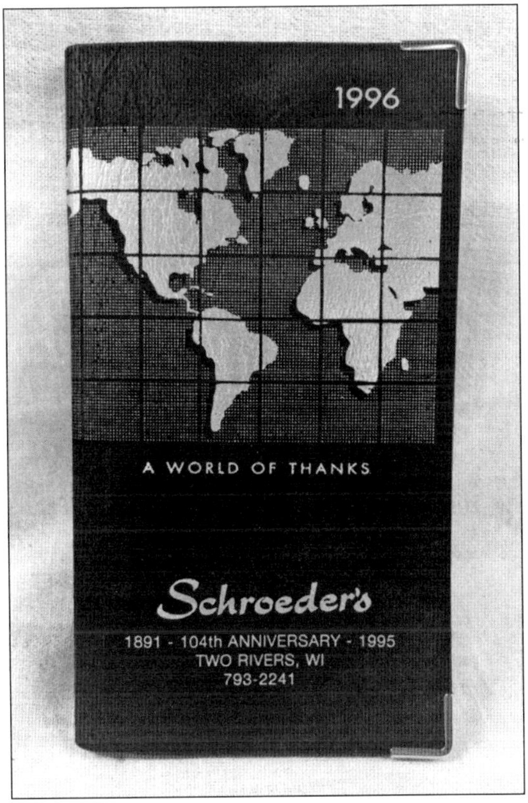

In 1995, pocket calendars were given as gifts to celebrate the 104th anniversary. This was another form of a calendar that the Schroeder family gave out over the holidays. Some years, wall calendars were handed out, but this year, they decided to give out pocket calendars. (Courtesy of Schroeder's Department Store.)

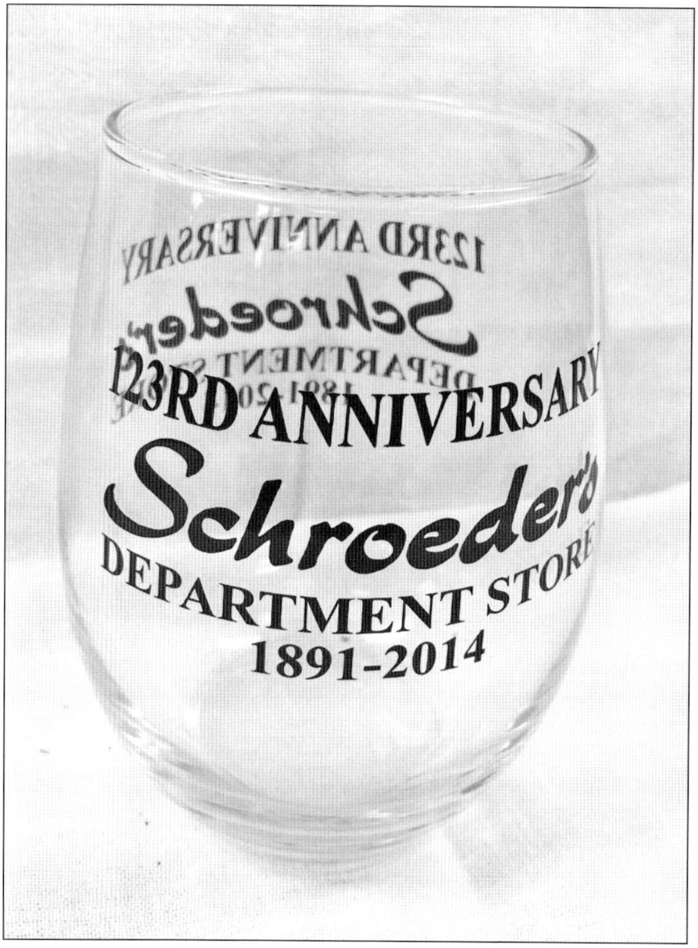

In 2014, the 123rd anniversary gift was stemless wine glasses. During this anniversary sale, Schroeder's invited 3 Sheeps Brewery and Cold Country Winery to serve beer and wine to invited guests. Guests shopped and enjoyed hors d'oeuvres during the evening. (Courtesy of Schroeder's Department Store.)

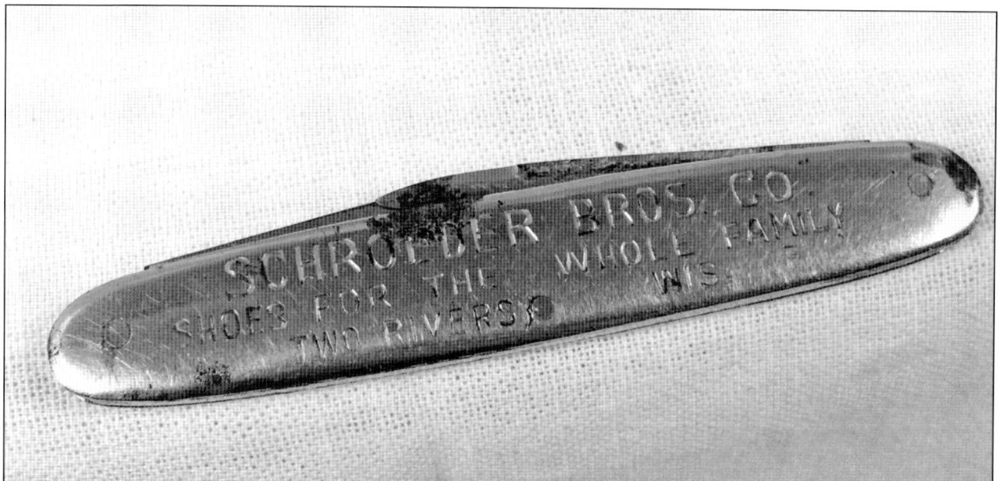

Pictured is a pocket knife promoting shoes for the whole family. Back in the 1960s, many companies offered co-op dollars to purchase promotional items for a customer giveaway. Schroeder's bought pocket knives for this giveaway. (Courtesy of Schroeder's Department Store.)

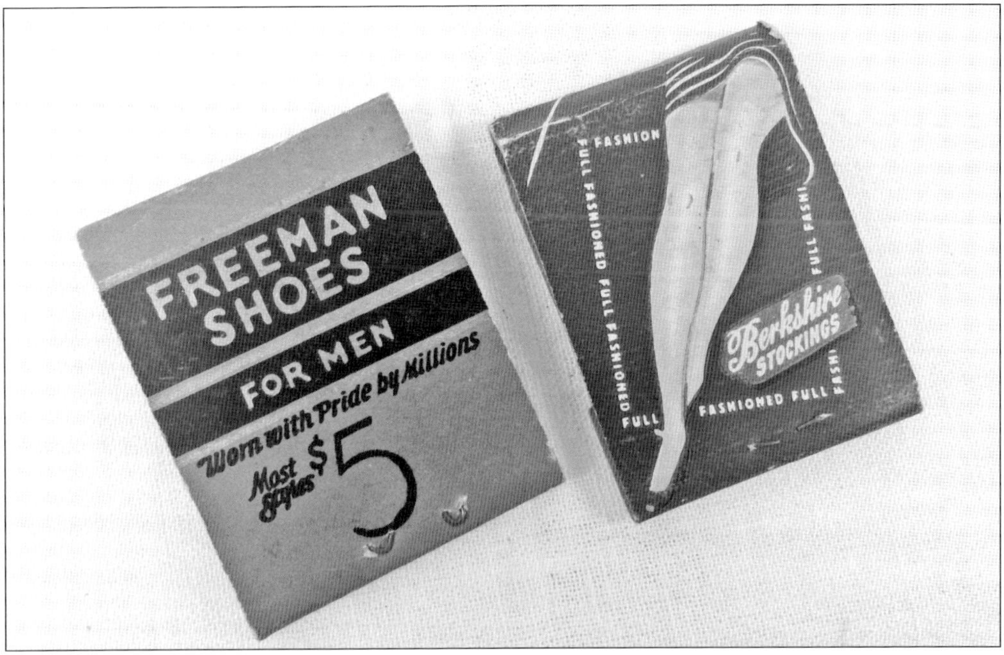

These are matches from Freeman Shoes and Berkshire Stockings. Companies sent promotional items to businesses to hand out to customers. For a while, many companies gave away books of matches. Freeman Shoe Company was in business until the 1990s. Berkshire stockings is still in business. (Courtesy of Schroeder's Department Store.)

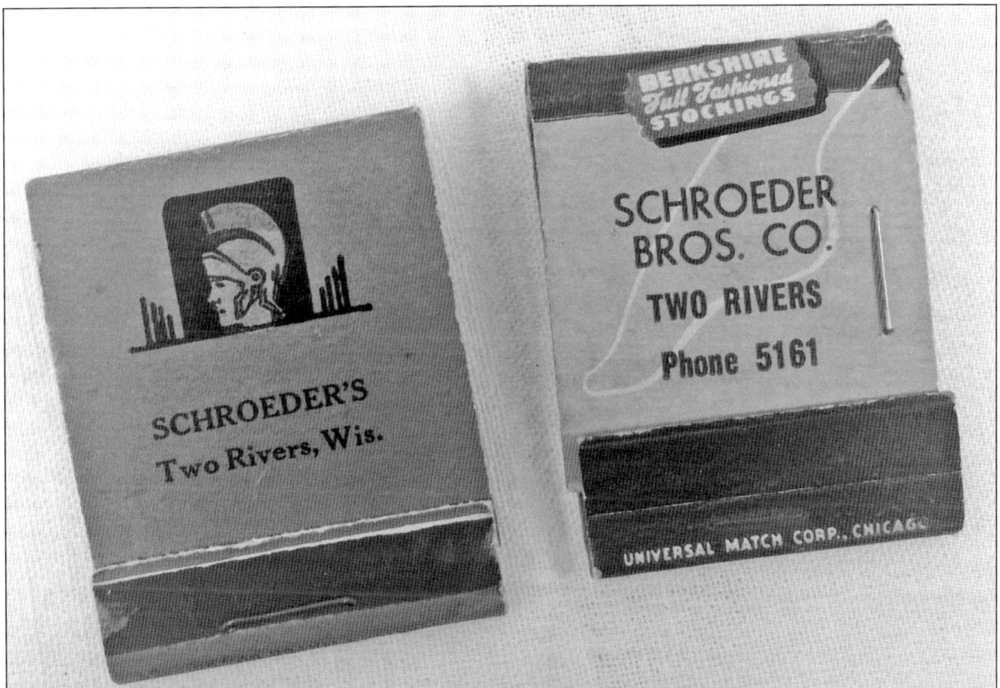

The back of the matches shows Schroeder's business name with the Berkshire Stockings logo and Schroeder's phone number: 5161. (Courtesy of Schroeder's Department Store.)

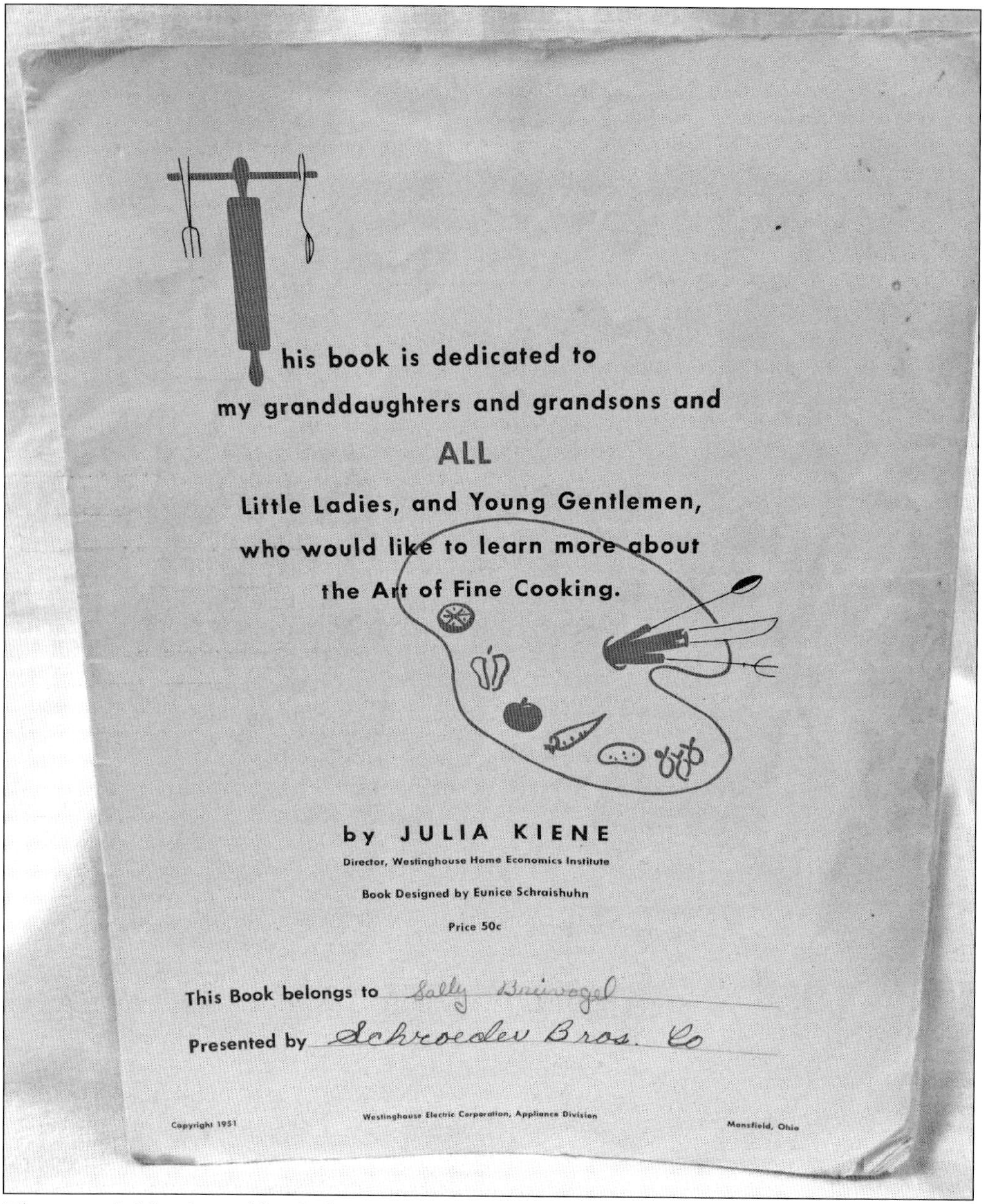

This is a children's cookbook from Westinghouse Electric Company. Schroeder's appliance partnership with Westinghouse helped Schroeder's purchase children's cookbooks in the 1950s. A customer brought her copy to the store for display. (Courtesy of Schroeder's Department Store.)

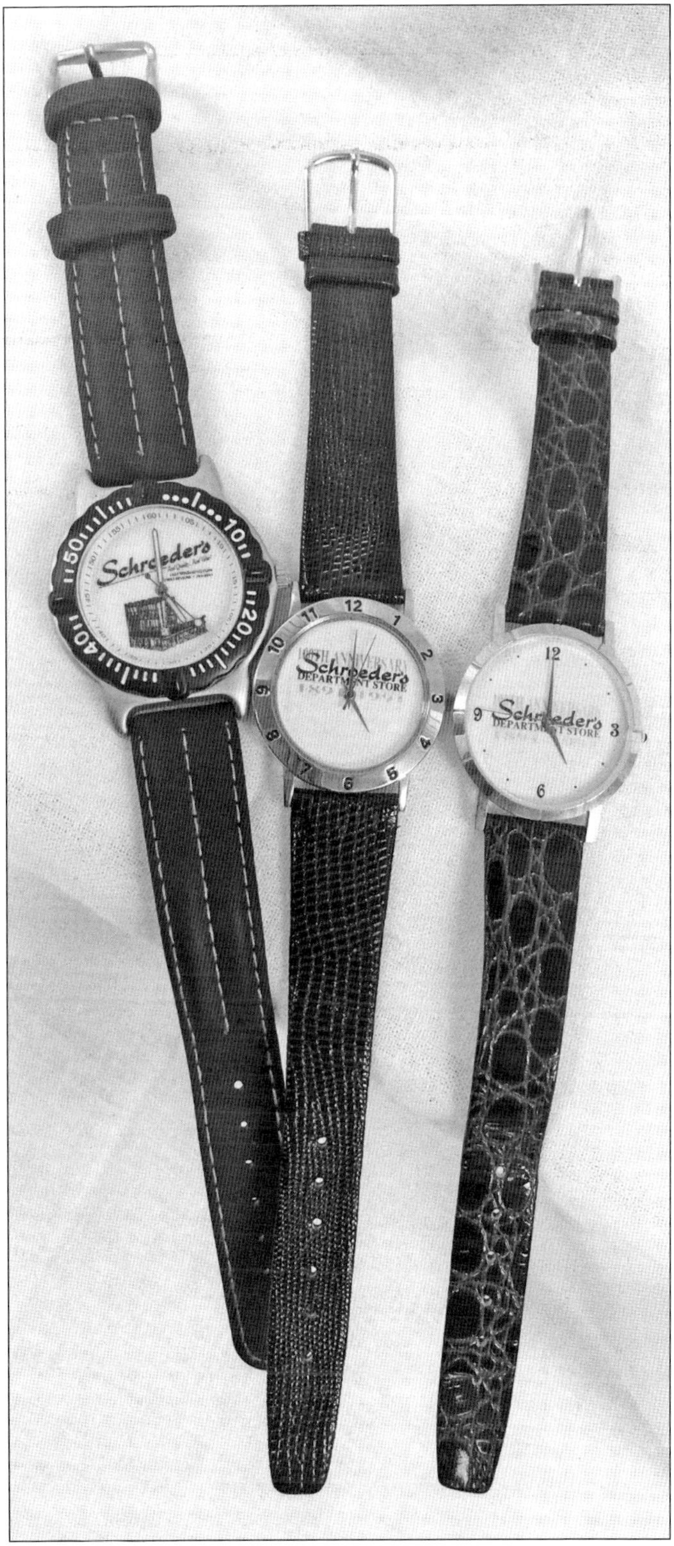

John C. Schroeder would receive watches in the mail. He never ordered any as a giveaway, and he never wore them either. While cleaning drawers in the men's shoe department, A.J. found them and put them on display. (Courtesy of Schroeder's Department Store.)

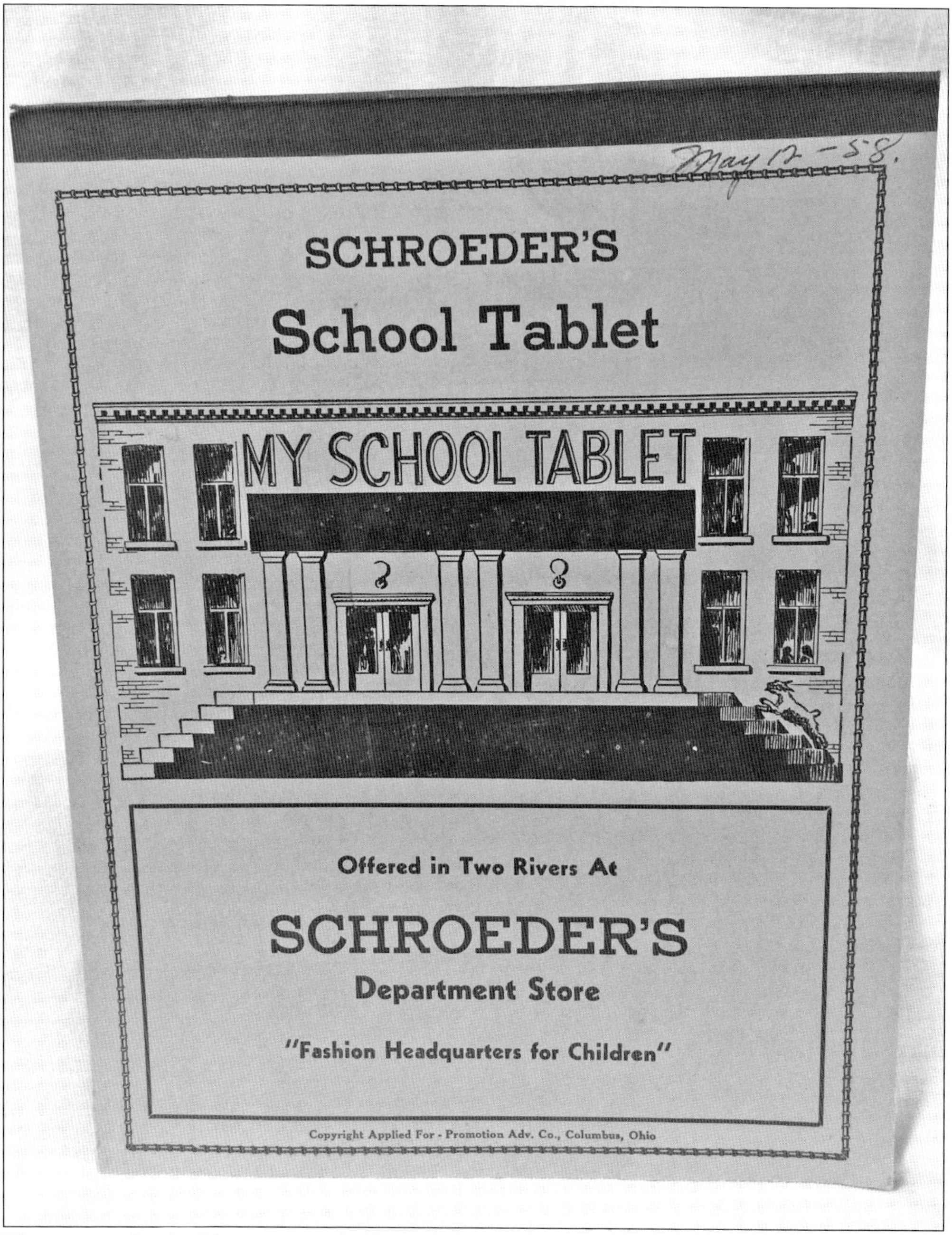

This was a school tablet given to children in 1958 as children came in with parents for back-to-school shopping. This school tablet was given back to us by a customer. She remembers receiving it as a child. (Courtesy of Schroeder's Department Store.)

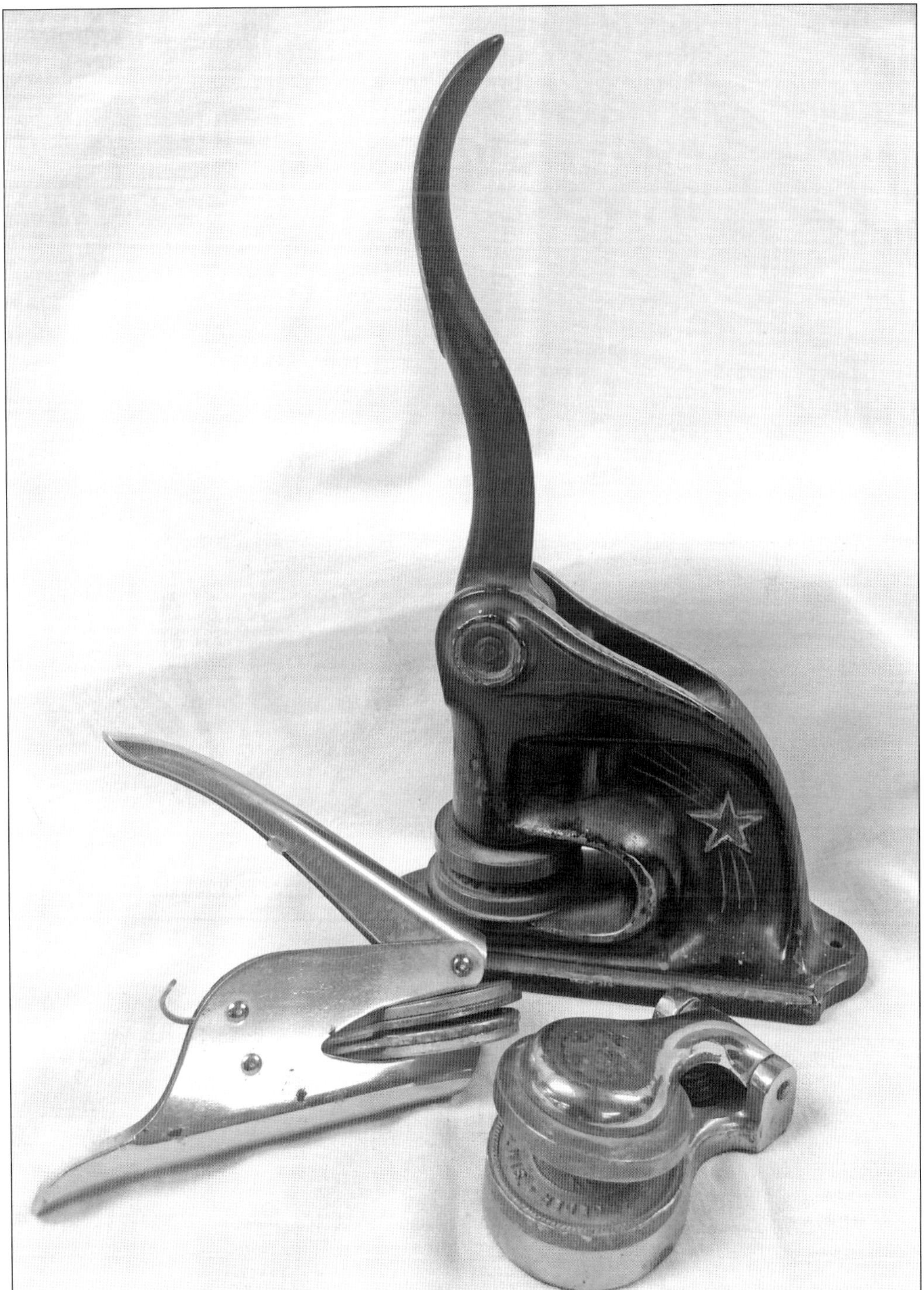

The seal pictured in the far back is the Schroeder Brothers Company, Inc., seal, far left is the Schroeder Building Corporation seal, and the front seal is Joseph S. Schroeder's notary public seal. Schroeder's still uses the corporate seals on all shares sold. (Courtesy of Schroeder's Department Store.)

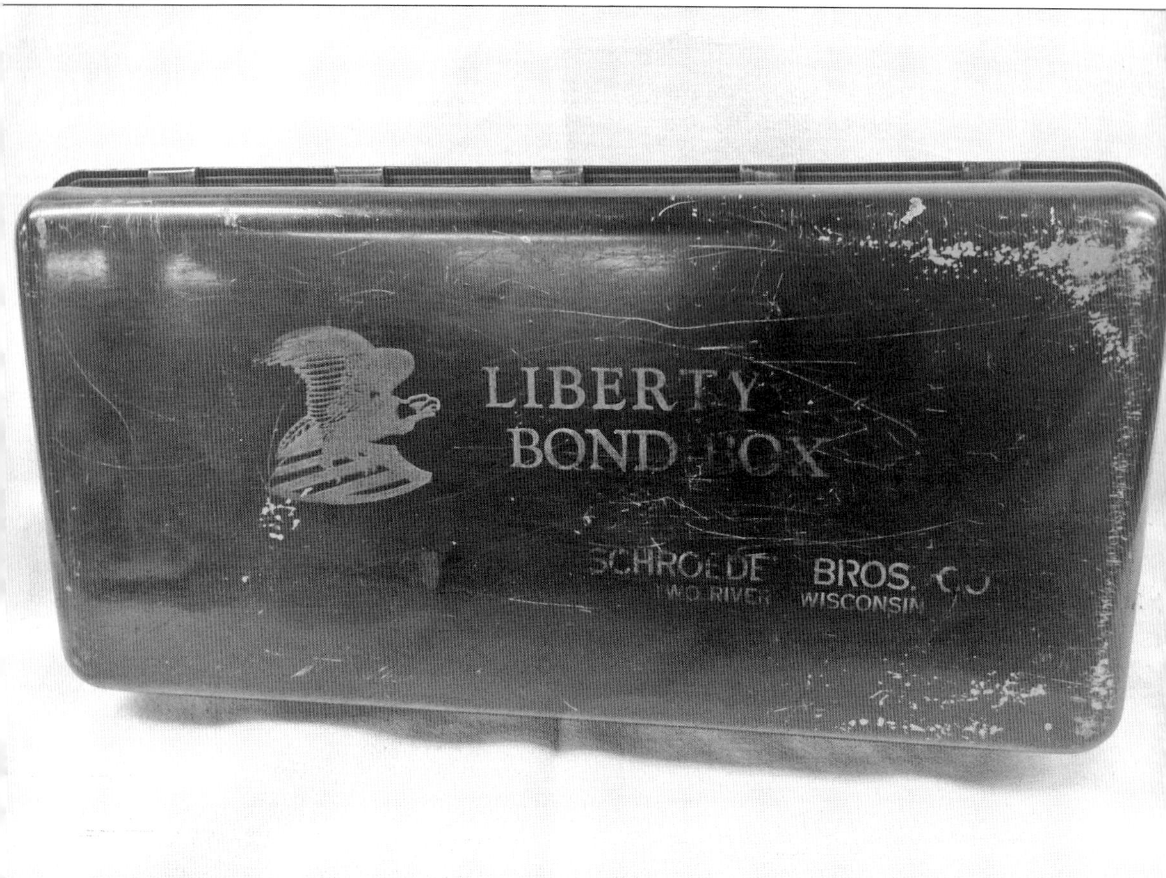

This is a Liberty Bond Box with "Schroeder Bros. Co." stamped on the top. These metal boxes were from the World War I era and sold to customers to hold their liberty bonds. (Courtesy of Schroeder's Department Store.)

Six

Advertising

Throughout Schroeder's history, the method of advertising has varied. Newsprint and radio were the primary methods driving the Schroeder message to consumers for nearly 100 years. When A.J. was in middle school, she attended St. Luke's School, which was a block away from Schroeder's. After school, she would go to the store, do her homework, and then watch her dad layout ads for the newspaper. For a brief time, A.J. worked for a newspaper, *Wisconsin Newspress*, in Plymouth, Wisconsin. There, she helped layout ads in the newspaper and even helped design ads. When A.J. was hired in 2002, however, online media such as Facebook, Twitter, Instagram, and their own website took the place of conventional marketing. The time she spent watching her dad and working for *Wisconsin Newspress* helped her with understanding the marketing for Schroeder's. In promoting the store via social media, A.J. blends old photographs in posts with new merchandise. In 2017, email marketing introduced Schroeder's to a much broader audience. Customers now receive emails with notification of sales and downtown Two Rivers events. Being versatile in delivery of any businesses marketing message is the name of the game. The Schroeder's message, though, remains the same: quality products and knowledgeable staff at reasonable prices.

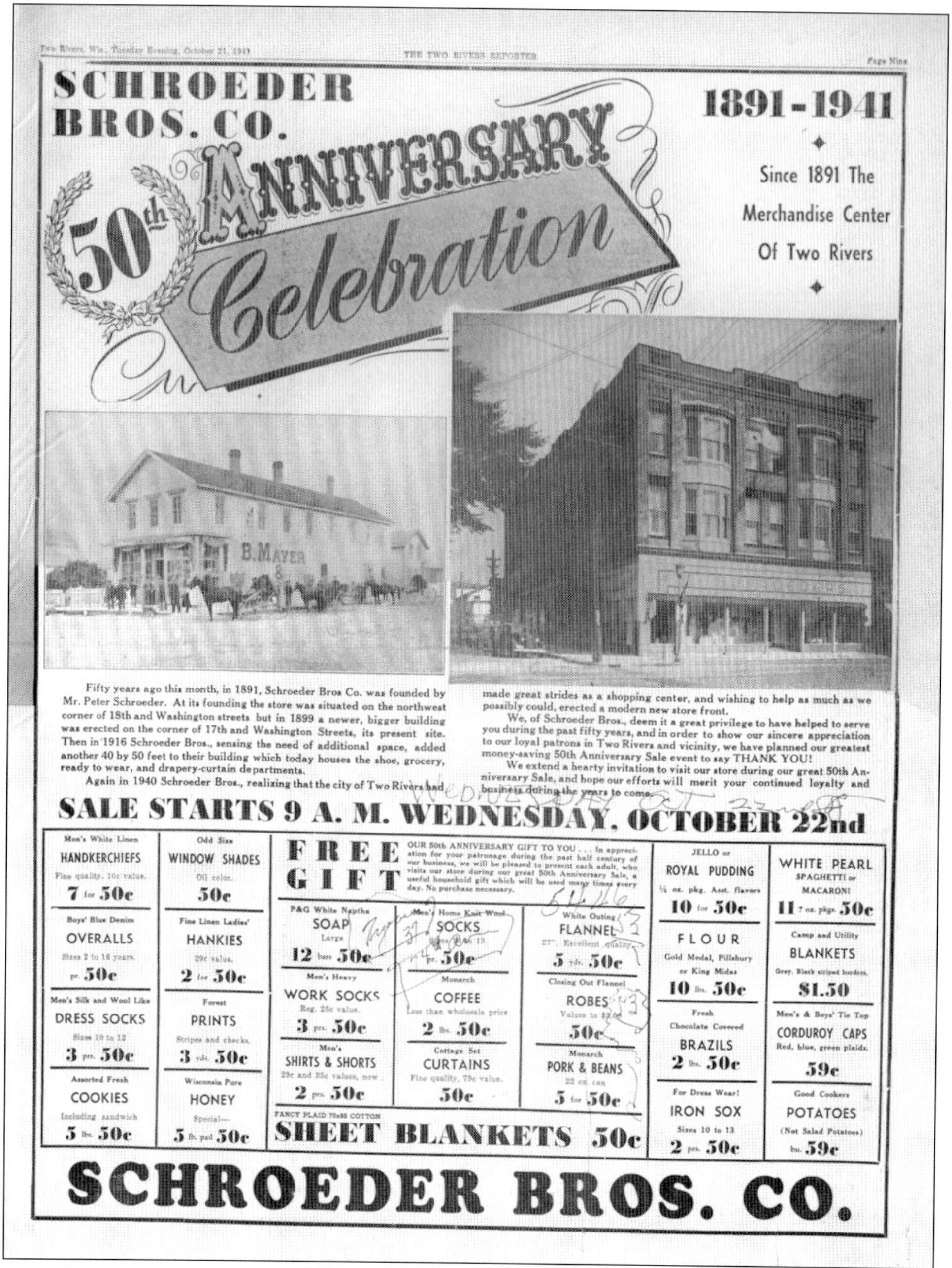

Two Rivers, Wis., Tuesday Evening, October 21, 1941 THE TWO RIVERS REPORTER Page Nine

SCHROEDER BROS. CO.

1891-1941

50th Anniversary Celebration

Since 1891 The Merchandise Center Of Two Rivers

Fifty years ago this month, in 1891, Schroeder Bros Co. was founded by Mr. Peter Schroeder. At its founding the store was situated on the northwest corner of 18th and Washington streets but in 1899 a newer, bigger building was erected on the corner of 17th and Washington Streets, its present site. Then in 1916 Schroeder Bros., sensing the need of additional space, added another 40 by 50 feet to their building which today houses the shoe, grocery, ready to wear, and drapery-curtain departments.

Again in 1940 Schroeder Bros., realizing that the city of Two Rivers had made great strides as a shopping center, and wishing to help as much as we possibly could, erected a modern new store front.

We, of Schroeder Bros., deem it a great privilege to have helped to serve you during the past fifty years, and in order to show our sincere appreciation to our loyal patrons in Two Rivers and vicinity, we have planned our greatest money-saving 50th Anniversary Sale event to say THANK YOU!

We extend a hearty invitation to visit our store during our great 50th Anniversary Sale, and hope our efforts will merit your continued loyalty and business during the years to come.

SALE STARTS 9 A. M. WEDNESDAY, OCTOBER 22nd

Men's White Linen HANDKERCHIEFS Fine quality. 10c value. 7 for 50c

Boys' Blue Denim OVERALLS Sizes 2 to 16 years. pr. 50c

Men's Silk and Wool Like DRESS SOCKS Sizes 10 to 12 3 prs. 50c

Assorted Fresh COOKIES Including sandwich 5 lbs. 50c

Odd Size WINDOW SHADES Oil color. 50c

Fine Linen Ladies' HANKIES 29c value. 2 for 50c

Forest PRINTS Stripes and checks. 3 yds. 50c

Wisconsin Pure HONEY Special— 5 lb. pail 50c

FREE GIFT

OUR 50th ANNIVERSARY GIFT TO YOU . . . In appreciation for your patronage during the past half century of our business, we will be pleased to present each adult, who visits our store during our great 50th Anniversary Sale, a useful household gift which will be used many times every day. No purchase necessary.

P&G White Naptha SOAP Large 12 bars 50c

Men's Heavy WORK SOCKS Reg. 25c value. 3 prs. 50c

Men's SHIRTS & SHORTS 29c and 35c values, now 2 prs. 50c

Men's Home Knit Wool SOCKS Sizes 10 to 13 pr. 50c

Monarch COFFEE Less than wholesale price 2 lbs. 50c

Cottage Set CURTAINS Fine quality, 79c value. 50c

White Outing FLANNEL 27". Excellent quality. 5 yds. 50c

Closing Out Flannel ROBES Values to $2.00 50c

Monarch PORK & BEANS 22 oz. can 5 for 50c

FANCY PLAID 70x80 COTTON SHEET BLANKETS 50c

JELLO or ROYAL PUDDING ¼ oz. pkg. Asst. flavors 10 for 50c

FLOUR Gold Medal, Pillsbury or King Midas 10 lbs. 50c

Fresh Chocolate Covered BRAZILS 2 lbs. 50c

For Dress Wear! IRON SOX Sizes 10 to 13 2 prs. 50c

WHITE PEARL SPAGHETTI or MACARONI 11 7 oz. pkgs. 50c

Camp and Utility BLANKETS Grey. Black striped borders. $1.50

Men's & Boys' Tie Top CORDUROY CAPS Red, blue, green plaids. 59c

Good Cookers POTATOES (Not Salad Potatoes) bu. 59c

SCHROEDER BROS. CO.

The world was engulfed in World War II, and the United States was cautiously watching from the sidelines. On October 21, Schroeder's highlighted the huge milestone and ran a three-page newspaper ad in the *Two Rivers Reporter*, announcing Schroeder's 50th anniversary sale. The ad featured the original location on the northwest corner of Eighteenth and Washington Streets and its current location on the southeast corner of Seventeenth and Washington Streets. In the ad, the management thanked the patrons and extended a "money saving 50th Anniversary Sale." Every department was featured in the impressive ad. Groceries, men's, women's, and children's apparel, curtains, and appliances. The store gave away 2,000 seven-inch mixing bowls with "Schroeder's 50th Anniversary" stamped on the inside. (Courtesy of Schroeder's Department Store.)

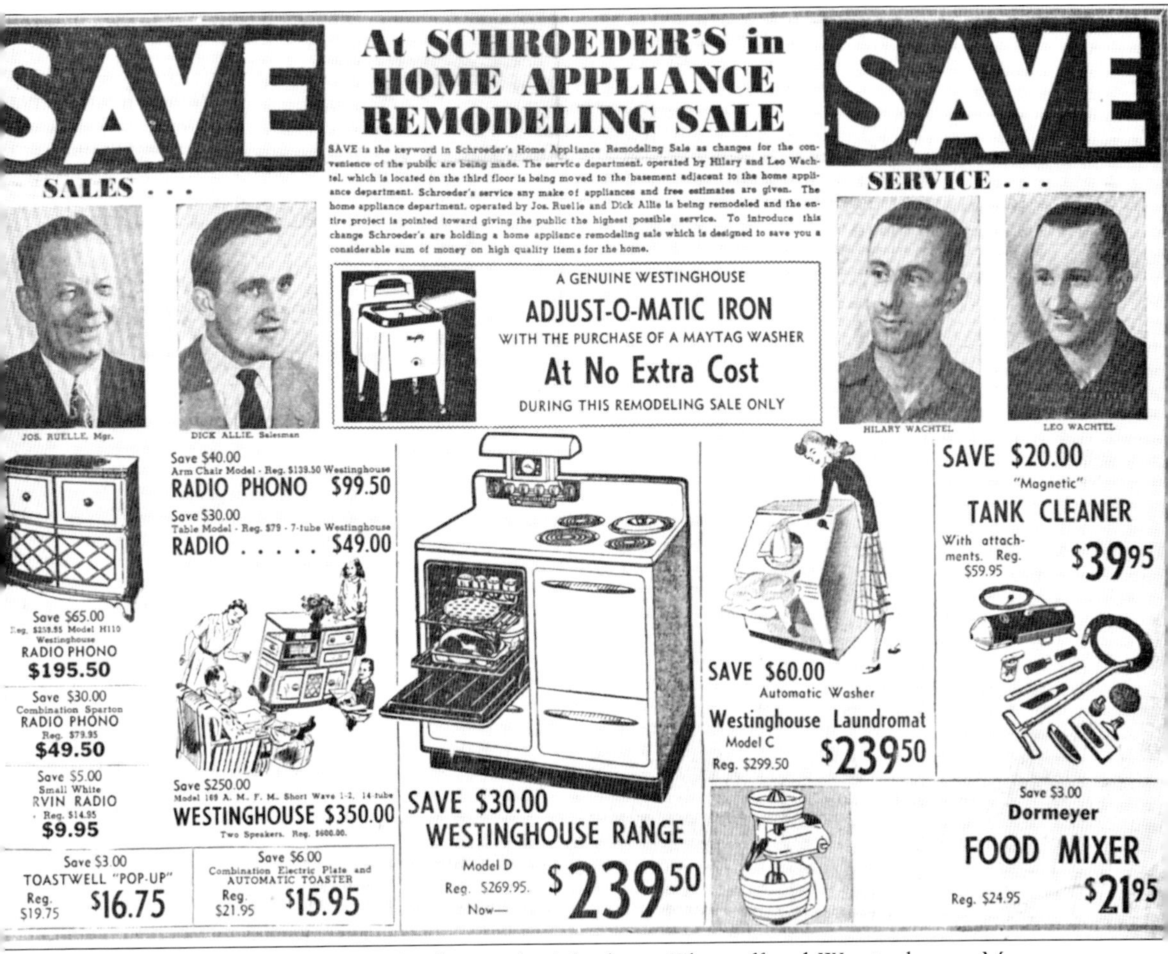

Schroeder's was an appliance leader on the lakeshore. They offered Westinghouse, Maytag, Hoover vacuum cleaners and other household items like mixers and radios. In the March 1, 1949, *Two Rivers Reporter*, a remodeling sale was announced. The Wachtel boys' photographs were included to announce they were on hand to service all the customer's appliance needs and that they were moving from third floor of the Schroeder Building to the lower level adjacent to the newly remodeled appliance department. The home appliance department was managed by Joseph Ruelle, and Dick Allie was the salesperson. (Courtesy of Schroeder's Department Store.)

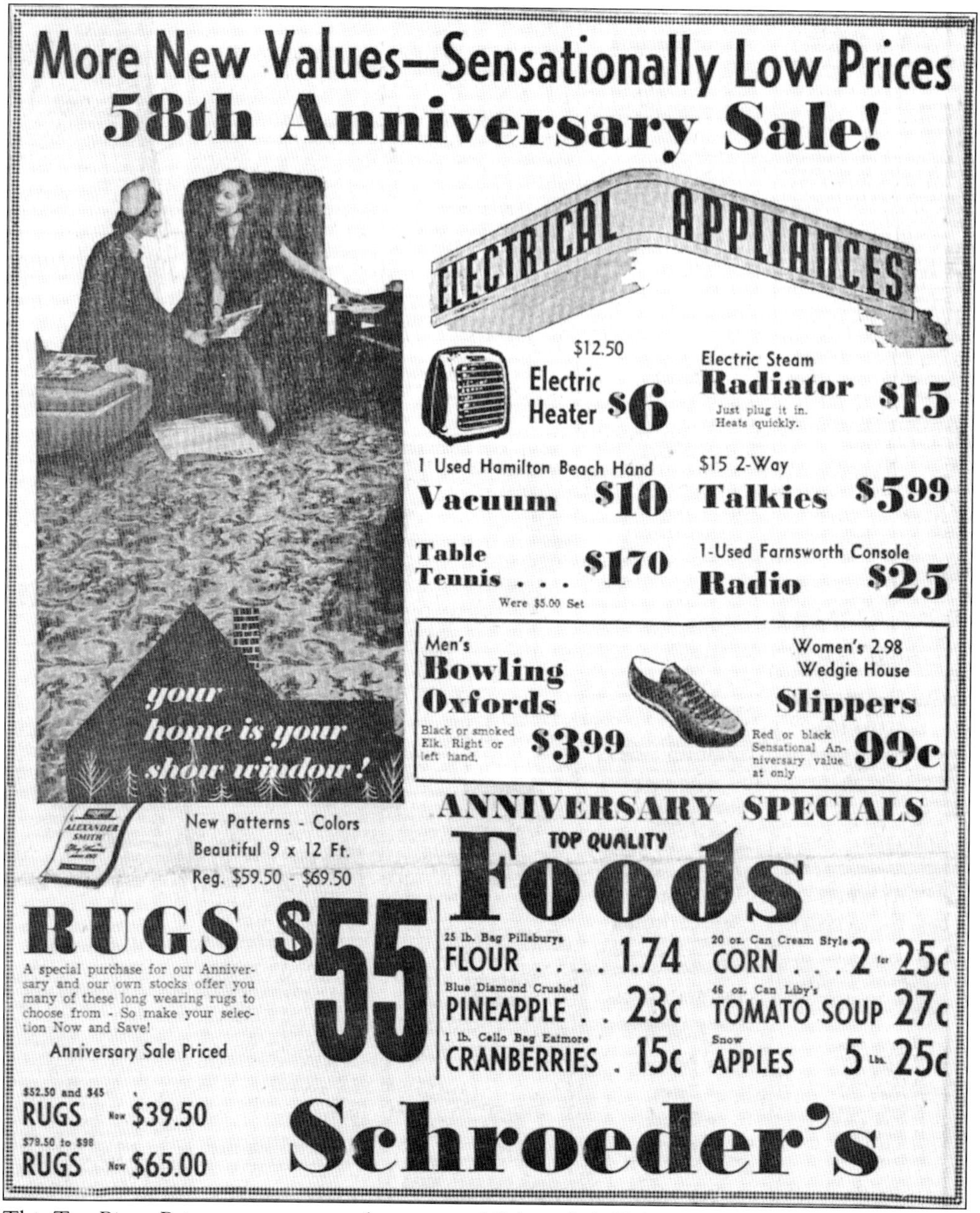

This *Two Rivers Reporter* newspaper ad announced Schroeder's 58th anniversary sale in the October 26, 1949, paper. Slippers were only 99¢ and apples were five pounds for only 25¢. Alexander Smith rugs were specially priced at $55. Alexander Smith Company was based in Yonkers, New York, and later was merged with the Mohawk Corporation. (Courtesy of Schroeder's Department Store.)

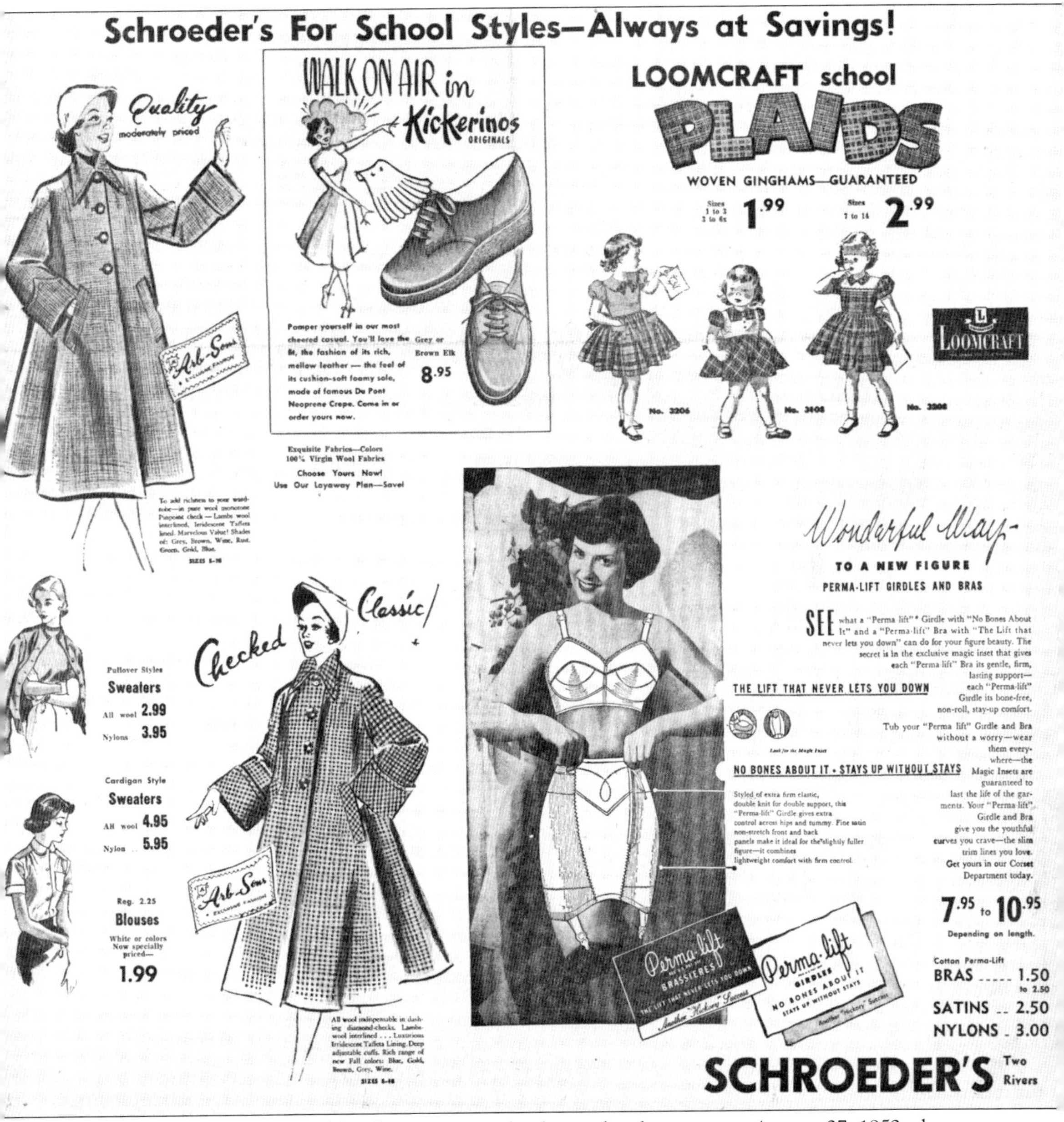

This *Two Rivers Reporter* ad for the upcoming back-to-school season on August 27, 1952, shows plaids, swing coats, and girdles featured in the ad directed toward a female audience. Shoes by Kickerinos tells moms to "pamper yourself in our most cheered casual." Kickerinos, a shoe company famous for the Alaskan boot, made casual shoes with soft buttery leather and DuPont Neoprene Crepe. (Courtesy of Schroeder's Department Store.)

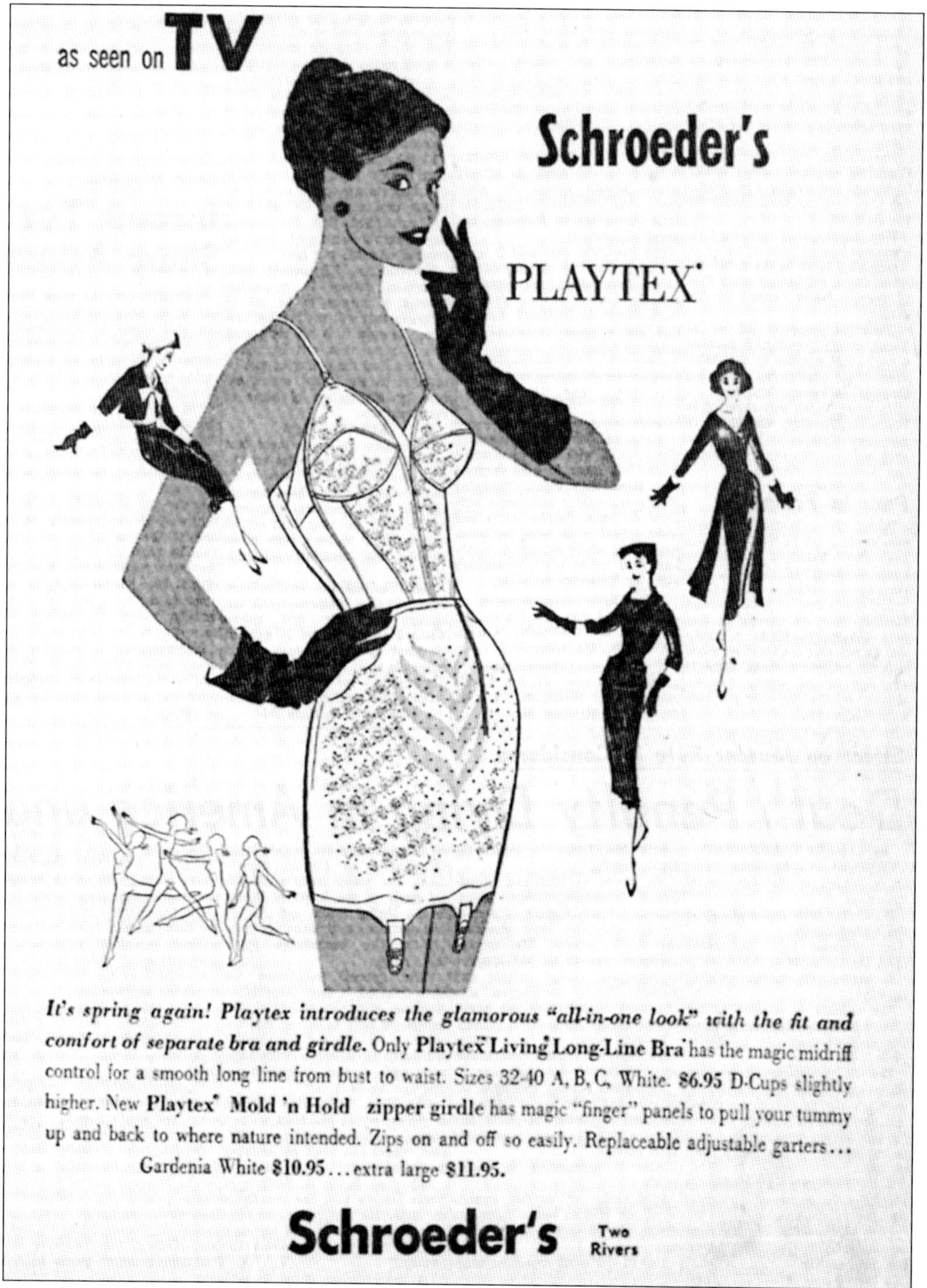

Playtex began making undergarments for women in 1947. Playtex was the first to advertise undergarments on national television in 1955, and the Schroeder's ad from April 10, 1957, makes mention of it being seen on TV. The women's apparel and lingerie departments were located on the second floor in 1957 and featured ready-to-wear women's apparel, lingerie, and hosiery. (Courtesy of Schroeder's Department Store.)

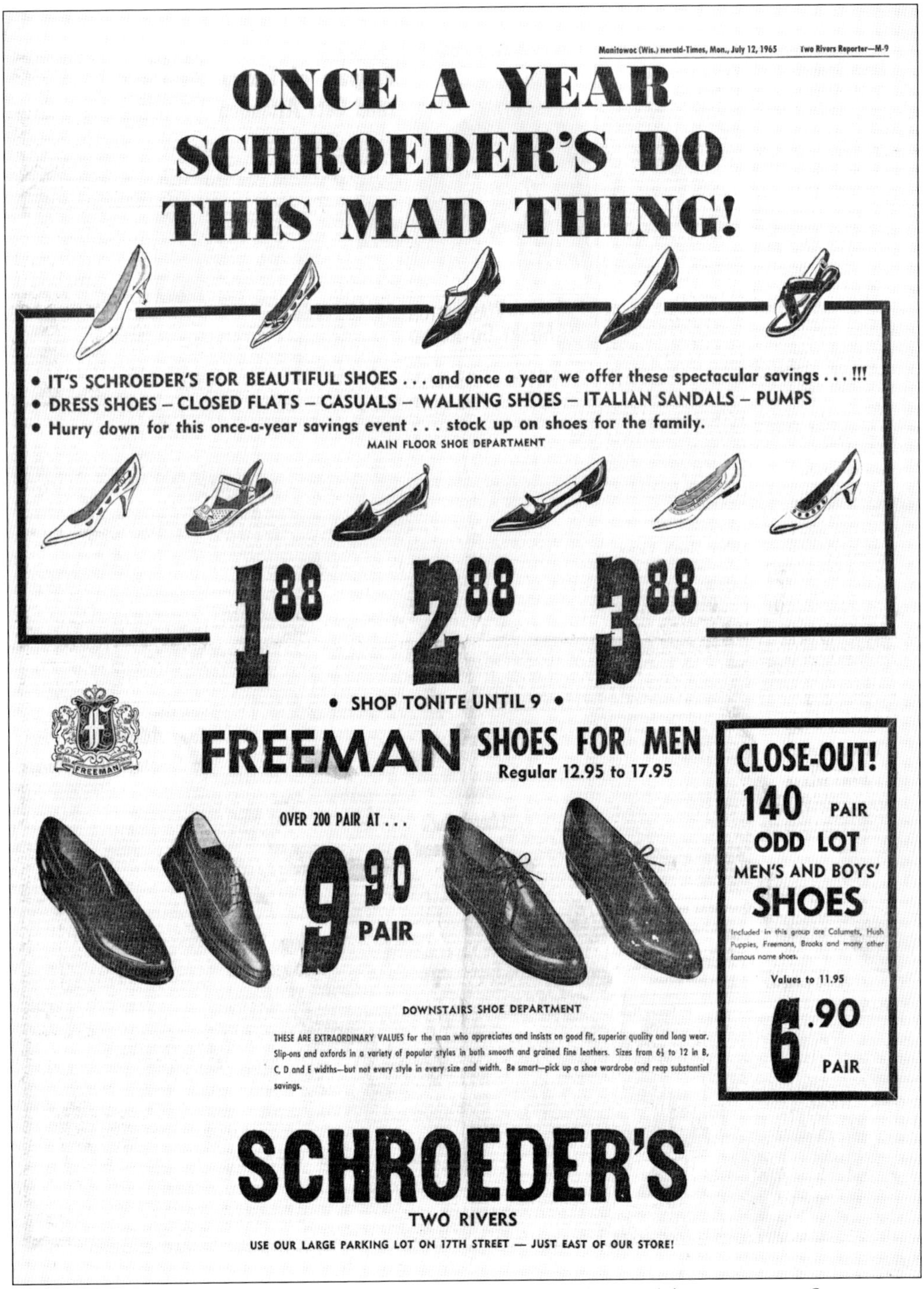

Schroeder's offered substantial savings in the July 12, 1965, edition of the newspaper. Once a year, Schroeder's "do this mad thing" and price men's and women's shoes at crazy low prices. Women's shoes, located on the main level, were priced $1.88, $2.88, and $3.88. While the men's shoes, located on the lower level, were $9.90 a pair, with 200 pairs for sale. (Courtesy of Schroeder's Department Store.)

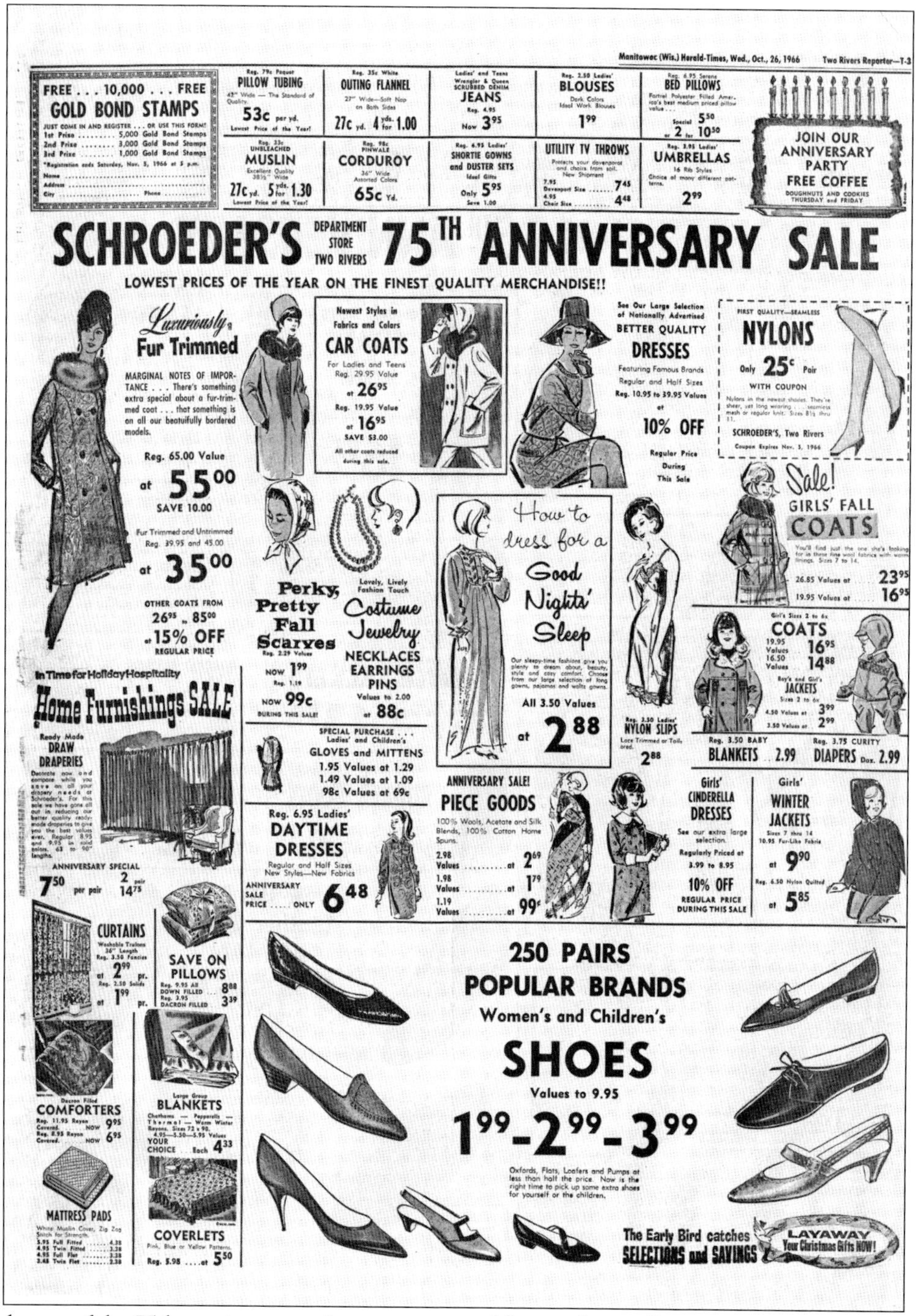

In honor of the 75th anniversary sale, customers could enjoy free coffee and donuts on Thursday and Friday, October 27 and 28, 1966. On the two-page advertisement from October 26, 1966, Schroeder's features Maytag's "May" the go-go girl and ringer washers as low as $108.75. Freeman shoes were on special for $11.99 in the downstairs shoe department. Men's, women's, and kid's clothing were marked at the lowest prices for the year, and home furnishings were also on sale. (Courtesy of Schroeder's Department Store.)

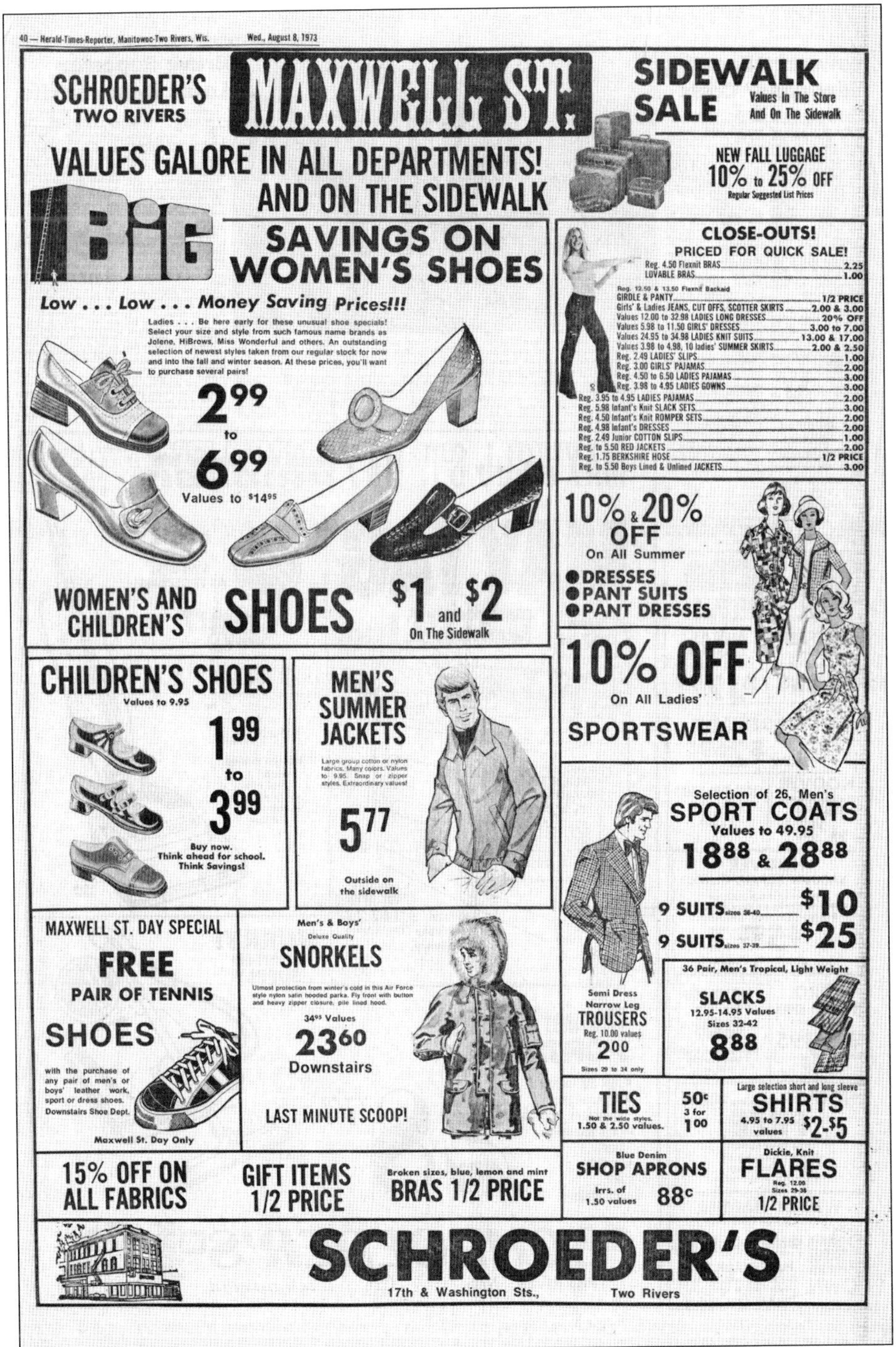

40 — Herald-Times-Reporter, Manitowoc-Two Rivers, Wis. Wed., August 8, 1973

SCHROEDER'S
TWO RIVERS

MAXWELL ST.

SIDEWALK SALE
Values In The Store And On The Sidewalk

VALUES GALORE IN ALL DEPARTMENTS!
AND ON THE SIDEWALK

NEW FALL LUGGAGE
10% to 25% OFF
Regular Suggested List Prices

BIG SAVINGS ON WOMEN'S SHOES

Low . . . Low . . . Money Saving Prices!!!

Ladies . . . Be here early for these unusual shoe specials! Select your size and style from such famous name brands as Jolene, HiBrows, Miss Wonderful and others. An outstanding selection of newest styles taken from our regular stock for now and into the fall and winter season. At these prices, you'll want to purchase several pairs!

2^{99} to 6^{99}
Values to $\$14^{95}$

WOMEN'S AND CHILDREN'S SHOES \$1 and \$2
On The Sidewalk

CLOSE-OUTS!
PRICED FOR QUICK SALE!

Reg. 4.50 Flexnit BRAS	2.25
LOVABLE BRAS	1.00
Reg. 12.50 & 13.50 Flexnit Backaid GIRDLE & PANTY	1/2 PRICE
Girls' & Ladies JEANS, CUT OFFS, SCOTTER SKIRTS	2.00 & 3.00
Values 12.00 to 32.98 LADIES LONG DRESSES	20% OFF
Values 5.98 to 11.50 GIRLS' DRESSES	3.00 to 7.00
Values 24.95 to 34.98 LADIES KNIT SUITS	13.00 & 17.00
Values 3.98 to 4.98, 10 ladies' SUMMER SKIRTS	2.00 & 2.50
Reg. 2.49 LADIES' SLIPS	1.00
Reg. 3.00 GIRLS' PAJAMAS	2.00
Reg. 4.50 to 6.50 LADIES PAJAMAS	3.00
Reg. 3.98 to 4.95 LADIES GOWNS	3.00
Reg. 3.95 to 4.95 LADIES PAJAMAS	2.00
Reg. 5.98 Infant's Knit SLACK SETS	3.00
Reg. 4.50 Infant's Knit ROMPER SETS	2.00
Reg. 4.98 Infant's DRESSES	2.00
Reg. 2.49 Junior COTTON SLIPS	1.00
Reg. to 5.50 RED JACKETS	2.00
Reg. 1.75 BERKSHIRE HOSE	1/2 PRICE
Reg. to 5.50 Boys Lined & Unlined JACKETS	3.00

10% & 20% OFF
On All Summer
● DRESSES
● PANT SUITS
● PANT DRESSES

10% OFF
On All Ladies'
SPORTSWEAR

CHILDREN'S SHOES
Values to 9.95
1^{99} to 3^{99}
Buy now.
Think ahead for school.
Think Savings!

MEN'S SUMMER JACKETS
Large group cotton or nylon fabrics. Many colors. Values to 9.95. Snap or zipper styles. Extraordinary values!
5^{77}
Outside on the sidewalk

Selection of 26, Men's
SPORT COATS
Values to 49.95
18^{88} & 28^{88}

9 SUITS sizes 36-40 \$10
9 SUITS sizes 37-39 \$25

MAXWELL ST. DAY SPECIAL
FREE
PAIR OF TENNIS
SHOES
with the purchase of any pair of men's or boys' leather work, sport or dress shoes.
Downstairs Shoe Dept.
Maxwell St. Day Only

Men's & Boys'
Deluxe Quality
SNORKELS
Utmost protection from winter's cold in this Air Force style nylon satin hooded parka. Fly front with button and heavy zipper closure, pile lined hood.
34^{95} Values
23^{60}
Downstairs

LAST MINUTE SCOOP!

Semi Dress
Narrow Leg
TROUSERS
Reg. 10.00 values
2^{00}
Sizes 29 to 34 only

36 Pair, Men's Tropical, Light Weight
SLACKS
12.95-14.95 Values
Sizes 32-42
8^{88}

TIES
Not the wide styles.
1.50 & 2.50 values.
50¢
3 for 1^{00}

Large selection short and long sleeve
SHIRTS
4.95 to 7.95 values
\$2-\$5

15% OFF ON ALL FABRICS

GIFT ITEMS 1/2 PRICE

Broken sizes, blue, lemon and mint
BRAS 1/2 PRICE

Blue Denim
SHOP APRONS
Irrs. of 1.50 values
88¢

Dickie, Knit
FLARES
Reg. 12.00
Sizes 29-38
1/2 PRICE

SCHROEDER'S
17th & Washington Sts., Two Rivers

The Maxwell Street Sidewalk Sale was announced in the August 8, 1973, newspaper. Sidewalk sale day was always on the first Thursday in August. This was an opportunity to buy back-to-school items at low prices. In this Schroeder's ad, kids could get a free pair of tennis shoes with any purchase in the men's shoes department. On the reverse side of the paper, even Maytag and Hoover were marked at low, low prices. (Courtesy of Schroeder's Department Store.)

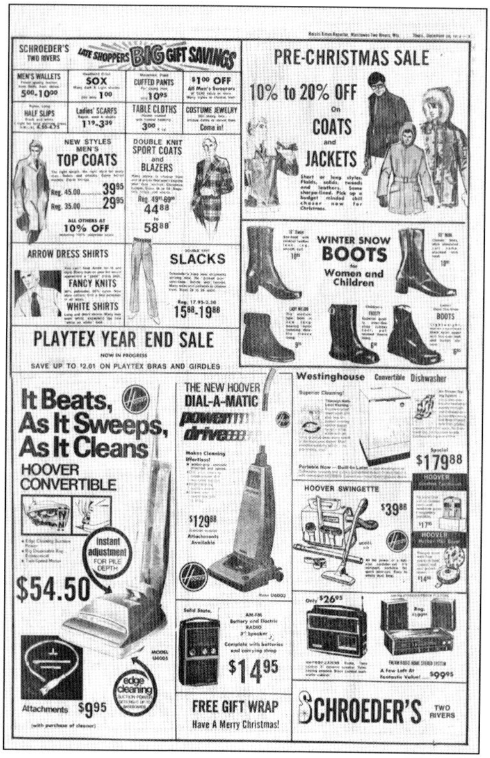

Five days until Christmas, and this December 20, 1973, *Herald Times Reporter* advertisement reached out to last-minute Christmas shoppers. The Schroeder's ad reminded people that wallets, slacks, boots, and coats were all pre–Christmas sale priced. Cordless Hoover vacuums and radios were also on sale. Plus, free-gift wrapping was offered on all Schroeder purchases. (Courtesy of Schroeder's Department Store.)

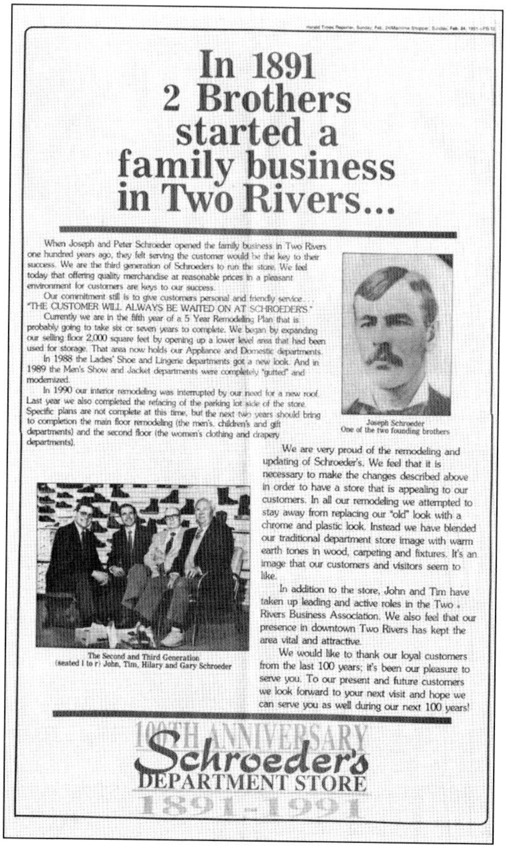

Schroeder's celebrated their 100th anniversary sale on October 16, 1991. Schroeder's had huge savings on winter coats, sweaters, and kids' wear. Chuck Conroy, Soft Spot Shoe Company sales representative, was also on hand to help customers. In a previous ad from February 24, 1991, Schroeder's reaffirmed their commitment to give customers personal and friendly service. "The customer will always be waited on at Schroeder's," the ad declares. (Courtesy of Schroeder's Department Store.)

Seven

Transitions through the Generations

Transition of management and ownership never happened as planned. A manual on how to run a family-owned business never existed for the Schroeder family. Parents encouraged their children to work in the business, and some loved the day-to-day retail operations while others did not. Each generation of the Schroeder family has memories of working at Schroeder's. Rocky and smooth, transitions happen by no choice of the current regime. The first transition of Schroeder's took place during a pivotal time in history and is a very complicated story. It all happened during the Great Depression. Joseph Schroeder died in early 1929, and during that time his wife, Isabella, was not allowed voting rights with his Schroeder shares. She gave her three sons—Hilary, Neal, and Gary Schroeder—all the shares in the business. Hilary worked in the men's apparel department, Gary was in men's footwear, and Neal was in the office. In addition to the three sons working at the store, many other Schroeders were also receiving paychecks. Because too many Schroeders were living off the store, Frank Schroeder had the honors of firing many of the extra Schroeders not pulling their weight. Those leaching Schroeders were kicked out, shares were bought back and redistributed. The second generation to third generation was less tumultuous. Neal passed away in 1985, but his four daughters were not interested in working at the store. His shares were bought back and moved into treasury stock. Hilary had two sons and two daughters, and all of which had followed different career paths. Tim Schroeder, son of Hilary, was teaching English in Illinois and came home on request of his father in 1973. Over time, Hilary gave his kids all shares in the business. Gary had two daughters and five sons, and all seven children followed different career paths, as well. John Schroeder, son of Gary, was away at University of Wisconsin–Madison studying pharmacology. One day, he watched *It's a Wonderful Life*, and something with George Bailey stuck with him. He wanted to come back home and work at the family store. He started working in the men's shoes and jacket department in 1972. Tim and John did not assume management rolls until the early 1980s. In place of monetary compensation, shares in Schroeder Brothers Company were given to the cousins. In 2015, Gary Schroeder passed away at the age of 104, and his shares were distributed to the surviving six children.

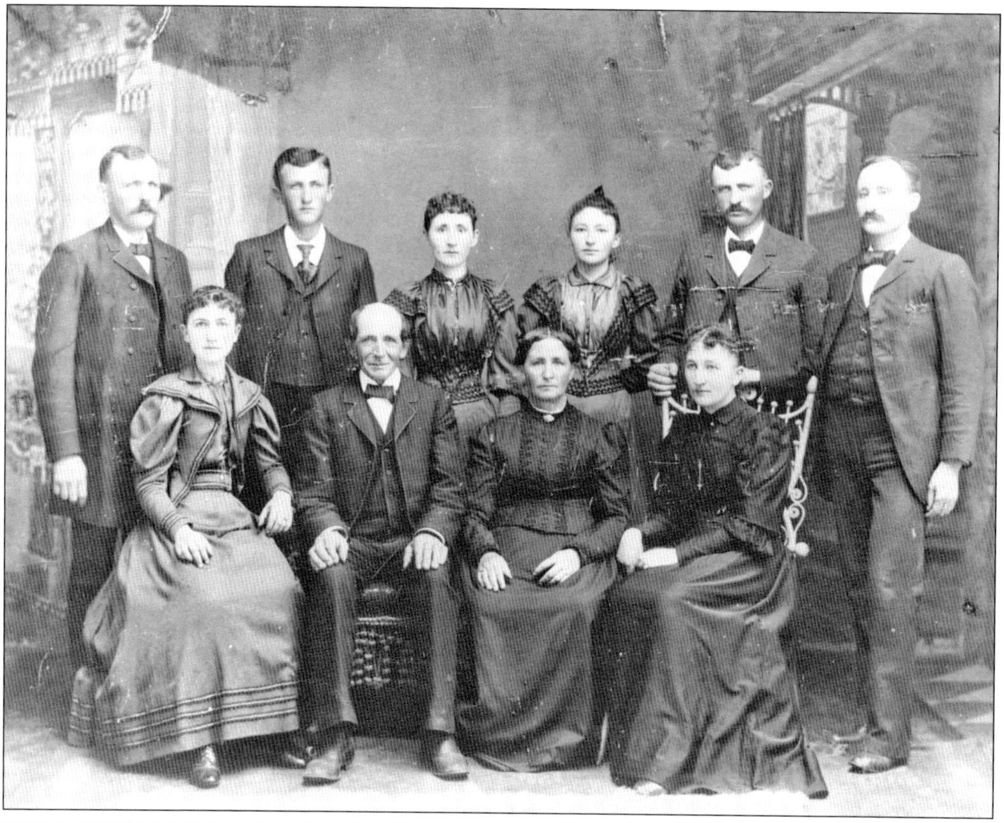

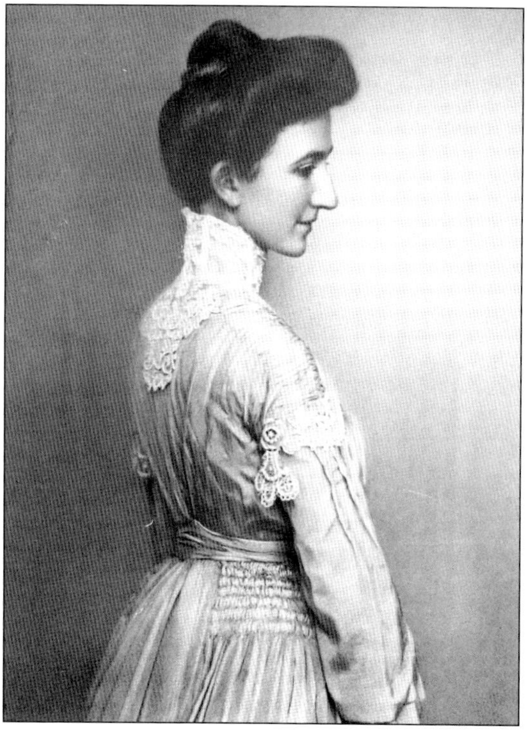

Pictured is the first-generation Schroeder family in an unknown year. Seen here are, from left to right (first row) Frances, Peter, Angeline (Rollinger), and Sister Mary Hubert Peter Schroeder; (second row) Joseph, Frank, Catherine, Theresa, John, and Peter Schroeder. (Courtesy of Julie Schroeder.)

Frances Schroeder, born in Two Creeks, Wisconsin, on May 30, 1876, lost her life off the coast of California on July 21, 1907. While sailing aboard the steamer *Columbia*, tragedy struck the ship, and it sank. Frances went overboard into the Pacific Ocean without a life preserver, was struck with an item, and drowned. She was director of the Two Rivers Kindergarten from 1899 to 1907. Her portrait hangs in Schroeder's with her memorial plaque. (Courtesy of A.J. Ashenbrenner.)

Joseph S. Schroeder was born on April 12, 1862, in Two Creeks, Wisconsin. He married Mary Ann Short in 1890. She passed away on May 8, 1898, after giving birth to a baby girl: Helen Theresa Schroeder. On October 28, 1900, Joseph married Isabella Wolf, and together, they had seven children. Joseph died February 23, 1929, of typhoid fever. (Courtesy of Schroeder's Department Store.)

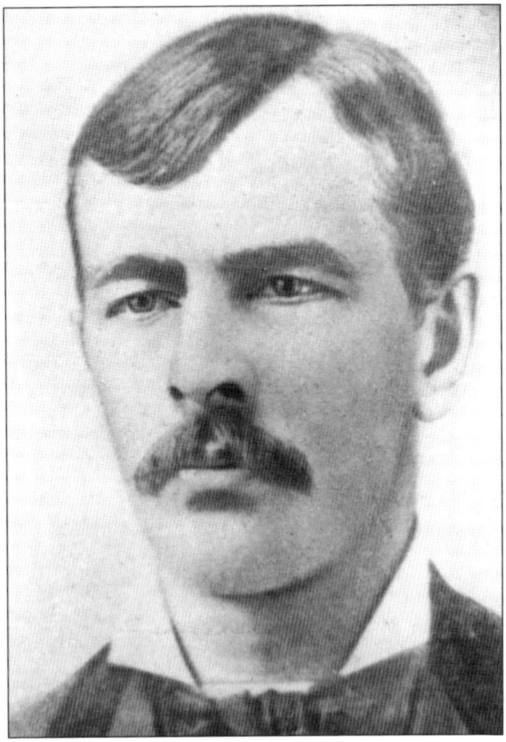

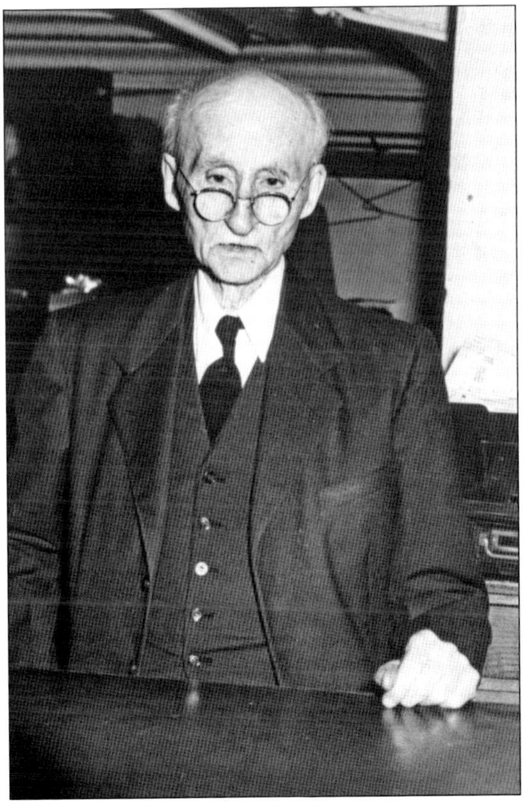

Peter Schroeder is the fourth child to be born to John and Catherine (Graef) Schroeder. Peter was born on June 27, 1860. He married Ida Schwantes on November 23, 1920. They never had any children. He died on April 8, 1954. He is pictured here in the Two Rivers Savings Bank. (Courtesy of Schroeder's Department Store.)

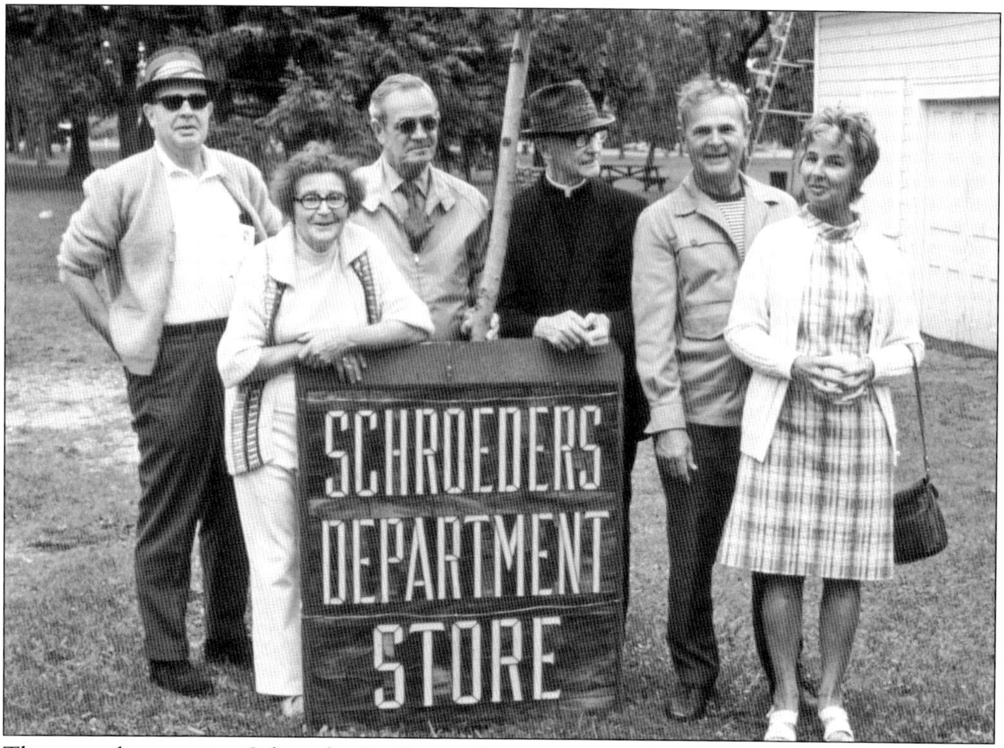

The second-generation Schroeder family members are pictured at a Schroeder family reunion in 1973. Pictured from left to right are Hilary, Helen (Suettinger), Neal, Father Peter, Gary, and Kitty (Doleschal). The Schroeders still have family reunions in Two Rivers. (Courtesy of Schroeder's Department Store.)

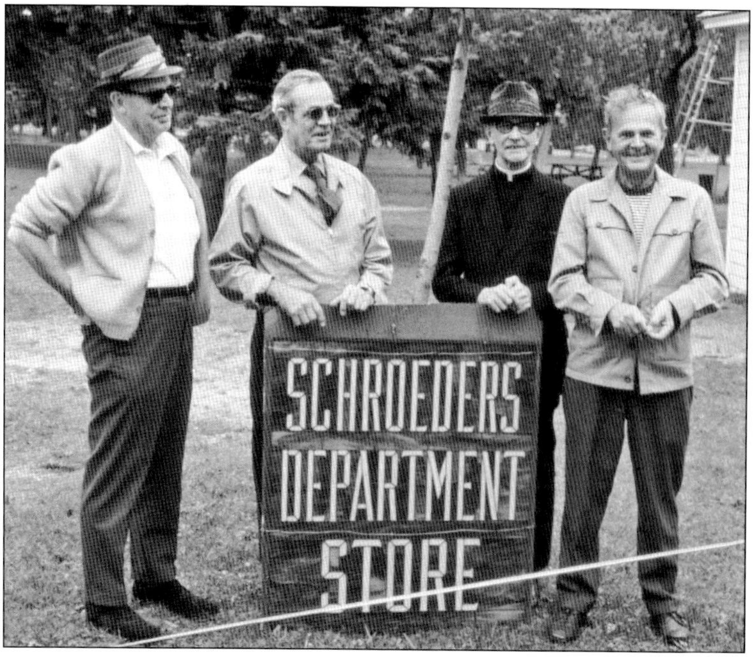

The boys of the second generation gather at the annual Schroeder family picnic. Pictured from left to right are Hilary, Neal, Father Peter, and Gary Schroeder. The store had two stained-glass windows with Schroeder's Department Store. One is still intact, and the second one is in pieces but in storage. (Courtesy of Schroeder's Department Store.)

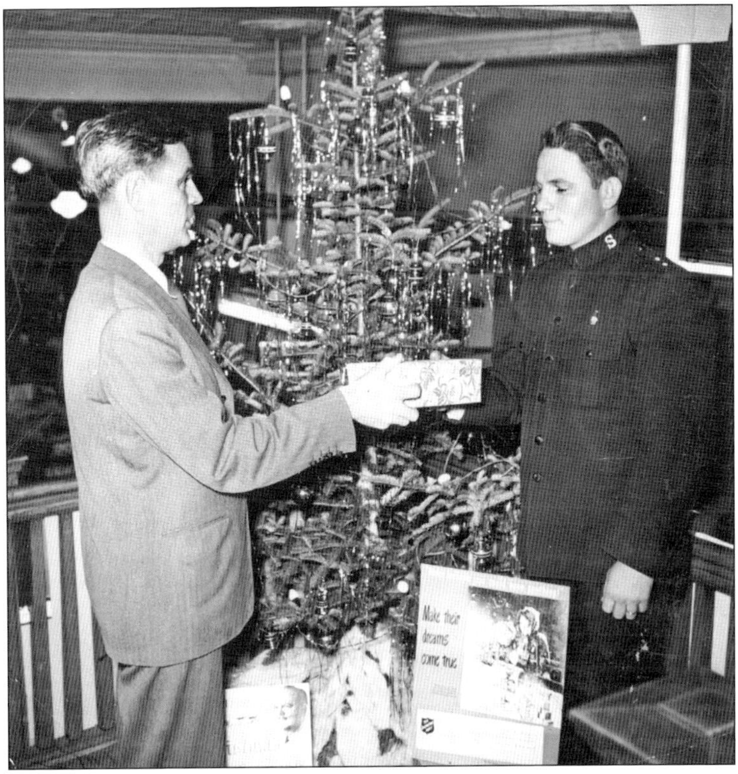

Neal Schroeder is presenting a gift to the Salvation Army on the mezzanine level at the Schroeder Building. The Schroeder family believes in helping when and where they can, whether in donation of time or money. (Courtesy of Schroeder's Department Store.)

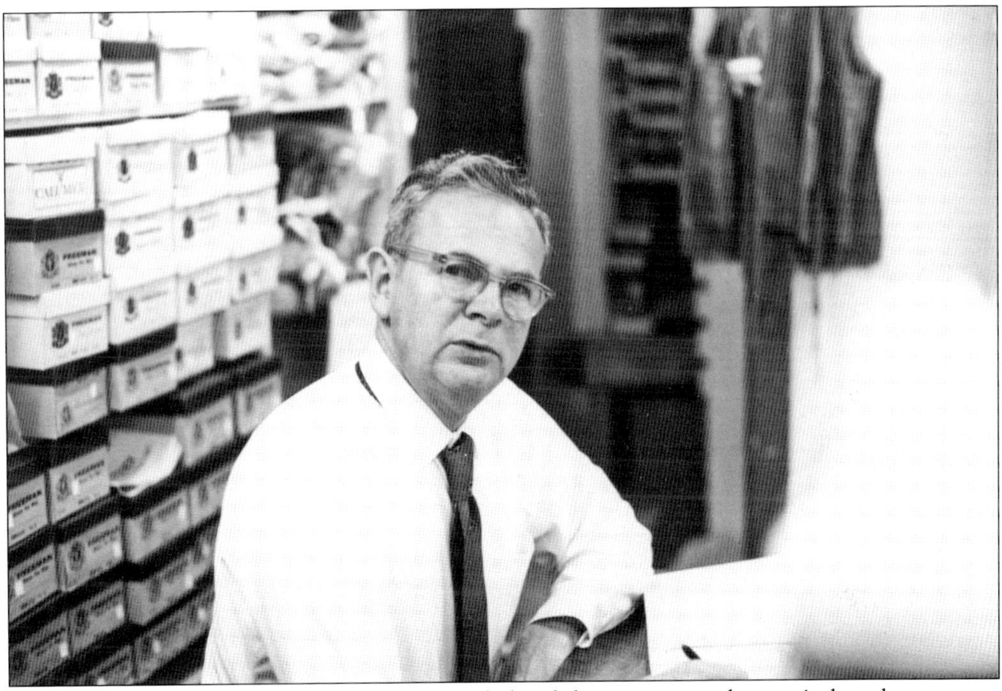

Gary Schroeder, son of Joseph Schroeder, sits behind the counter in the men's shoe department. He was the manager of the men's and women's shoe departments while he worked at Schroeder's. (Courtesy of John Schroeder.)

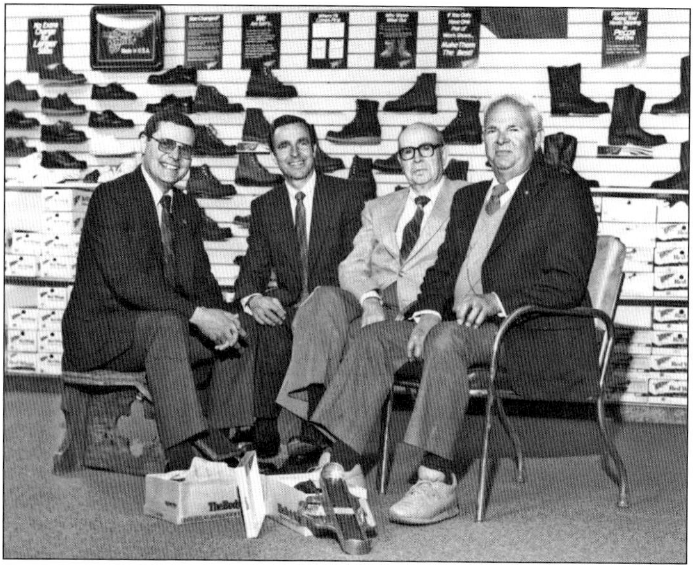

The second and third generations are seen here during a photography shoot for a GTE ad. Pictured from left to right in the newly remodeled men's shoe department are John, Tim, Hilary, and Gary Schroeder. The GTE ad stated, "We've kept up with the Schroeder's for generations." GTE used a different photograph in the ad that was featured in 1990. (Courtesy of Welnetz Studio and the Schroeder Brothers Company.)

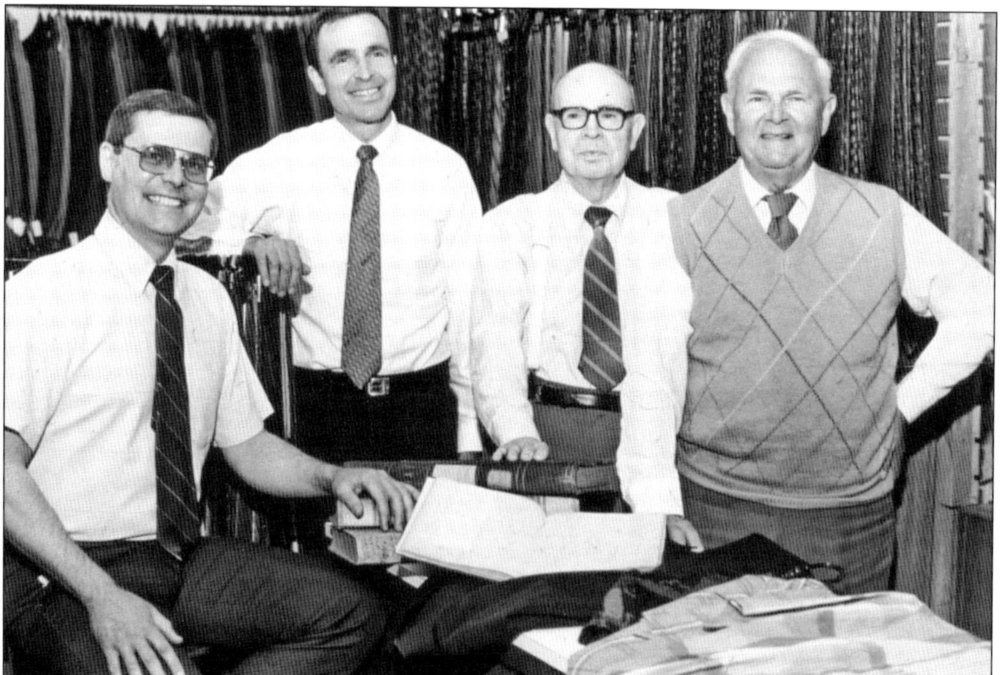

This photograph was used in the GTE ad, stating, "We've kept up with the Schroeder's for generations." The ad was featured in 1990 in anticipation of Schroeder's 100th anniversary. Pictured from left to right are John, Tim, Hilary, and Gary. (Courtesy of Welnetz Studio and the Schroeder Brothers Company.)

Tim Schroeder is pictured in the men's clothing department during the 100th anniversary sale in October 1991. Tim managed the men's and women's clothing departments while working as the general manager of Schroeder's Department Store during his time there. (Courtesy of Schroeder's Department Store.)

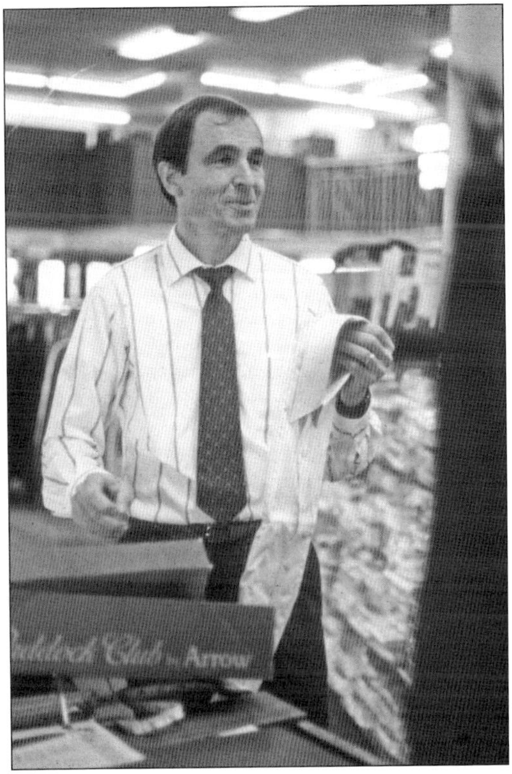

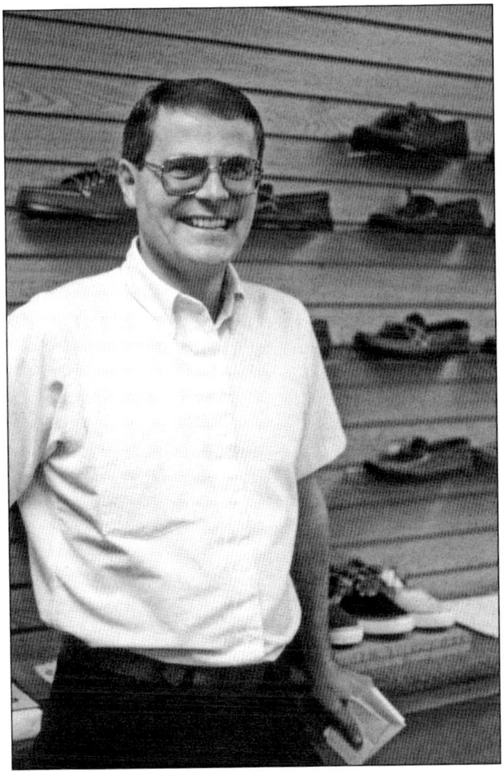

John Schroeder, 43 years old in this photograph, managed the men's and women's footwear and alterations departments while working as general manager for Schroeder's. He also worked with the marketing of Schroeder's. (Courtesy of Schroeder's Department Store.)

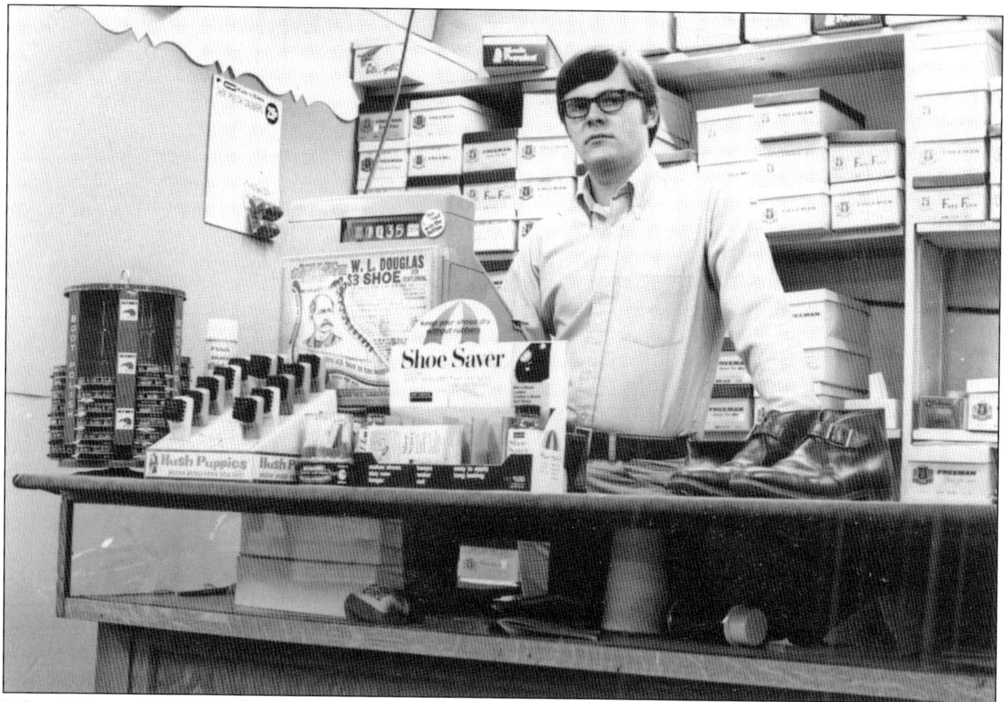

John Schroeder, son of Gary Schroeder, came back to the family business in 1970. While John was away at school, he watched *It's a Wonderful Life*, and he promptly came back to work for the family business. (Courtesy of Schroeder's Department Store.)

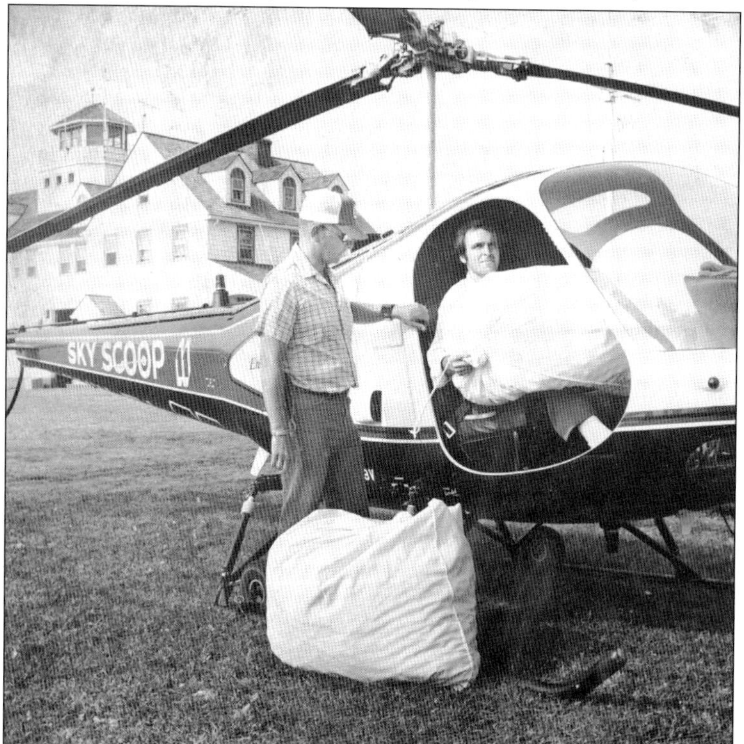

Tim Schroeder, third-generation owner/manager, getting ready to shower Two Rivers with the annual Ping Pong Drop in 1981. This image was captured at the Coast Guard Station with Two Rivers in the background. The Annual Ping Pong Drop was held in August during the Maxwell Street Sidewalk Sale. (Courtesy of Schroeder's Department Store.)

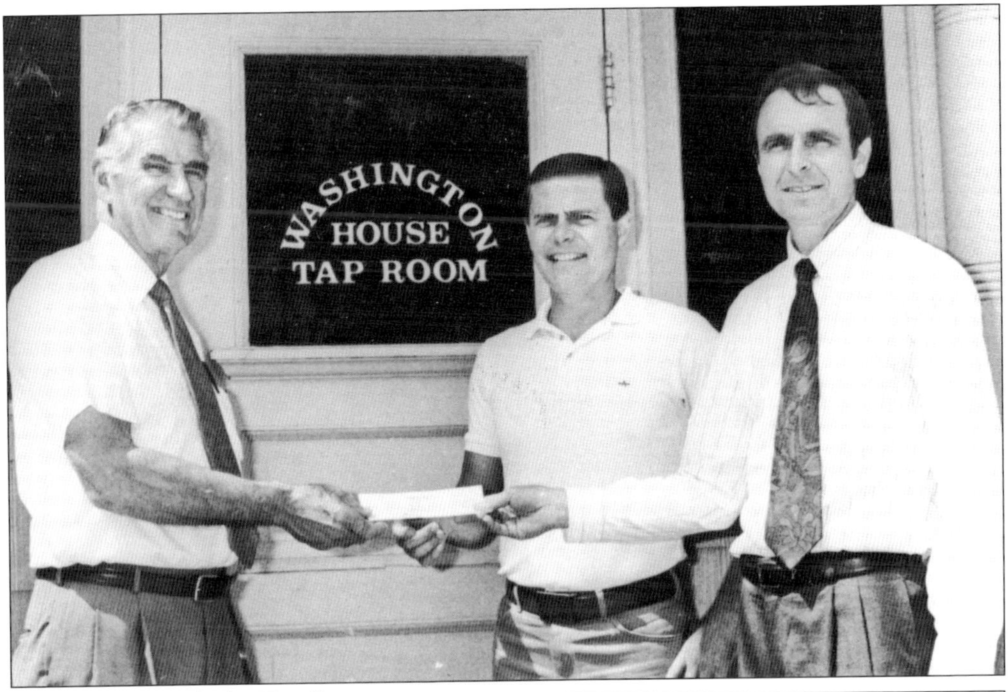

Walter Vogel (left), the Two Rivers Historical Society director, is pictured with John (center) and Tim Schroeder. John and Tim presented the historical society with $500 to help renovate the Washington House. (Courtesy of Schroeder's Department Store.)

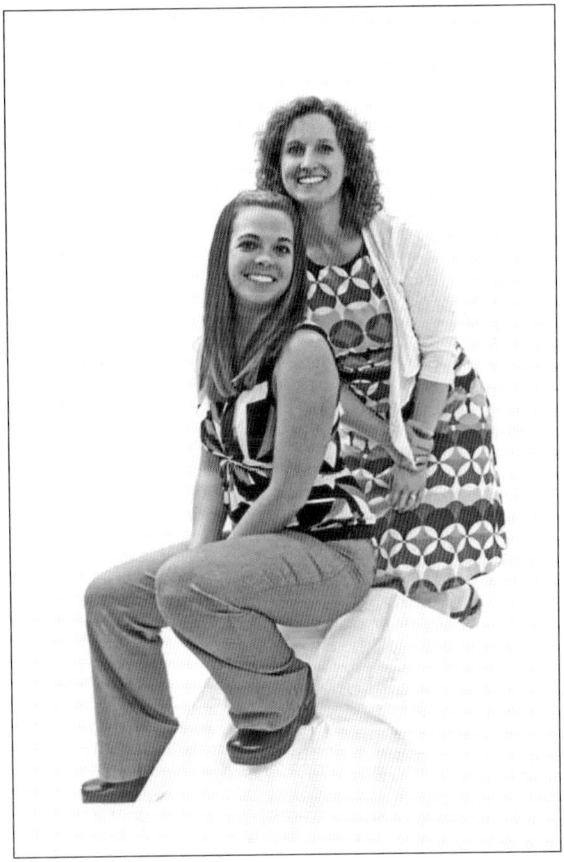

Two brothers started the business in 1890, and two sisters continue the family tradition. Now in fourth- and fifth-generation ownership, the daring duo are making bold changes to put the store on financial success and a stable course for the future. Pictured from left to right, Theresa Kronforst and A.J. Schroeder are successful professionally and personally. "The Girls," as they are often referred to, are enjoying life, raising a family, volunteering, and working for the family business. (Courtesy of Julie Schroeder.)

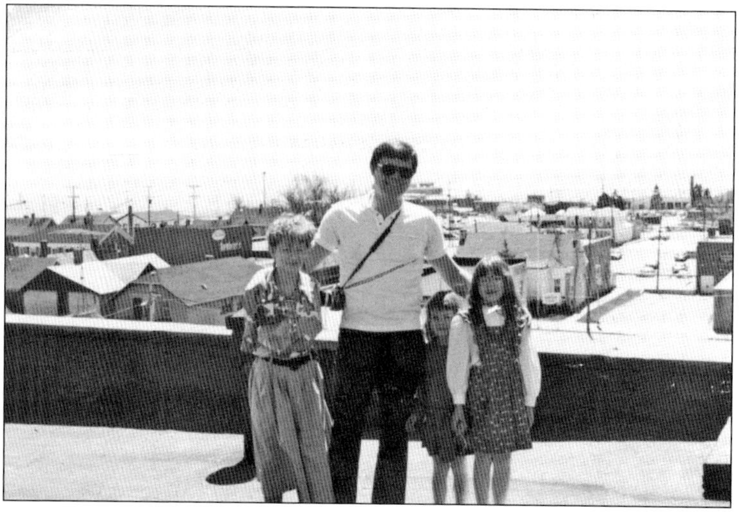

The Schroeder girls are with their dad, John, on top of the Schroeder Building in spring 1989. The girls would visit Schroeder's on a Sunday after church and head up to the roof to see the sights of Two Rivers. Pictured from left to right are A.J., John, Liz, and Theresa. (Courtesy of Schroeder's Department Store.)

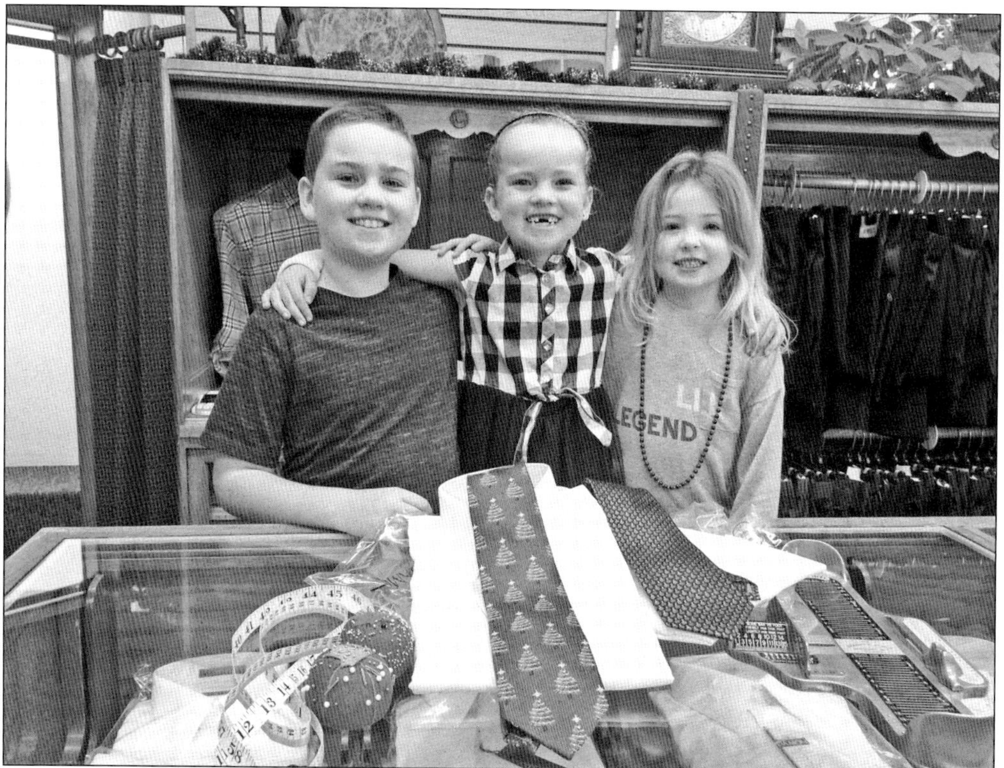

In 2014, another generation was brought into the fold. Fifth-generation children to A.J. and Theresa—Connor and Norah Ashenbrenner and Clara Kronforst—all received shares of ownership to Schroeder Brothers Company, Inc. This photograph of the fifth generation was taken in the men's clothing department in 2017. Pictured from left to right are Connor Ashenbrenner, Norah Ashenbrenner, and Clara Kronforst. Connor can be found cleaning windows, delivering packages, and dumping garbage. Weekends during the year, Norah and Clara play in the office while their moms work the sales floor. (Courtesy of Schroeder's Department Store.)

Eight

Carrying on the Tradition

Since 1891, three transitions of ownership have taken place. Each transition was unique like the people managing. The fourth generation of ownership is marked with sadness after the passing of John Schroeder in December 2008. A.J. was working full-time managing marketing and the women's apparel and footwear departments. Tim was offered a teaching job in the summer of 2008 and decided it was a good time to let the next generation take over. Training the new generation started at the annual sidewalk sale and was the Schroeder form of baptism into the retail life. The year 1987 was A.J.'s first official year of working. A.J. enjoyed working at Schroeder's; she dreamed one day she would be able to work with her dad, but it was tough working for family. She had to work smarter, harder, and faster than regular employees. In September 2002, her dad hired her back to manage marketing and work the retail floor. A.J. developed Schroeder's first website, with help from Veronica Schroeder, Tim Schroeder's daughter. From there, other social media followed. A.J. and her husband welcomed a son in 2006, and A.J. continued to work, bringing him in daily. Three generations of Schroeder's were at the store daily for two years. Theresa started working in women's lingerie and footwear in 1991. Her story is similar to A.J.'s story. Theresa tried a variety of jobs, and at A.J.'s suggestion, she started part-time in the Red Bank Coffeehouse in 2004 while going to school to be a court stenographer. In 2007, she took a part-time position in the office at Schroeder's. After the death of their dad, the girls were now in charge but never really worked together. "We spent many lunch breaks at Kurtz's Pub in 2009 with a notepad and chatted over lunch and a beer," A.J. recalls. They were learning how to run a century-old business while learning about each other. In 2009, Theresa finished her father's term on the Two Rivers Main Street Board. Since 2009, she has been the president, vice president, treasurer, and interim Main Street director. She became the coffeehouse manager in 2009, as well. She married Nathan Kronforst and became an instant mother to his two daughters, Madison and Samantha, in 2011. Her daughter Clara was born in 2012.

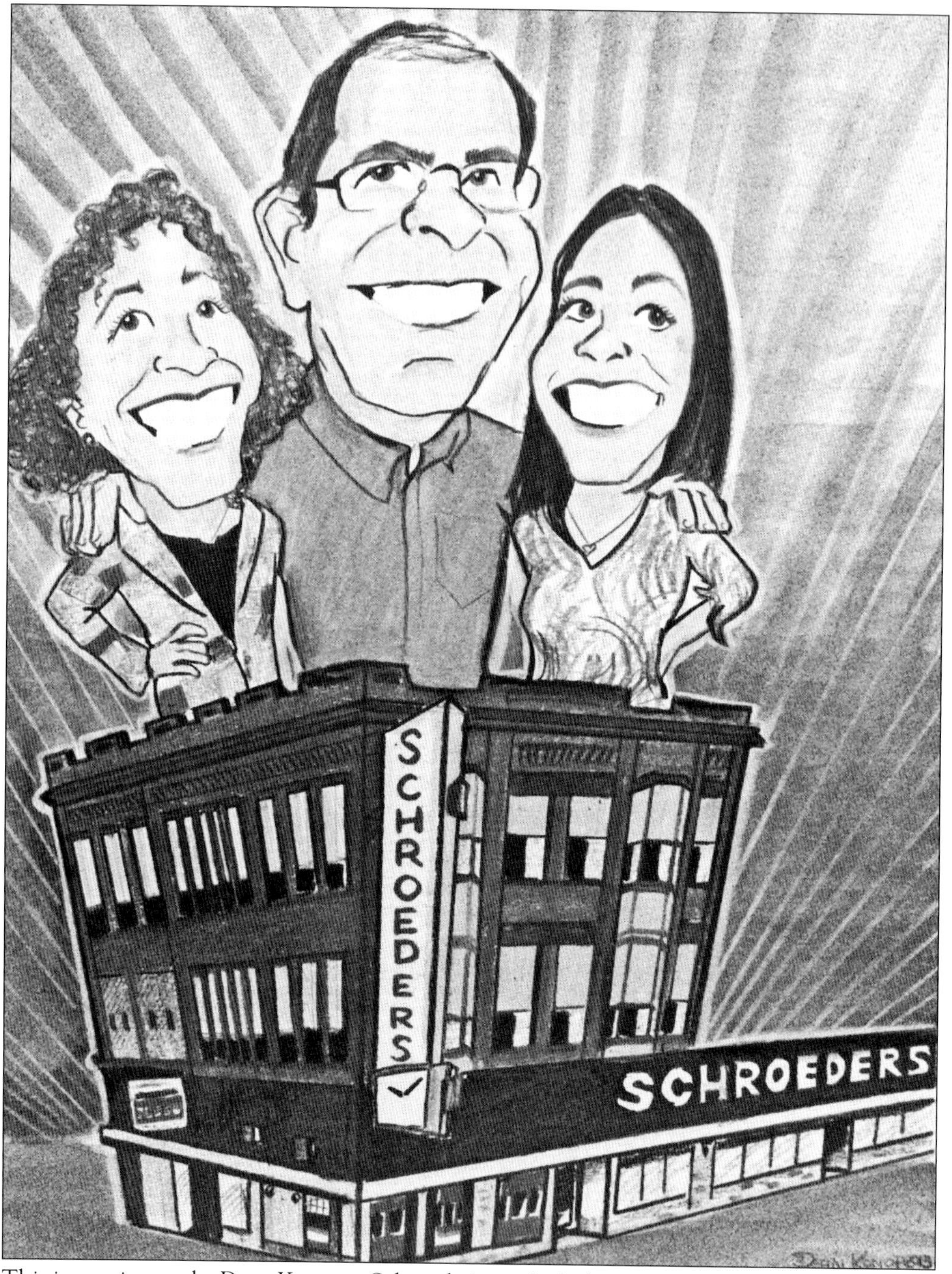

This is a caricature by Dean Konop, a Schroeder's men's clothing and footwear employee, of A.J. Schroeder, John Schroeder, and Theresa Kronforst, standing on top of their kingdom. There was no ceremony like the one pictured. The girls lost their dad to cancer in December 2008, and 2009 was the start of a new generation taking ownership of Schroeder's Department Store. (Courtesy of Schroeder's Department Store.)

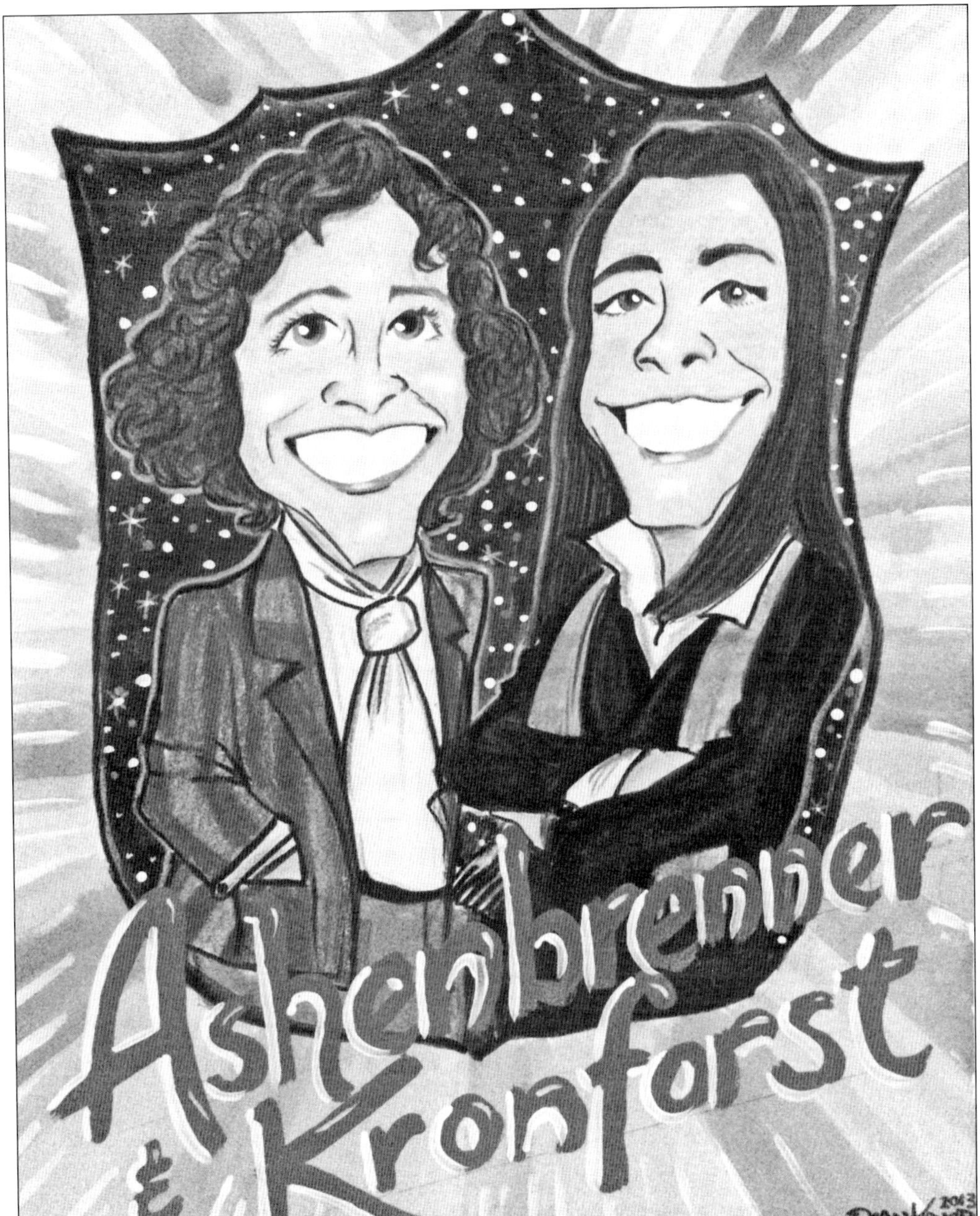

This is a caricature of A.J. (left) and Theresa by Dean Konop, who wanted to capture their partnership and mimicked the *Cagney & Lacey* television show. The year 2009 was a tough year at Schroeder's, and the Schroeder girls needed to make some big changes at the store to really make a financial difference. In the beginning management years, A.J. changed how marketing was handled at Schroeder's, and Theresa became the men's clothing manager/buyer. The Schroeder girls were finally starting to make their stamp on the store. (Courtesy of Schroeder's Department Store.)